From the book...

For me, the instruments of nostalgia are more capricious—like the phantom itch of an amputated limb. While the slightly dissonant twang of a sitar makes me smile . . . sirens always catch me off guard—frozen out in the open, as it were. They set off an air raid inside me, probing the painful ambivalence that has strained my attachments since leaving Pakistan. More recent memories have become entangled with the fear that sirens trigger, evoking the same dread and confused sense of guilt. The childhood source of these emotions has blended with other wars—with my father, with school teachers, with failed love, and with the many merchants of God who have preyed upon my desire for spiritual truth by bribing my hunger for community. And sirens never let me forget that I am still a refugee in my own country.

Many of us feel guilty that our grief is trivial in comparison with the "real" suffering in the world—in Bosnia, Rwanda, or America's inner cities. But a child doesn't make these comparisons, and long after we have intellectually gained some perspective on the particular traumas we experienced while growing up, it is the child's emotional scars that remain. . . . There is something powerful, of course, in hearing your own private story articulated by someone else. It is a healing revelation, one that moves us from isolation to a bond with the rest of humanity.

We all need to tell our stories, for we long to be assured that we are not alone.

The West and the Wider World Series

The West and the Wider World Series features works that describe the historical processes of inter-cutural relations using Europe as a point of reference and those that deal with the influence exerted on Western Civilization by other major civilizations.

Paper Airplanes in the Himalayas

The Unfinished Path Home

Paul Asbury Seaman

The West and the Wider World Series, Volume XIII

Cross Cultural Publications, Inc.
CrossRoads Books

Printed in the United States of America. *First Edition*

Grateful acknowledgement is made for permission to reprint excerpts from the following works:

"Dweller on the Threshold." Written by Van Morrison and Hugh Murphy. Copyright © 1982 Essential Music. Used by permission. All rights reserved.
"Leaving the Harbor," by Nanci Griffith. © 1989 Irving Music, Inc. and Ponder Heart Music (BMI). All Rights Reserved. Used by Permission, Warner Bros. Publications U.S., Inc., Miami FL 33014.

"Like a Prayer," by Madonna Ciccone and Pat Leonard. © 1989 WB Music Corp., Bleu Disque Music Co., Inc., Webo Girl Publishing, Inc. and Johnny Yuma Music. All Rights o/b/o Webo Girl Publishing, Inc. & Bleu Disque Music Co., Inc. administered by WB Music Corp. All Rights Reserved. Used by Permission, Warner Bros. Publications U.S., Inc., Miami FL 33014.

"Train in the Distance." Copyright © 1981 Paul Simon. Used by permission of the Publisher: Paul Simon Music.

Epigraphs on page 7 and page 163 and quotation on pages 176–177 © 1992 by Frederick Buechner. From *Listening to Your Life* (Harper Collins). Permission granted courtesy of Harriet Wasserman Literary Agency, Inc., NY.

Epigraph on page 207 © 1981 by Patricia Hampl from the book *A Romantic Education* (Houghton Mifflin Co., Boston). Permission granted courtesy of Rhoda Weyr Agency, NY.

Epigraph by Jon Robin Baitz on page 121 is from an Associated Press wire story, "Books and Authors: From Lonely Boy Abroad to Acclaimed Playwright," by Nita Lelyveld, January 14, 1994.

The quotation by Samuel Shoemaker at the beginning of chapter 15 ("Obscure Paradise") is from *A Young Man's View of the Ministry* (New York: Association Press, 1923), p. 38.

An earlier version of chapter 11 ("Sirens") was published in *The Global Nomad*, Washington, DC, 3:2 (March-April 1993).

Library of Congress Catalogue Number: 97-066689

Seaman, Paul Asbury.
Paper Airplanes in the Himalayas: the Unfinished Path Home — 1st ed.
       p. cm.
            ISBN 0-940121-44-1
1. Children of Missionaries—Autobiography. 2. Third Culture Kids (TCKs)—Global Nomads—Adult TCKs. 3. Re-entry—cultural readjustment. 4. Pakistan—Travel and History. 5. Author (1957-). I. Title.

Cover art by Karin Tunnéll

To Margie, Eileen, and Raymond

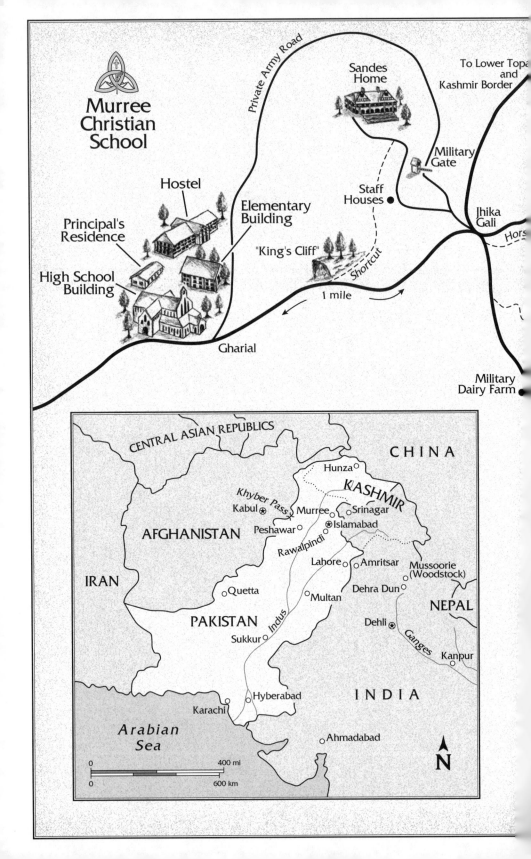

The Town Of
MURREE
AND MURREE CHRISTIAN SCHOOL
Elevation: 7,500 feet

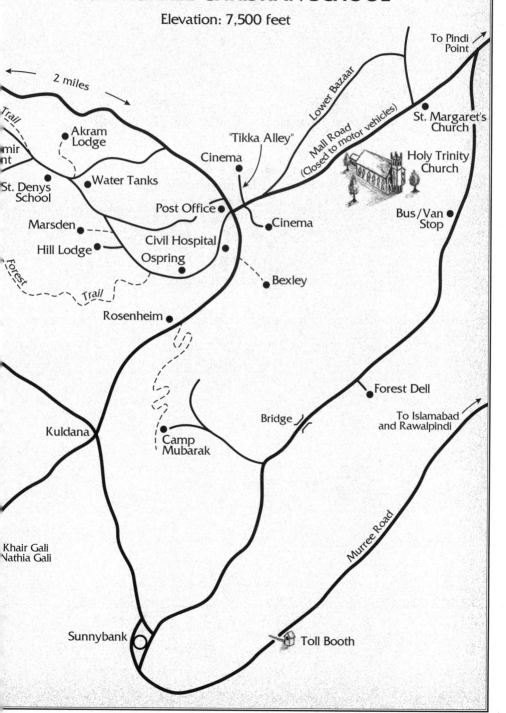

To Pindi Point

2 miles

Trail

Lower Bazaar

Mall Road (Closed to motor vehicles)

St. Margaret's Church

Akram Lodge

"Tikka Alley"

Cinema

Holy Trinity Church

mir nt

St. Denys School

Water Tanks

Post Office

Cinema

Bus/Van Stop

Marsden

Hill Lodge

Civil Hospital

Ospring

Bexley

Forest

Trail

Rosenheim

Forest Dell

To Islamabad and Rawalpindi

Bridge

Kuldana

Camp Mubarak

Khair Gali
Nathia Gali

Murree Road

Sunnybank

Toll Booth

Map: LOUIS J. SPIRITO

Obscure Paradise (An Expatriate Childhood)

Paper airplanes, matchbox trains
Take me home — all in vain.
Himalayan Range, memories strange
I only suspect what they claim.
Fog and damp obscure the lamp
Of something more than earthly gain.

We thought it paradise —
But would not live it twice.

— PAS, 1994

Contents

SUPPLEMENT: The Alumni Letters

Prologue

I grew up in the mountains of northern Pakistan. One summer when I was eight my family took a weekend outing to the home of friends several miles outside the town of Murree. I recall nothing of the visit, but remember the journey vividly. My two older sisters and I sat in the very back seat of the old Ford station wagon that belonged to the missionary couple we were traveling with. The road grew more narrow and less paved, while at the same time the sheer drops on the cliff side became ever more bottomless, descending precipitously to scenic valleys that seemed to be on some other continent. Only in the Himalayas would this area be referred to as "foothills."

I glanced out the window with a feeling akin to what you experience when a roller coaster reaches the top of its slow, methodical climb and you are suddenly confronted with how far up you are, where you are about to plunge, and how totally, stupidly helpless you are.

"Can't you please slow down!" I pleaded, heedless of the impertinence of speaking to an adult this way.

And then came the driver's patient, if slightly exasperated reply: "I'm only going ten miles per hour."

As in this outing, most of my childhood was contained within a few miles either side of the boarding school I attended and the larger area of Murree, from which the school took its name. Even weekend camp-outs were rarely more than twenty or thirty miles away. Yet, it seemed an endless kingdom, a secret garden still full of mystery after ten years of active exploration—and one that only hinted at the terrors and wonders of the larger world just over the next hill.

❂

Murree Christian School (MCS) was established in 1956 to provide an education for missionaries' children comparable to what they would get back in the States. My sisters and I spent half of each year—every spring and fall—in boarding, raised by "aunties" and "uncles" who shared responsibility for a hundred and fifty kids in twelve grades. This communal foster care arrangement freed our parents to focus on their ministry; the rigorous religious training we received was a bonus, at least for the parents.

Our families lived in isolated villages and in modern cities; as the only expatriates in the area (like mine) or in communities of other missionaries. Our parents worked with tribal people and with large institutions; they were literacy campaigners and Bible translators, technical advisors and evangelists, doctors and nurses, teachers and administrators; but mostly, they saw themselves as "witnesses" to the love of Jesus, and as colleagues and friends to the Pakistanis they had come to serve.

In the 1960s and '70s the majority of our families were from the United States. A great number also came from England and Scotland and other Commonwealth countries, and from Germany, Sweden, Finland, and Norway as well, representing the major Protestant denominations—Baptists, Presbyterians, Lutherans, Anglicans, Methodists—and a host of independent mission boards. The Roman Catholic missionaries working in Pakistan were priests, nuns, or members of religious orders which all required celibacy.

There were three American international day schools in Pakistan, but these were all in major cities and therefore impractical for the many missionary families who lived in remote areas. This situation, together with the long tradition among expatriates on the Indian subcontinent of sending their children to private boarding schools, was the reason Murree Christian School existed.

The great Himalayan range piles up along the bottom of Tibet, stretching from Afghanistan all the way to Burma. Its vast, frozen crescent forms the northern contours of the Indian subcontinent, linking the borders of Nepal, China, Kashmir, Pakistan and the Central Asian republics of the former Soviet Union. Here, the four highest mountain ranges on earth come together in a knot of hymn-compelling peaks known as the Roof of the World. Second only to Everest, Pakistan's K-2 towers over the valleys of Gilgit and Hunza —the real Shangri-la that inspired James Hilton's modern fable, *Lost Horizon*. A thousand years before the time of Christ, trade routes found their way through these secret valleys and hidden passes, later becoming the legendary Silk Road that first linked Western civilization to the Orient. The Chinese called this section of the route "the Suspended Crossing."

Monumental forces of change came through this region, channeled between the barren hills of the Khyber Pass with its swashbuckling Pathan warriors and the pastoral beauty of Kashmir. Here, in the fourth century B.C., confronted by the unexpected fierceness of local resistance, Alexander failed to expand his Macedonian empire into India. Instead, this encounter led to the rise of the great Gandharan civilization that flourished here, in what is now northern Pakistan. Two thousand years ago, its distinctive mingling of Roman, Greek, and Indian cultures drew philosophers, royalty, and spiritual pilgrims from both Europe and Asia. Marco Polo passed through here on his way to the courts of Kublai Khan. The "Middle Way" of Buddhism, though founded in India, achieved its greatest articulation at this crossroads, spreading religious reformation into Tibet and China.

A famous cross dating back to the second century A.D. found in the ruins of Taxila—the capital of Gandhara—confirms the early influence of Christianity; and local tradition asserts that one of Christ's own disciples, St. Thomas, visited this ancient city.

In the sixth century A.D., while their cousin Attila was sacking Rome, the White Huns pillaged the Persian Empire, plunging India into its own Dark Ages. Then, early in the eighth century, invaders from Iraq and Syria brought much of the subcontinent under Muslim rule for nearly a thousand years, with various dynasties (mostly of Mongolian and Turkish descent) battling, ascending, and being overthrown. Bubar the Tiger followed Tamurlane the Earth Shaker. In 1526, Bubar took Delhi and became the first of the great Mogul emperors whose dominion would extend from the Persian border in the west to the Bay of Bengal, and from the Himalayas to the Indian Ocean. It was the richest empire the world had ever seen and it lasted for just two hundred years, until the British—the last foreigners to subjugate the region—began building railroads and mapping the Indian subcontinent for Queen Victoria.

Beginning with a small tea company and a few trading settlements on the coast, the English moved steadily inland for almost two hundred years until reaching this northern frontier in the nineteenth century. Here, the British Empire pressed uneasily against the boundaries of czarist Russia and imperial China. When India became independent in 1947, missionaries in the new nation of Pakistan needed a place to educate their children on their side of what quickly became a hostile border.

Those of us who grew up at Murree Christian School—less than sixty miles from present-day Taxila—were neither pilgrims nor conquerors. We too were foreigners; yet, nestled in this narrow crucible through which so much history had funneled, we never questioned our sense of belonging. The peculiar conditions of our being there created a spiritual geography we simply called "home."

Murree sits in the shadow of the great mountains, whose peaks stretch impossibly three or four times higher than Murree's gentle slopes, a mere 7,000 feet above the plains. During the colonial period, its scattered collection of hill villages grew into a minor resort town, developed by the British as a summer haven from the heat of the Punjab. Following the partition of India into two countries when the British left, Murree took on greater significance. While it would never rival Simla, Srinagar, or Darjeeling, it was the only such "hill station" on the Pakistan side of the border. The quaint stone cottages and two-story bungalows were cold and damp, but offered spectacular views of the Himalayas, glimpsed through a break in the evergreens. After Independence, a number of these estates were purchased or rented by missionary organizations.

In June, when the wilting heat of the plains became almost unbearable, most of our parents came up to Murree from their mission stations across the country and took us out of boarding for the summer. They studied Urdu at the Murree Language School, or just rested and enjoyed the luxury of fellowship with other missionaries. And for three months we got to go to day school, like kids "back home." A real school bus came rattling around the hill to pick us up.

With our families together, attending the big church in Murree, and having dinner with other families, summers provided the closest thing to a normal community. Still, we often experienced even those months as "single-parent families," when our fathers were too busy to leave their work on the plains for more than a few weeks. And all too soon, all of the parents returned to their mission stations and we went back into boarding for the fall term of school. It wasn't possible to keep the facilities heated during the winter months, so we took our long vacation in December, January, and February.

We were a curious tribe, a scrabble of diverse national origins and local circumstances, united by our common lot and the larger purpose that had brought us to Murree Christian School. Like nomads, we moved with the seasons. We grew older and we came and went, compelled not by the calendar or the school year, but by the weather. Four times a year we packed up and moved to, or back to, another temporary home. As with the seasons, each move offered something to look forward to, and something was lost.

We learned early that "home" was an ambiguous concept, and wherever we lived, some essential part of our lives was always someplace else. So we were always in two minds. We learned to be happy and sad at the same time. We learned to be independent, and we learned that things were out of our control. We learned the reassuring familiarity of routine and the comforting exactness of being able to pack everything needed for life into a single footlocker and a bedroll. We had the security and the consolation that whenever we left one place we were returning to another, already familiar one.

"Home" might refer to the school dormitory or to the house in Murree where we stayed during the summer, to our parents' mission station on the plains, or more broadly, to the country of our citizenship. And while we might have some sense of belonging to all of these places, we felt fully at home in none of them. Boarding life seemed to have the most consistency, but there we were separated from our siblings and shared one "parent" with twenty other kids. As it grew colder we looked forward to being with our real parents for the holidays.

Each annual cycle began and ended with a ritual passage—a children's caravan called the Train Party. Forty or fifty of us from MCS traveled together in specially designated coaches on a public train, back to our various homes "down the line." For some boys and girls, the journey lasted twenty-eight hours, spanning the length of the Indus River—from Rawalpindi at the foot of the mountains, a thousand miles to Karachi on the Arabian Sea. After the winter break, another "train party" gathered us together like the Pied Piper and took us away from our families again. We were always eager to be reunited with our parents, but after three months of separation from our friends, we were just as eager to go back. Every time we got on the train we experienced both abandonment and communion.

So too, in the larger cycle of furloughs—every three or four or five years, depending on the leniency or economic ability of the various mission boards: Our families went home to Canada or the States or New Zealand for awhile and then our parents left their home countries for another term abroad, and we *came* home to Pakistan. And yet, soon after we got there, we dreamed about going "home"! (Our parents shared this ambivalence: when they were home on furlough they felt like visitors, anxious to return to the place of their calling. It has been said that missionaries only feel at home on the airplane in between.) The train party stitched together our patchwork sense of belonging until eventually, when our parents changed jobs, or there was a medical crisis in the family, or we graduated from high school, the cycles stopped.

But the ambiguity did not. For our parents, life on the mission field was an occupation; they would eventually resign or retire and become "former missionaries." But we would never be former "missionary kids"; being an "MK" is our inheritance. As MKs we grew up straddled between worlds, not fully reconciled to one or the other. Only much later would we become aware of the chasm our circumstances had created for us.

PART ONE

Reconstructing a Missionary Childhood

Listen to your life. See it for the fathomless mystery that it
is. In the boredom and pain of it no less than in the
excitement and gladness: touch, taste, smell your way to
the holy and hidden heart of it because in the last analysis
all moments are key moments, and life itself is grace.

FREDERICK BUECHNER
Listening to Your Life

Interior of Murree Christian School, 1967.

1

The Leaving Season

Going off to boarding school as a young child is like parachuting: the second time is actually much worse than the first. The first time you are distracted by the anticipation of a novel experience. Excitement is mixed with the fear; you are fooled by the lure of the unknown, and by well-meaning older siblings with their tales of great adventures waiting to be had. You are naive to the true dangers. But the second time, you know full well what it means to leave the solid platform of all that is familiar and safe and drop into bottomless space.

I remember nothing from my first year in Pakistan except that second time of saying goodbye to my parents when I entered boarding again for the spring term. I can only conjecture about what the several months previous to that must have been like. My family moved constantly during the year prior to arriving in Pakistan: from a small town in Pennsylvania to missionary orientation training in Indiana and New Jersey and finally Stony Point, New York. I do remember one trip to New York City where, as an eager five-year-old, I boarded the wrong subway train and was temporarily separated from my family.

We crossed the Atlantic on the original *Queen Elizabeth;* saw London and the Buckingham Palace Guards, the Suez Canal; finally arriving at the port at Karachi late one suffocatingly hot night in May, 1963. All the new smells, repellent and mysterious, the rush and revelry of strange-looking people speaking unfamiliar languages, were disorienting and frightened me. A smothering heat permeated the darkness like a claustrophobic dream.

We took a train up to Lahore and then another one out to the village where Dad would be working. No sooner had I been told that this was our new home than a few days later I found myself on a train again, headed with my family for a place called Murree. High in the mountains, Murree was not so hot but it rained all the time. The dampness and the mildew smell were so foreign, so completely unfamiliar; and there was no refuge, no "time out," no getting back to the comfortable habits and knowledge of my former life.

There must have been day school and then entering boarding in the fall—and the sudden, lurching realization, again and again, of the incomprehensible fact that my parents were not with me anymore. I turned six that November, and still had a hard time distinguishing between three months and forever.

Then, just before Christmas, my family was finally reunited, and some reassuring routine and secure relationships were restored. But I don't remember any of this. Only the confusion of being sent away again. It turned out I was only being fattened up for sacrifice to the hungry "train party" god. I knew my parents loved me, but they did it anyway.

We arrive at the place where the terrible act is to be performed with plenty of time to spare. The temple is already packed for the occasion and we jostle our way through the press of unfamiliar bodies, to the chosen altar on one of the Lahore train station's twelve platforms. My family stops in a breathless huddle before the high doorway of an enormous green-and-yellow train carriage. On a small blackboard fastened to the side of the car are chalked the words, "RESERVED: Murree School." I stand there, dressed in starched khaki shorts that are too big for me, clean-scrubbed under a new white shirt, and clutching a "Road Runner" lunch box. I cannot actually read the sign, but stare at it anyway, knowing it announces my fate.

Inside, I file past parallel rows of slatted wooden benches, still mostly empty. The compartment smells like a public restroom. Khushi, our Pakistani cook, has accompanied us and he clucks at me, shaking his head, as I plop down by the window. He takes a rag and swats at the dust on a lower bunk before allowing my sisters to sit down. BANG! The floor trembles as another footlocker drops from a coolie's head and is slid under the seats; my father stuffs bedrolls overhead. It is hotter in here than on the platform, but I do not want to move again, anxious to be going.

Alas, this is not to be a mercifully swift separation, the single slice of a sharp sword. The train party god is not content to swallow me whole; I must be slowly torn to pieces first, courtesy of that exquisite tester of patience—Pakistan Western Railways. The up-country express is an hour late. And our lifeless row of carriages waits to be attached to that train.

My mother tries to fill the awkward time by ordering snacks and chatting about what a good time I'm going to have and that I should be a good boy and make her proud of me. But I am not listening and taste only something like ashes in my mouth. My chest hurts and I can barely swallow. My father is practicing some of his newly-learned Urdu on would-be passengers who, either illiterate or ignoring the signs, try to push their way into our compartment. *Muaf karo, Babuji, yih dibba mahfuz hai.* "Pardon, sir, but this compartment is reserved." Dad and some of the other parents busy themselves barricading the doors with luggage and shutting all the windows so people won't climb through them.

It gets even hotter. My skin sticks to the varnished armrest, sucking like a Band-aid coming off when I lift my arm. The stirred-up dust is already caking on my legs. Several more kids get on but I scarcely notice them.

With a huge shriek and clatter of metal, the train lurches and begins rolling forward. My heart leaps into my throat. At last we are leaving! Both relief and terror. My dad is beside us now, the family united once again—for a moment. Mom begins kissing each one of us good-bye. Then the train lurches to a stop. The executioner's blade is suspended mid-stroke. It is a false departure. Our complement of cars is being added to the main train. Each time the train moves forward my heart sinks. This is it. We're off. But no. Reprieve. We're stopping. More waiting. Reverse. SMASH! Forwards and backwards again and again as each section is coupled and uncoupled and shunted together again in some mysteriously designated order. This is the last opportunity for us to be together as a family. The thrill of motion stumbles over other emotions. Assurances of love and last-minute instructions mingle with tears and hugs and silence. There are friends to be greeted, new adventures waiting in the mountains, but now I cling to the moment, the closeness of my parents, even the heat.

The rolling and bumping and screeching seem unending, and yet I dread the quiet smoothness that will mean we are finally on our way. Inevitably, the moment does come and the reality of leaving must be confronted. The engine's shrill whistle sends out the alarm and the station master's bell triggers a final frenzy of boarders. Mom kisses and hugs us all good-bye again and is gone. Dad hugs my two older sisters and then me. His shirt, soaked with sweat, presses against my face. He leans down to kiss me, pushing his hat back on his head. "Goodbye, son. Remember, you're the man of the family in boarding school. Take care of your sisters. . . . Don't neglect to write. . . . I'll miss you."

Any response I want to make sticks in my throat. I am not going to cry. *Buck up, self; don't be a baby. You're six years old.* I panic with a new thought: I hardly know how to write! I don't know how to mail letters. How will Mom and Dad know how I'm doing? That I miss them? Suddenly I have a lot of questions, but no words come out.

Second whistle. The train heaves against the greater weight, pauses, catches its breath and then moves slowly forward. Mom is outside the window, squeezed among the press of vendors and well-wishers. She waves and wipes her eyes, each one alternately with her handkerchief. Then she disappears, swept away by the outgoing human tide, lost in an undertow of grief. Wait! I think I could tell her now all that I wanted to earlier, but she is gone.

Suddenly I am aware of my father's hand still on my shoulder. "Dad, you'll have to get off!" We're gaining momentum. Lots of faces flop past the window. We're going faster. This is a long platform. The crowd is thinning. "Dad, come on; get off!" We're going faster. "Daddy!" He has jumped out, running apace. There are tears in my eyes. There are tears in his. He's running close by the window, squeezing my hands on the sill. He falls back to the next window, touching my sisters' hands as they pass. Then, instantly, he's snapped away, as if by a hangman's rope; he's come to the deserted end of the platform and stops and we race away. He snatches the big felt hat from his head and waves it wildly. All admonitions to keep heads and arms safely inside are forgotten: we all wave frantically, as if trying to swim back to the platform where his diminishing form still beckons. His face is obscured by distance now, but I can still see a tiny white speck waving a black hat.

Twelve hours later, in the cold embrace of a far mountain night I fall exhausted into sleep and dream—the same dream I would have many times over the next several weeks: A figure, dark behind a haze of steam and soot, stands at the end of a train platform waving his hat. What is he trying to say? I see him mouth the words, "I love you, son"—those words I only heard from him when he was sending

me away, so bittersweetly attached to that other word: "good-bye."
Does he know how much I miss him? All I want is to be pulled
around in the little red wagon we had to leave behind in Pennsylvania; and to smell the cold, clean smell of his cheeks like when he used
to get home late and come in to kiss me goodnight. I didn't mind
the rough prickliness of his whiskers. In my dream, I see him in the
far distance, waving his black felt hat as if to flag down the *Khyber
Mail* and welcome me home.

2

The Mother of All
Kissing Fights

A lot seems to have happened when I was in second grade
—maybe because I experienced it twice. During that time
the new hostel was built, I got saved, and Auntie Inger
broke her nose in a kissing fight. Auntie Inger was fifty years old
when she came to Pakistan to be housemother for the first-through-
third-grade boys; grandmotherly plump, already white-haired, and
recently widowed. She had enough energy, though, to take on all
twenty-three of us—with the exuberance of a camp counselor and
the tenderness of a real mother.

It was my class that invented the "kissing fight." On privileged
nights, which were more often than not, we played this game when
we were being tucked in: Auntie Inger would try to kiss us good
night and we would try to stop her. Of course, eventually, she
always won. Even the littlest boys, aching for a mother's affection,
would pretend to be shy and duck under their blankets when Auntie
Inger got to them, and some of the third graders half-heartedly
claimed they were getting too old for such games, but every one of us
played; Auntie Inger knew that really we all wanted to.

My first two years with the Little Boys department were spent
in one of the houses above Sandes Home, the old boarding hostel,
and we had to walk a mile to school every day. I remember the 1964
elections, when a rousing chorus of senior high boys sang *"We're all
for Goldwater . . .,"* accompanied by an impromptu brass quartet. It

was no wonder he got the most votes, at Murree Christian School, anyway.

The week before the elections I snuck up to the senior boys' house at the top of the hill looking for someone to talk to about it. Paul Gardner kindly invited me into his room and I sat on his bunk and we talked about my man, Lyndon Johnson, and also what were the best kinds of marbles and sneakers. (My marble collection was pretty dull, but I did have a brand new pair of PF Flyers.) Paul was Auntie Inger's son and everybody called him Moose because he was so tall. His friends started calling him Mouse, but I never did. Not that I was scared, or anything; it just didn't seem nice.

Failing second grade wasn't too upsetting. Tim Old and Dale Stock were put back, too. And besides, we all remained in the same boarding department with our old friends. In the fall of 1965 Pakistan and India went to war for a few weeks and I learned about "blackouts" and "evacuations," and what a foxhole was. These air-raid trenches remained in our back yards long after the cease-fire and were a great place to play with a homemade periscope or dig for buried pirates' treasure.

By the spring of 1966, with five boarding terms behind me, I felt pretty grown up for an eight-year-old. Now, when the jackals howled in the forest outside our bedroom window, I didn't get scared; I just howled back. I shared a room with five other boys, and one night all of us were howling together after lights out. Auntie Inger came in and told us to be quiet and go to sleep. As soon as she left we howled out the window again and giggled when she came back. She didn't turn on the lights this time, but scolded us from the doorway and her exasperation was clear when she added, "and I *mean* it!"

"But I can see the twinkle in your eyes, Auntie Inger," I said.

"No you can't, Paul Seaman. It's dark in here," insisted Auntie Inger through pursed lips that gave her words a kind of nasal squeak. She was trying to sound stern, but I could hear the twinkle creep into her voice.

"I see it too," Tim Old said from the top bunk by the door, "Aaaa-ee-aaaah!" She was outflanked.

"All right, boys, that's enough! You'll wake the whole hostel. If you don't get to sleep, you'll have to stay home and rest instead of going on the birthday hike tomorrow."

"Ooooow," David Hover sighed reverently, shrinking into his covers.

Maybe she meant it, and though tomorrow was a long time away, there was no point in making her really mad. None of us wanted to do that. So we were quiet and then we were alone again.

I couldn't stand it. I got out of my bunk and stepped onto the ledge of the full-length louvered windows. Standing there in my BVDs I swiveled my butt in a mock belly dance and sang in a loud whisper:

> In the land of France, where the alligators dance
> One wouldn't dance so they shot him in the pants.
> The pants she wore cost a dollar-fifty-four PLUS TAX!

The old French folk tune had a nice snake-charmer's swirl to it. I had no idea what the original words were, but this is how it had been passed on to us in the school yard:

> In the land of Mars, where the ladies smoke cigars
> One wouldn't smoke so they shot her in the tope.
> The tope she wore . . .

"Seaman, get back in bed and shut up!" Dale growled from the top of the bunk I shared with him. Dale had a temper like Dr. Jekyll and Mr. Hyde and I lay down again without protest.

For breakfast every morning we had toast and *chappatis* (Pakistani flatbread, like tortillas), with butter and jam and cream ("J.C." was a popular mixture to put into a rolled-up *chappati*). For hot cereal, we had *suji* or *dahlia* (made from whole or cracked wheat); plus *chai* (ready-mixed tea) and eggs—usually over-boiled hardboiled ones. The milk always tasted awful, even when it hadn't been watered down by the milkman, and we could hardly stand to drink it. Auntie Inger had brought a couple of big cans of Strawberry Quik out from the States with her and she would spoon a little into our milk each morning for as long as it lasted.

We took our lunch cafeteria-style, on pre-formed metal trays, and ate in the courtyard right behind the hostel dining room. If you weren't careful, monkeys would swoop down and steal your food. A low wall around the edge of the courtyard overlooked the hillside below and the mountains beyond. This was a favorite place to sit because if you didn't like your food you could dump it over the "khud" without being noticed. For tea time after school, we got cookies and watery *chai* in enameled tin mugs.

We ate well. Full course, meat-and-potatoes meals and dessert every night. At least twice a week we had rice and curry or other Pakistani dishes—which were usually better than Khan Zaman's efforts to imitate Western cooking. We had our own names for these efforts—"monkey grits" for the finger-shaped hamburger patties, "fish-eye sauce" for gooseberry pudding—and we told each other gross stories about the origins of "yellow jello" and other mystery dishes.

After supper and a short free time for outdoor games, we climbed the stairs back to the Little Boys department for a bedtime story and "devotions." We sat on the carpet in the playroom while Auntie Inger read us a chapter from a Hardy Boys mystery, or some other children's adventure book. Before praying together, there was an inspirational reading and something from the Bible. Then we were all encouraged to make prayer requests. There was a certain status in having the most dire situation that needed to be "lifted up" in prayer, whether it was an illness in one's family or a problem at one of our parents' mission stations. Maybe a new hospital wing needed funding or permits from the government had been delayed; and, of course, there was the over-arching goal of getting the Pakistanis saved. Sometimes our parents wrote about one of our Pakistani friends who was sick and we prayed about that. I always felt the other kids had much more exciting prayer requests than I could come up with. My dad was just an agriculture teacher; he wasn't urgently saving lives or saving souls.

One boy got to lead off the time of voluntary, out loud prayers and then Auntie Inger closed. She always began, *"Our gracious heavenly Father . . ."* and ended with, *". . . in the name of your precious Son, Jesus, Amen."* I learned to be thankful, as well as asking for God's help, and to be concerned about the needs of those far away, as well as for those "near and dear." These times of prayer closed our daily routine with a comforting reminder that even in our most private moments we were not alone.

(APRIL 8, 1966)   M.C.S., UPPER TOPA,
                              MURREE HILLS
     DEAR MOM AND DAD. I HOPE THAT YOU
ARE FINE. I AM FINE HOW IS MIRIAM. WE
PLAYED SPACEMAN IN THE HOSTEL ON A
RAINNY DAY. WE DREST IN OUR RAIN COTES
AND LIED DOWN ON THE BOCK'S AND HAD

THE COUNT DOWN AS YOU KNOW, AND THEN
WE PRETENDED TO GO UP. WIN WE RECH
THE MOON WE GOT OUT AND STARED TO
WALK WIN A MOON MONSTER CAME AFTER
US AN CHASTE US ALL THE WAY TO EARTH
AND THAT WAS THE END OF THAT GAME.
                                LOVE, PAUL

We had to write home every week. I loved getting letters from Mom and Dad, but writing to them was a real bother. I usually only wrote as much as the teacher made me, then filled the page up with Xs and Os for "hugs and kisses." Lots of things happened in boarding, of course. Some, maybe it was better if my parents didn't hear about. Some, I didn't know how to put into words, anyway. One week went like this:

On Monday I pooped in my pants because I couldn't get them down fast enough. They were the kind I was supposed to grow into and to keep them up I had to wrap the belt—also way too big—around one of the beltloops several times. But when I had to go it knotted stuck. Boy, was that embarrassing!

Tuesday, I got my mouth washed out with soap for lying. The teacher took me over to the numbered rack where all the tin drinking cups hung in rows just inside the front entrance of the school. First she told me that this was good, clean American soap, so it wouldn't hurt me, then instructed me to stick out my tongue. After she rubbed that nice white bar of American soap across my tongue a couple of times she told me to rinse my mouth out. Of course, that made it worse as the soap sudsed up.

On Wednesday during recess I was playing on the wooden monkey bars between the principal's house and the new basketball court. I was trying to skip *two* bars on every swing going across—a real accomplishment—but going through the middle I slipped and tore my knee on a long bolt that fastened the center braces together. It gouged my knee so deep, I could see white stuff that I thought was the bone. And it really hurt. My sister Ruth got me cleaned up and took me to the school nurse, and I was back in class the same afternoon. The teacher told the other kids not to feel sorry for me because I hadn't asked permission to use the monkey bars so I shouldn't have been up there.

On Thursday afternoon an unfamiliar woman showed up at the hostel with some of our missionary parents—an event in itself, in the middle of a term. It was *Major Goodman's* wife, and the school was all abuzz about her visit, as if the U.S. ambassador had dropped by, or something. A while back, one of our mothers had written about an American Army major, a friend of the family, who had been captured in Vietnam. For a year now, gathered in our pajamas and bathrobes close around Auntie Inger, we had prayed almost every night that "our" POW would be released. Then Mrs. Goodman had come, and in chapel Friday morning she announced that her husband had died in prison; she was traveling to Vietnam to reclaim the body.

We sat on the long wooden pews, our feet barely touching the floor of that big, cold room—half sanctuary, half gymnasium—and did not comprehend.

"But why, Auntie Inger?" we asked in devotions that night. "You said that God answers prayers."

"Well, you prayed that he would get out of prison," she told us in her unflappable way, "and he did. He's gone to be with the Lord."

Fridays were always supervised game night and we played Kick the Can, Run Sheep Run, or Flashlight Beckon out in front of the hostel, with boys and girls playing together. But this April week-end had started out cold. Snow flurries on Friday afternoon confined us to the playroom.

Our favorite indoor game was Blowout! Whoever was picked as leader went around the circle and whispered the name of some part of an automobile in each boy's ear. Then he started walking around the outside of the circle telling the story of a road trip and the many mishaps that would invariably occur. When he spoke the name of an auto part, the boy who had been given that part got up and followed him. This went on till nearly all of us were following the leader around, waiting for him to say it, and around some more, and then he would suddenly yell "BLOWOUT!" and we all jumped into a pile on top of each other.

Tonight David Churnside, who was a "big" third grader but actually smaller than most of us, got to be leader. This was a pain because, being from Scotland, he always used the British names— like "bonnet" instead of hood—and it was hard to keep it all straight listening to his story. Being kind of shy he didn't talk very loud, either, but he always wove the most elaborate adventures and it took forever for him to get to the big moment. When it came, instead of jumping in first, David squealed, "*blowout!*" and quietly stepped back so that he wouldn't be crushed in the heap. Some of us thought this was unfair and wanted to tackle him anyway, but David was popular so he got away with it, and stood to the side smirking to himself.

After game night all the grade school kids gathered in the dining room for a special treat of hot chocolate and—if we were really lucky—homemade fudge. Gene Stoddard agreed to polish David Churnside's shoes in exchange for his piece of fudge. Gene hid the extra piece under his pillow to eat later, but forgot about it till the next morning. All that remained was a big brown spot on the sheet and on the underside of his pillow. This amused us all terribly.

"Aaaaa-eeee-aaaah," cried Tim Old, "Stoddard pooped on his pillow!" Even Dale couldn't help smiling.

Saturday, after morning devotions and breakfast, we did our chores. Each of us had a special assignment such as sorting the laundry or cleaning the bathroom. We kept getting distracted, though, with contests to see who could peel the most skin off someone else's back. The Saturday before, because of the water shortage, we had taken the bus down to the Jhelum River for a bath and a swim. The Little Girls department had gone, too, and on the trip down their boarding mother led us in singing folk songs. Auntie Eunice sang really sweetly—we could hear her down the hall in the hostel; and we all wanted to marry her when we grew up because she was so pretty.

Two of the best songs Auntie Eunice taught us were "The Happy Wanderer" (*I love to go a-wandering along the mountain track . . .*), with the chorus that goes, *Valderi, valdera-hah-hah-hah, my knapsack on my back,* and "The Little Dutch Boy":

Oh Mister, Mister Johnny Rebeck, how could you be so mean?
Now all the neighbors' cats and dogs will never more be seen
They'll all be ground to sausage meat in Johnny Rebeck's machine!

We sang this one gleefully, enjoying the change from boring Sunday School choruses like "Jesus Loves the Little Children," and "Do Lord"—which was fun, but we sang it *all the time.*

And soon we were at the river. The school bus pulled off to the side of the road just past the big stone bridge that marked the halfway point between Murree and Rawalpindi. With the bus leaning so close to the hillside, there was barely room to get out. We hiked down a steep rocky trail into the ravine about 150 feet below the road. The terrain was different on this side of the bridge, barren and rocky with dry grasses and prickly scrub. And it was hot.

Here, the river's head-long rush out of the mountains slowed into wonderful deep pools and rapids that weren't dangerous but offered plenty of thrills for seven- and eight-year-olds. The chilly water took some getting used to. We climbed big boulders along the shore and jumped into the river from rocks higher than we were tall. We played in steep backwater crevices. And we all got thoroughly sunburned. For some reason, the trip back up to the bus always seemed three times as far.

A week later we were ripe enough to be flayed alive. We competed to see who could peel the biggest patch of dead skin off someone else's back—a far more interesting project than cleaning up your room on Saturday morning. The largest strip was almost a foot long.

Eventually we got our bedsheets changed and our rooms properly dusted and swept. Then Auntie Inger came around to inspect, wearing a white glove to check for dust on top of closets and over the door. "White glove inspections" were standard procedure every Saturday throughout my time at MCS. Auntie Inger awarded points to each room and to each individual for clean hands before dinner, for how neatly clothes were folded in our drawers, for how carefully our beds were made up, and for remembering to brush our teeth. At the end of the term the room with the most points got an ice cream party. That spring our room won and I got a special individual award, a toy derringer pistol. I cherished that prize—a real working cap gun with an engraved handle of polished metal—till I lost it or traded it away for something that seemed more important at the moment.

Trading stuff was an important ritual at MCS. Comics, marbles, candy, and matchbox cars were all high-traffic items, supplemented by things we bought at the summer barter sale: a toy bow-and-arrow set or a compass. You got in trouble, though, if you "gypped" someone too obviously, like getting a bicycle speedometer for three sticks of licorice. A "feastings" exchange had the advantage of "no give backs"—you could eat it all before someone complained about an unfair deal.

"Feastings" were the special treats our parents sent to boarding with us, like homemade peanut brittle, fudge, and cookies. "Care-package friends" were common at MCS. The afternoon a parcel of edibles arrived from home, kids who'd sneered at you in the morning would hover around promising to be your best friend for at least a week, and some of us were hungry enough for such assurances to let ourselves be taken advantage of.

In a way, it was because of feastings that I got saved. It had happened one Sunday afternoon the previous fall. Robert Lotze had a huge stash of goodies that he kept in the bottom drawer of his dresser. My feastings were long since gone and, besides, he had real candy bars and American Tootsie Rolls. I waited till the other kids had all gone out to play after nap time, then slipped open the drawer. It wasn't the first time I had helped myself, but today Auntie Inger walked in and caught me chocolate-handed. As punishment—while the other boys were out playing Three Feet in the Mud Puddle or building "dinky towns" for their matchbox cars on the hillside behind the hostel—I had to stay on my bed for an extra half hour. Afterwards Auntie Inger called me into her room and asked me if I'd ever accepted Jesus Christ as my personal Savior. I wanted to, but was too shy to do it in front of her so I went back to the scene of my guilt, kneeled down beside my bunkbed and said the magic prayer: *Dear Lord Jesus, please wash away my sins and come into my heart. Amen.*

The next day, when it was time to compose our weekly letters home in class, I wrote:

DEAR MAMMY AND DADDY ON HOLWEN WE
HAD FUN. WE WINT TO THE HOSTEL FOR A
SPOK-HOUSE. ON SUNDAY I ACCEPTED THE
LORD. WE HAD SALT-METE IT TASTE LIKE
HAM AND IT LOOKS LIKE HAM. THE IND.
xxxxxxxxXXXXXXXooooooooooOOOOOOOOOOO.

My usually-mean second grade teacher got very tender with me when she read this letter and wanted to know if it was really true. I can't say if there was much outward sign of my "conversion," since our daily routine involved morning and evening devotions, Bible lessons during the school day, chapel services every Friday morning, Sunday school, church, *and* "singspiration" on Sunday evenings. But we were brought up to understand that being born again was *the* critical event of our lives. So I had passed an important milestone; the sudden approving attention from adults was nice, too. Otherwise, I didn't feel any different.

The weather had warmed up by lunch time—much to our relief—and Auntie Inger said we could skip our usual Saturday afternoon nap time so we could get an early start on the hike. Today was a special picnic "tea" for all the boys who had birthdays that month. The boarding cooks had made a big cake and filled a couple of big plastic containers with Kool-Aid, which we lugged with us. Auntie Inger was usually the only adult to accompany these hikes, but she never had any trouble. Sometimes we took the main road down to the golf links by the old Golf Hotel, but usually, like today, we went up "around the hill."

Sandes Home, the high school boys' dorm, was on the other side of this hill, up in the woods; in between—strictly off limits—were some of the officers' quarters for the Pakistan Army's summer training camp next to our school. The roads to Murree on the other hill and to Rawalpindi on the plains, the one to the Kashmir border and the main road to MCS, all came together in Jhika Gali, a run-down bazaar just a mile from the school. But a three-mile private road serving the Army camp wound around the other side of the hill behind the school and connected again at Jhika Gali. This was "our" road.

We spread out for almost half a mile along the winding lane that rose into the forest, each with a best friend, while Auntie Inger and the littlest boys brought up the rear. Every once in awhile some bossy goody-goody would be sent to tell the ones out front to wait up.

We brought along old copies of *Life* magazine and old school notebooks, and when we reached "lookout point," our favorite cliff, we stopped to make paper airplanes. From the retaining wall at the edge of the road the hillside fell away sharply into a steep, rocky meadow with pine trees crowding on either side. We made jets and gliders and stunt planes—there weren't that many different designs, really; the trick was in the weight of the paper or the slight curl of a wingtip. Gliders were best; I made them exactly the same way every time—lining up the edges of the paper and making sure the folds were even—so it was a mystery why some flopped and some floated so beautifully. But when the launch was good and the wind was right, that little paper plane would hang over the valley like a kite, soaring for an endless moment before tipping into a slow spiral and making a near-horizontal landing.

After we each threw some, we scrambled down the steep "khud" around the side of the big overlook to pick up our scattered aircraft, noting the most successful ones to throw again. After three or four rounds of this, we headed on for "Birthday Rock," a huge boulder beside the road that was one of our landmarks. We called it that because it was roughly round and flat on top and, well, looked like a big cake. Our actual destination was another flat rock down in the woods where we gathered to eat our real birthday cake.

The forests around Murree, filled mostly with huge old pines, were scavenged by woodcutters and goat herders; there was almost no underbrush. Beneath well-spaced trees—except for the occasional thicket of saplings—rolling grassy slopes were broken by rocky outcroppings. Where the woods were more dense, dry pine needles covered the ground—often as slippery as wet moss or the clay edges of underground springs. In the dip between every couple of ridges a stream coursed its way down toward the valley far below.

We set up our birthday picnic beside one of these streams and after wolfing down the cake we set about making dams. We used loose rocks and pebbles, twigs, dry grass, and thick sludge from the stream bed. The prime spot for a dam was a narrow rocky gap at the top of a twenty-foot drop. There was already a small pond here with another little waterfall feeding into it. The older boys claimed this spot and set to work. After a while four or five "locks" had been created in a chain going back a hundred yards upstream. Auntie Inger wandered back and forth giving advice, breaking up quarrels, or hunting for flowers with those who didn't want to get muddy. Tim and Dale and I smoothed our dam over with clay and along the top molded a road for our dinky cars. We placed plastic soldiers at either end as sentries and put toy boats in the miniature lake that had built up.

When all the dams were finished, we gathered eagerly by the two furthest upstream and, with ritual deliberation, busted them open. The sudden release of water rushed down upon the other dams like a great natural disaster: tiny boats swirled around furiously; hapless soldiers were flung over the edge; and cars tumbled into the swollen torrent. We all ran along the stream, watching one dam and then another give way. The master dam slowly cracked as its carefully-packed clay began to slide against the onslaught, then crumbled all at once. With a tremendous gush, the combined backup of water and accumulated debris burst into the chasm below.

It was hairy cool as all get out.

The whole business had taken only a couple of hours and we pleaded with Auntie Inger to let us hike in the woods some more. She consented, and we walked and walked, exploring the terrain in private adventures or in a group pretending together: Tarzan and pirates and the last of the Mohicans. William Tell, with his famous crossbow, was my own favorite hero. We hiked down to a lower road where we'd never been before. On the way back we were scattered pretty thin and some Pakistani boys stole David Hover's and David Churnside's sweaters. Hover and "Churnsey" had left their sweaters on a rock while they played and saw them being taken. The Pakistani boys didn't seem to be much bigger than us and we tried to go after them, but they threw rocks at us. I got hit by one. I wasn't hurt, but it was enough to turn us back—though we still talked big about what we would do if we caught the dirty thieves.

Auntie Inger scolded us for trying to follow them—it might have been dangerous. She sympathized about my getting hit, though, and said I was brave. That made me feel important, and it seemed like it would have been okay if I'd been hit harder. Auntie Inger was angry about the sweaters getting stolen, but wouldn't tolerate any of our name-calling. She said we should have a Christian attitude toward those who wrong us, and reminded us that the Pakistanis were a lot poorer than we were.

We got back late for supper. It felt cool to "break a rule" and not get into trouble for it. Promptness was a priority in boarding and our lives were regulated by the bell that hung on a tree in front of the hostel. At the sound of the dinner gong we reluctantly would leave our play and go in to wash up. Then we lined up to have our hands inspected and, at the second bell, raced back downstairs. Dinner often began with a stern lecture—especially if a guest visiting the school happened to have the misfortune of passing through the hall at the moment of our blind dash for the dining room. *You ought to be ashamed of yourselves, charging down the stairs like a herd of buffaloes; is that any way for Christian children to act?* I never saw a guest buffeted by our "stampede," but the staff member on duty convinced us that our reckless behavior had put the school's reputation in jeopardy—to say nothing of our "Christian witness."

Saturday night was movie night. The whole school gathered in the dining room and we got to sit with our older sisters or brothers. We didn't see much of them during the week because they were in different boarding departments. Mostly, we watched educational films from the United States Information Service, documentaries about the Guinness Book of Records, the wheat fields of Kansas, or climbing Mount Everest. The most violent feature we saw was a crazy cartoon about the body's war on germs.

Afterwards we returned to our separate departments for bedtime devotions. Because it was so late after the movies we just had a quick prayer together and then Auntie Inger said, "Okay boys, I want you to go to the bathroom, brush your teeth, fill your hot water bottles and get right to bed. It's been a long day."

"Does that mean no kissing fights, too?" someone asked.

"That's what it means. You've probably had enough fun for one day."

"Aaww, Auntie Inger, but we didn't have one last night," I said, hoping she wouldn't remember.

"Boys, you know I'm really tired. And it's late," Auntie Inger repeated. "Now get going."

Instead, Tim jumped on her back. "Aaaaa-eeee-aaaaa!" he said, "Giddee-yup!" Before she had time to get cross, suddenly there were several of us at her feet, pulling at her legs. Another boy jumped on her back. "Wait! My glasses . . ." was all she could think of to say, and Dale carefully took them from her outstretched hand. Then she was on the floor. Someone yelled "DRAG OUT!" and the whole department was there, grabbing an arm or a leg. We dragged her down the hall—all the way to the next department and back to the playroom.

After that, whenever someone yelled, "DRAG OUT!," Auntie Inger was a goner. Another tradition had been born. Like kissing fights—just one more nice, quiet way to get ready for bed.

It was about a month later that Auntie Inger broke her nose. And we didn't do it. She was taking care of the sixth grade girls one night when their boarding mother had the night off. They had heard about our famous kissing fights and Suzy Pietsch asked if they could have one. A little girl from New Zealand got too exuberant, and before Auntie Inger had gotten properly up onto the upper bunk, she charged her head-first. Auntie Inger was knocked off the bed and fell on her face.

We'd never seen a nose cast before. We felt bad for Auntie Inger, of course, but we also worried that the boarding supervisor might ban kissing fights—there were rules against every other imaginable danger or corruption; but Auntie Inger was back at it less than two weeks later. "I was having too much fun," she told me years later, "to let a little thing like a broken nose stop me."

❁

Auntie Inger remained close in our hearts long after we left her department and was famous throughout the school for her energy and affection. When I was in seventh grade, the school had the best game of Capture the Flag that I've ever been in. One Saturday afternoon the entire junior and senior high departments got together, including several staff members. Auntie Inger participated too.

A young Mennonite named John Unrau was the new boarding father for the high school boys that term and had the misfortune to be on the opposing team to Auntie Inger's. He was astounded by her spunk and skill in avoiding capture, even if she couldn't run fast. "I hope I can be as good at this as you are!" he exclaimed.

Around that time Auntie Inger started taking piano lessons from Auntie Rosie Stewart and that spring she was a special participant in the student music recital. After she finished her selection—something, I'm sure, not much more complicated than "Chopsticks"—she gave a little bow, and brought the house down. It was the biggest standing ovation the school had ever seen.

In 1976, the graduating class from our original group held an "Auntie Inger Day." Auntie Inger was no longer a boarding mother then; she was working at Bach hospital in Abbottabad. When she came up for the event, they relived those old walks up the road, around the hill, throwing paper airplanes off our special point, then going down into the woods to make a dam. I had left Pakistan by then, but heard about the event later.

The girls had come along this time and, watching the high school boys building an intricate dam at the edge of a deep and dangerous-looking drop off, one of them said to Auntie Inger, "It's a good thing you didn't let them build dams here when they were little!"

Auntie Inger laughed and replied: "This *is* the exact same spot where they built their dams when they were my little boys."

3

Train Party

My parents worked in a Punjabi village-turning-town called Raiwind, thirty miles south of Lahore. My mother was a nurse; my father taught agriculture at the Christian mission school and ran an experimental farm that was an outpost of the Green Revolution then sweeping the Third World. Our red brick ranch-style house was about a mile from the main railway line —just close enough to hear the faint, breathy chugging of freight locomotives and the clickity-whisk of passenger trains making their way across the landscape. The deep sigh of their whistles tracked the passage of time, day and night, a wistful counterpoint to the muted pounding of diesel-driven wheat mills, the squeaky see-saw sound of Persian wheels pumping water into neatly-squared irrigation ditches, and the slow circling of oxen or camels tramping round and round the threshing floor. These slow rhythms filled the days and nights, filled the green, near-treeless plains of mustard fields and rice paddies, and each train passed by like a lazy horsefly through a room full of softly creaking rocking chairs.

It did not seem exotic. Maybe the vast deserts of Sind had a kind of severe beauty, as did Baluchistan's barren mountains that stretched all the way up to the Khyber Pass, creating a natural border between Pakistan and Afghanistan; but the Punjab was all farmland and bureaucracy. A sophisticated network of canals—the largest irrigation system in the world when the British built it—stretched between proud Moghul cities, weaving the remnants of dead empires into "the breadbasket of Pakistan."

As a major railway junction, Raiwind station was a popular bombing target during both wars with India. For passenger trains it was just another whistle stop; and express trains, if they stopped there at all, did so for only momentarily. Once, when my three sisters and I came back from boarding, we hadn't gotten all our luggage off when the train started pulling out. Dad was frantically throwing footlockers off the train all the way down the platform till finally leaping off himself. After that, when it was time to return to school in March, we took the mission Land-Rover the hour's drive into Lahore to connect with the MCS train party in a slightly less hectic way.

On trips to Lahore we sometimes got stuck at the level crossing just outside the city, where the train tracks crossed the Grand Trunk Road. The "G. T." Road was a national highway that followed the main rail line from Karachi on the coast up to Peshawar in the North-West Frontier Province. Once, stuck behind a gate that had been closed prematurely, we watched the train we were trying to catch pass by. But most of the time these delays were merely a sweltering nuisance. The "level crossings" were never actually level, usually consisting of a sharp "S" curve and an incline that brought the road up to the raised track bed at a proper right angle. A heavy backup at these places seemed more often like a carnival than a traffic jam. Zealous vendors came around to all the waiting buses and cars, selling pretty bangles and pocket knives, and all kinds of sweets. But at night—especially on less-traveled secondary roads—you prayed not to encounter a closed level crossing. Sometimes the gatekeeper locked the gate and went to bed, and Dad had to go and find him. Even though the trains usually ran an hour or more late, the gates were faithfully locked according to the printed schedule.

Lahore is the capital of the Punjab, Pakistan's most populous and powerful province. A thousand years old and renowned for its Islamic art and architecture, Lahore is also the cultural center of Pakistan. Beyond its ragged hem of beggarly tenements, the city boasts prestigious universities, women's colleges, technical schools, and music academies. The conspicuously-manicured lawns of Gulberg's Western-style suburbs blend into the busy-thick bazaars of Old Anarkali. Moghul monuments stand beside glass-walled banks, and both are dwarfed by the gleaming white, space-age sweep of the power company's new office building.

The last empire to rent Lahore was the British, and its aggressive tenancy is evident in the dusty Victorian architecture of government and academic buildings, more functional versions of the "gingerbread" palaces of Bombay and Calcutta. Further out the tree-lined sweep of Mall Road are the polo fields, racecourse, and country clubs of colonial leisure that have so smoothly slipped into the hands of Pakistan's elite. "Kim's Gun," named for the young hero of Rudyard Kipling's famous novel, still sits across from the Lahore Museum, where Kipling's father was curator. The celebrated cannon is now isolated on a narrow traffic median, almost lost among the pressing urban scramble; but to a ten-year-old boy it still had the power of great adventures, and Dad took a photograph of me sitting astride its long brass barrel.

The Lahore Railway Station, its castle towers rising behind the black-and-silver shrubbery of a thousand parked bicycles, faces a busy downtown roundabout. Horn-blaring buses, screeching taxis, horse-drawn *tongas* form a crazy carousel. Little motor rickshaws, with their deviously tiny two-passenger seats, dart in and out; an entire family, seemingly with half their worldly belongings, is packed into the cloth-flimsy cab of one of these three-wheeled scooters; five white-turbaned farmers cling to each other in another, balancing an assortment of seed bags and a goat.

When our big, cream-colored Land-Rover pulls up to the station entrance we are swarmed by beggars and insistent coolies. Inside, the air is thick with the warm smell of deep fried *pakoras* (vegetable pastries) and *samosas,* sweaty bodies, dirty clothes, and exotic perfumes. Color and motion fill the station, filtered through smoke and bright shafts of morning sunlight. The creams and grays of village dress jostle with Western suits on Pakistani businessmen; brown military jerseys highlight khaki against a cluster of green and white private school jumpers fastened to shiny smart girls; black full-length *burkas* cover traditional Muslim women observing *purdah;* and the dull flame of soiled coolie uniforms flickers in swirling red lines along the platform.

A couple of coolies carry our trunks and suitcases piled high on their heads, well-cushioned under great scarlet turbans. My father has prudently copied down the porter number from the brass badges on their arm bands. I race ahead to find Tim Old. As soon as we spot each other we go wild, leaping at each other, hugging and pounding and kicking with mock hostility. But even the urgent tales and well-practiced banter eventually wind down, giving way to the restless limbo of waiting for a train that is all-too-reliably late.

Finally the *Khyber Mail* arrives, pulled proudly by a great, puffing steam engine. The huge black barrel of its boiler swells into the station, hissing and clicking importantly as it passes us on the platform. Carriages bang and clatter against each other as the train squeals to a stop.

We push into the doughy mass, all urgent and inevitable, till we find relief in the sanctuary of our reserved compartment. After eight train parties, going to boarding or coming home, it is a familiar routine. On the platform, vendors cry out in their hoarse, nasal drone: *Chai, garum chai! Ice cream wallah; eyezzzz ka-reem wallah!* Tea, hot tea . . . ice cream, while beggars pester for *baksheesh.* The greatest show on earth: right here—fresh fruit! Step right up. See strange and wonderful things—nowhere else. You there! Buy something? Bye-bye. The train pulls out while the vendors are still haggling, insisting, hurriedly exchanging rumpled paper packets of sweet *jalabees* or salty nuts for rupees or paisa. Tea cups are handed back, empty or not.

This time, I do not get up when Dad reaches out to say good-bye and he leans awkwardly under the overhead bunk to give me a hug. I smile reassuringly and turn my gaze back to Mom who is already waving from the platform. I don't want to seem clingy. What would the guys think of Dad's emotional farewells? Once again, Dad jumps off at the last minute, landing awkwardly at a stumbling trot so as not to lose his balance. At the end of the platform he stops and waves his hat, the one he bought to wear to funerals, but it's really too hot for Pakistan. I watch till he fades into the city haze then pull my head in. Leaning back into the seat, I wonder for the first time how long my father stood there after the train had gone.

The train picks up speed, *thkk-thkk . . . thkk-thkk . . .* SHEW-WOOOOO, TOOT-TOOT! And with the whistle's signal we glide away into our own separate world. This year, my parents had taken us to Karachi for a week's vacation at the beach just before it was time to go back to boarding. We took camel rides, collected shells, and followed turtle tracks. We saw giant sea turtles minding their eggs, and watched brand new baby turtles push out of their sandy cradles and scurry down to the ocean. I couldn't wait to tell the guys all about it. And when the station master rang the big brass bell announcing our train's departure it reminded me of the dinner gong at school.

It would be cold in Murree. Maybe there would still be snow on the ground, and the *chowkidar* would have to shovel a path to where the bell hung from the big tree in front of the hostel, so one of the cooks could come out and ring it. I wonder how many times a day the bell was rung: wake-up call, breakfast, start of school, lunch, the five-minute-wash-up warning that called us in from play, and then the dinner bell . . . Even if there is no fresh snow, the huge drifts or piles that always slid off the roof of the school would provide ample material for building a fort.

The thought of snow-ball fights melts into the dusty heat of the train. In early March, the plains are already summer-hot. By habit, I watch the landscape slip by: wall after wall of dirty white-washed tenements with small, barred windows and courtyards facing the tracks, where children and women come up to the railroad embankment to defecate, turning their exposed bottoms away from the city as if *we* were not there. At the main level crossings traffic is backed up two miles: cars, tongas, buses, and wildly painted trucks, end-to-end with bullock carts stacked with hay to impossible heights.

Outside of Lahore we cross the Ravi River on a stone arch bridge that looks like a Roman aqueduct. Looking back, I can see the massive red clay towers of the famous gate to Lahore Fort. Then the endless salt plains . . . wheat fields . . . and a horizon as wide and flat as the ocean.

A couple of hours pass, and just before Gujrat we cross the Chenab River, almost a mile wide. Day or night, there is no mistaking the loud clatter of the long metal bridge: crossed support beams whip by like a passing train, as if all the windows and doors of the train had suddenly been flung open. Tim and I jostle with other boys for the thrill of sitting on the steps of a gaping doorway and looking down to the river below. Beyond the shoulders of older boys and the fast-flicking racket of bridge girders, the rusty stone pilings of an old bridge glide past above pale mud flats. The dry-season river, shrunken into sluggish brown fingers, winds through a splotchy green flood plain laced with winter wheat; then solid ground again, up close, and the quiet rush of air.

Lunch consists of dry sandwiches and fruit, and Kool-Aid out of big blue dispensers that tastes of plastic, even through the sweetening.

When the afternoon reaches the restless side we cross the Jhelum River. Shortly after that the train stops, to wait for another train to pass we suppose. We idle in the dry countryside for an hour and then another. It turns out the train has hit a water buffalo. Tim Old and I wander along the track, seeing how far we can go before one of the staff chaperons calls us back.

"Let's put some coins on the track!" I suggest. This was a favorite pastime whenever a few of us found ourselves near a railroad line. Then we'd wait for a train to come by and press our one-paisa or ten-paisa pieces into foil-thin ovals of tin or copper. Some of the boys said that putting coins on the track might cause a train to derail, but we did it anyway—with a slightly guilty thrill.

"We'll be gone when the train runs over them, stupid," Tim says.

"On the other track—*stupid*," I reply, pointing to the second line a few feet away. But Tim thinks this is a boring idea—probably because he didn't suggest it first.

Not really old enough to get permission, we risk defying the rules and walk up to the front. The great locomotive towers over us, trembling with power. Hissing in restless bursts. Steam sweats down its sides, glistening from the mass of black metal pipes, valves, cranks, and pistons. The engineer looks down like a knight from his horse. He wears a tattered brown military jacket over pajama-like Pakistani pants. His sinewy face and long white beard carry more authority than any uniform might have. Today we are lucky and he lets us climb up into the cab, which is suffocatingly hot from the boilers. The novelty quickly wears off.

And the dead buffalo is starting to stink. We head back to our own carriage. Eventually we are off again.

The thick yellow light of late afternoon tints the rolling grass-lands and little canyons with an antique glow. The rising, broken terrain offers the first sign of the approaching mountains, not yet visible. Snaked through with dry creek beds, these badlands always make me think of cowboys and Indians. I wish I could be down there exploring secret gullies, climbing the castle-like outcroppings of weathered rock and eroding earth. But we pass by.

Because of the delay, darkness falls while our destination is still three or four hours away. The order comes down from the adults that all the elementary children should unroll their *bister-bunds* and take a nap—or at least lie down on them. Some of us chafe at this slight to our maturity, but the small band from the Sind are only too happy to turn in. They have been on the train for twenty-four hours already, through desert heat and dust, some of them all the way from Karachi. Among each other, their superiority to those of us who have been on the train less than eight hours, is a given. But this elite camaraderie, born of mutual hardship, will last only as long as the circumstances that give it relevance. Tomorrow morning, when the train party is forgotten, other interests will effortlessly re-shuffle relationships and loyalties.

Bister-bunds are the Pakistani version of sleeping bags. A thin mattress, sheets, and blankets all fit into a canvas covering with a tuck of pockets at each end for pillows, pajamas, and toiletries. Slept in or not, they are an inseparable part of the train party ritual. I lie on the lower bunk next to the window, feeling the familiar rocking of the train, back and forth; the slickety-clack of the tracks almost merges with the whir of the overhead fan. Suddenly, the roar of a passing train, barreling through the night in the other direction, breaks the quiet, steady pitch of the carriage: WHHOOOSSHHH! The windows rattle loudly as shadows whip across the ceiling— *rumble-rumble-rumble-rumble*—then the roar fades abruptly, leaving an imagined echo in the vacuum.

Snuggling securely into my bister, I listen to the soothing sound of the tracks, *thkk-thkk . . . thkk-thkk . . . thkk-thkk . . .*

After that everything is a blur of disembarking the train, someone shouting, jostling through another station, and being herded onto the school bus. And then another kind of sound and rhythm lulls me back to sleep as the bus rises into the mountains, pulling us through the night, up the winding road, shuddering around hairpin turns, climbing ever upwards, till we are home. I drift through the dreamy chaos of trunks and suitcases in the narrow dormitory halls, find my room assignment for the new term, select the bunk I want— or settle for the one that is left—and roll out my bister. Auntie Inger says that since it was so late we don't have to make up our beds properly, just for tonight. After a quick good-night kiss, I huddle into the blankets, which smell of mothballs from their recent storage. All I can think about is how cold it is! And I wish I had taken the time to fill my hot water bottle.

When the lights are switched off, silence falls with the darkness. Each bunk is set adrift, a world unto itself. Before the shivering stops and sleep closes over me a terrifying loneliness pours into the void. I feel abandoned. In the nights to come we will whisper excitedly about important things or nothing in particular, to put off this moment as long as possible; but now everyone, dead tired, seems to have switched off the instant their heads hit the pillow.

Wake up, wake up! I cry silently. *Let me show you what I got for Christmas; tell me what great adventures you had during the winter break.* In the days to come I will revel in the freedom of the woods around the hostel, the wide open hillside with its constant surprises —packs of monkeys, mysterious holes, secret clay "mines" that supply the construction of our "dinky towns." I will treasure the invigorating privacy of escaping into imaginary adventures without interruption. But now I long for the carnival atmosphere of the train party, where we were all too busy racing around and laughing and arguing to think about what we were leaving behind and what might lie ahead.

What will this term be like? Will old friends hold true? Will I make new friends? The rhythm of the train lingers—like the way roller skates remain heavy on your feet even after you've taken them off. *Clickity-clack* . . . the train rolls down the tracks; my body sways imperceptibly as the train rocks back and forth inside of me, like the pendulum of a clock. The tracks unfold before me, tie after tie, slipping over the gravel stream, rails telescoping in endless extension, like ladders in seamless connection.

The last thing I remember is the jackals howling in the woods, strangely human—like old ladies cackling, we always described it—laughing at some joke I am not in on.

4

A Spy in the House of Love

When my grandfather died I wrote a poem about the bag of marbles he once gave me. It was the only thing I could remember getting from him. My dad's parents had both died before I was born, but because I was a missionary kid I didn't have grandparents anyway. My parents' job effectively deprived me of them during the years when I could have appreciated them the most.

The few times we visited her, Grandma Kunz lavished attention, gifts, and food on my sisters and me, like a proper grandmother. But Edward Kunz, long separated from my mom's mother, was a stern and solitary man. He is the subject of my earliest memory, in which he chases me through the house threatening to whip me because I put my fingers on the clean white walls.

When I was ten my family came back to the States for our first furlough after five years on the mission field. Traditionally, this was a three-month combination of vacation and "deputation"—making the rounds to supporting churches to assure their continued interest in missions. However, my father had been accepted into a graduate program at Cornell University in Ithaca, New York. So, my sisters and I attended school in America for a year.

Before settling in Ithaca, we spent the summer traveling. My father, who believed in good stewardship in all things, felt that we should take advantage of the opportunities afforded from living overseas. So, "for the sake of the children's cultural education," our family returned to America by way of the Far East—completing a trip around the world begun five years before. After visiting Bangkok and Hong Kong, we took a ship to San Francisco, by way of Japan and Hawaii. In California my parents purchased a used Chevy-II and this little white car carried us through Death Valley—in July—and across the United States. Its small roof rack bulged with three months worth of luggage for the six people crammed inside: one six-foot-three Dad, one already emotionally exhausted Mom, my two pre-teenage sisters, Ruth and Martha, three-year-old Miriam who had been born in Pakistan, and one exuberant boy turned bratty by the boredom of too many long hours on the road.

In the summer of 1968 America opened hugely before us; but in the confined space of our limited means, some social upheaval was inevitable. Miriam, being the smallest, always got to sit in the front seat. Martha and I failed to appreciate the physical dynamics involved in this arrangement, and thought this was immensely unfair. After voicing our opinion a few times too many we were forbidden to use the word "spoiled" with reference to Miriam. Not to be deterred, I simply dubbed her "Deliops" ("spoiled" spelled backwards), a nickname which Martha seized upon with even greater relish.

Mom occasionally exploded into *I-can't-stand-it-anymore* tirades, producing a temporary lull in our bickering that was more a hushed awe at such a display of fury than any real penitence. But these were small moments compared to Yosemite Valley, the Grand Canyon, Dodge City, and the "the Gateway to the West" monument on the Mississippi River: a great steel arch soaring high above the city of St. Louis like one of the seven wonders of the ancient world. By the time we reached Ithaca, New York, several weeks later, I had collected flannel pennants from fifteen states. Dad had carefully mapped out our itinerary like a connect-the-dots picture, linking relatives, tourist attractions, and supporting churches.

My parents talked in Sunday school classes or at special evening meetings, showing slides and displaying handicrafts to give a sense of life in Pakistan. And I felt as though my life was on exhibit, like an entry in a hobby show. I reveled in the blue ribbon attention—until the hundred-and-fifty-fifth "It must be really hard for you" or "My, how you've grown!" I never got tired of the potluck suppers, though —I was actually *encouraged* to eat as much as I wanted, even of desserts! And at least people didn't pinch our cheeks like they did when we were guests in a Pakistani's home.

Sometimes Dad spoke at Sunday morning services in churches bigger than I'd ever seen before and I listened proudly as "the Reverend Alan Seaman" was introduced. Then Dad stepped up into the high pulpit, wearing the black minister's robe and red stole which he almost never wore in Pakistan, and spoke to the congregation about the vital work of missionaries with humbleness, conviction, and authority. Like somebody important; and I felt important too.

When we visited my grandfather in Louisville, Kentucky, he gave me a small canvas sack full of marbles. He said he had dug them up over the years while gardening in his back yard. What a treasure! Grandpa had no idea what a gift he was giving me. At MCS the boys played "marbs" every day at recess and after school. Even if you weren't any good at the game (which I wasn't), it was fun to collect and trade—if you had any marbles worth trading. All I had were ordinary green swirls or solids purchased in the local bazaar. But here in Grandpa's little sack were over a hundred of the best American marbles: peppermint swirls, cat's eyes, clambroths, cloudies, and solids of all colors. I couldn't wait to get back to Pakistan. Even the older boys would pay attention to me now.

That year in the States I got a crash course in American culture: big cars, hot dogs, root beer, department stores, McDonald's, and, of course, a completely different kind of school. I had *three* different teachers—and one of them was a *man*. It felt like high school! I got used to the classes, but making friends was hard. Even with the kids who tried to be nice, it was hard to find things in common. Television was the single greatest change from life in Pakistan, a window into American styles, obsessions, and lingo. (*"You can take Salem out of the country, BUT—you can't take the country out of Salem."*) TV provided both a refuge from other American kids and something to talk about with them. I immediately took to "Batman," "Star Trek," "The Rat Patrol" and "Speed Racer." Ruth was enchanted by "Dark Shadows" and Martha fought to watch "Gilligan's Island." Mom found most of our favorite shows to be morally suspect and when the tubes died on our second-hand black and white set it was not replaced. I soon had memorized all the lyrics to every Peter, Paul and Mary song in our small collection of records. The repetition necessary to accomplish this feat drove my mother just as crazy as my sisters fighting over the TV.

But I learned to swim at the local YMCA, thanks to Mom, and got to be a Boy Scout for a year, winning several merit badges for camping skills. And Mom made sure I got to go to a summer camp with the "Y"—the very last week before our ship back to Pakistan was due to sail.

This time we visited Italy—the Coliseum, the Vatican, the Catacombs, Pompeii—and Barcelona, Spain, where we saw replicas of the tiny ships in which Columbus sailed to the New World in 1492. And because the Suez Canal was closed from the recent war between Israel and Egypt, our voyage took us the long way back, around Africa. From the Canary Islands to Capetown, South Africa, meant almost three weeks at sea with no land in sight. And later, a stopover in Mombasa, Kenya, allowed my family to take a one-day safari with another missionary couple. It was just like the John Wayne movie, *Hatari!*, about lion hunters in Tanganyika. We saw giraffes, elephants, warthogs (lots of them), gazelles, rhinoceroses, and a big herd of zebras running across the savanna. And a group of lions crossed the road right in front of our rented, zebra-striped VW microbus.

Our ship had its own movie theaters—two of them! Some afternoons I would sneak into the one in the first class section where off-duty crew members watched Italian spy movies featuring James Bond-style gadgets and lots of shapely, sultry, scantily-clad women. This was naturally much more entertaining than the children's matinees being offered in economy class. I had a glorious time: playing and swimming and watching free movies all afternoon, and getting to "eat out" at every meal. I hardly noticed that Dad spent most of his time in his cabin, catching up on correspondence and organizing his research. It was amazing, though, that even without an office full of pressing responsibilities, he still didn't have much time for me.

When my sisters and I got back to Murree, the fall term had already begun. Mom had made sure we spent part of each day on the ship studying to keep up with our school work, but our late arrival put me behind in more important ways. Most of my old friends were gone. Some of them, now in seventh grade, were in another boarding department—far away at Sandes Home—and saw themselves as high schoolers now, making them even further removed; others had just left for furlough with their families. For months I had been eager to share my new collection of marbles with my old mates, but discovered that sixth graders weren't that interested in marbs anymore.

The Middle Boys department was ruled by a new staff member, Jim Hunter, whose cold British manner was a big adjustment after Auntie Inger. The now-seventh grade boys whispered horror stories about the scars left from Uncle Jim's canings. By the time I arrived, though, he had apparently been persuaded to limit his favored corporal punishment to a leather slipper.

As the oldest ones in the department, being in the sixth grade—and there were only seven of us—should have meant some advantage in respect and influence. But I wasn't any good at basketball, or interested in the card games that occupied the other boys, and I found myself returning to the imaginary adventures I had so relished in earlier years.

Behind the hostel was a large, open courtyard where we usually ate lunch. An eight-foot retaining wall—like the ones that kept most of the roads in the area from sliding down the mountain—separated the picnic area from the steep, forested hillside below. At the bottom of this stone wall was a big scrap pile of wood and other materials left over from building the hostel. Stuffy staff members, fearing we would injure ourselves, tried to forbid us from playing here, but it was too much to resist. This pile offered a complete stage with all the props for a pirate ship or a castle parapet, a colonial stockade from which to fend off Indians or a "Rat Patrol" jeep equipped with a top-mounted machine gun. The tennis rackets my mother sent to boarding with me served alternatively as carbines for jungle commandos and snow shoes for Arctic explorers. The wall, with just enough cracks and bumps for fingers and toe holds, became an intimidating rock face for brave mountain climbers.

A real mountain climber visited MCS that year, a British missionary who people said had climbed many of the Himalayan peaks, maybe even Mount Everest. One afternoon I came over the wall with a couple of my fifth grade followers close behind, and there was the famous mountain climber sitting at one of the picnic tables having tea, and he asked me why I had two tennis rackets tucked in my belt. I explained, only a little self-consciously, about the snow shoes, knowing that he would understand.

The other sixth-graders didn't think much of my pretend games, but they became more interested when, after consulting illustrations in the encyclopedia, I built a working model guillotine that could chop a carrot in half pretty impressively. And once they agreed to participate in a play I wrote and directed.

I had a recorded adaptation of the Walt Disney movie, "Zorro." Using a little plastic phonograph and the song-memorization technique I perfected with Peter, Paul and Mary albums, I scripted a scaled-down version that could be produced within our limited means. I fashioned a pair of Spanish fencing swords by nailing the spokes from a broken umbrella to a palm-size block of wood. A round piece of cardboard was slipped firmly over top of this handle to make a pretty convincing hand guard. Best of all, during my duels with the evil army Captain, the metal umbrella ribs swished dramatically and made a very satisfying clack when struck against each other.

We set up a stage in the dining room one Saturday afternoon, complete with a prison cell and gallows made from stacked cafeteria tables. In the climactic scene, I must rescue my trusty sidekick from being hanged. I sneak onto the gallows platform disguised as a monk come to offer last rites. I throw off my monk's robe, send the guards fleeing with a flourish of my sword, and quickly untie the mute Bernardo. A lengthy duel with "El Capitan" ends with him quivering beneath my blade. Then, before galloping off on Gene Stoddard's back, I raise my victorious rapier high and grandly pronounce: *"My sword is aflame to right every wrong, so heed well my name—ZORRO!"*

Auntie Inger said afterwards that it was the best play she had ever seen put on by boarding students.

For my classmates, the experience had been a novelty and they went back to their regular games—things for which I had about as long an attention span as they did for my imaginary worlds. Solitary adventures weren't just the response of someone tired of always getting chosen last for team games. They served me well during the long, three-month winter holidays when I was the only English-speaking boy at my parents' mission station.

Space travel and James Bond were the primary things that captured my imagination that winter. And compared with American presses, the British offered a far superior line of books geared toward eleven-year-olds, including a variety of *Boys' World* "Annuals." I saved up my allowance or birthday money and on the next family trip to Lahore eagerly visited the big English language bookstore downtown. I found a James Bond edition of one of these Boys' Annuals with comic versions of four of the 007 films as well as "Top Secret" files about secret agents and their gadgets.

I even created my own spy attache case. Mom let me have an old wooden silverware case with a red velvet lining, and the looped slots in its cover made perfect placements for a magnifying glass, Exacto knives, and other spy paraphernalia. I peeled out the inside lining of the bottom, cut out a piece of very thin, finished particle board (like clipboards are made of), that my dad let me have, and glued the lining onto the board. The result was a very effective false bottom where I could keep my rocket diagrams and code books. I wanted to get a rubber stamp made with the words "TOP SECRET" on it; but Dad didn't think that would be appropriate—because it might confuse the already spy-paranoid Pakistani bureaucracy and get us in trouble. So I settled for an imprint of a logo I designed for my own secret spy organization.

When I returned to boarding in March, the new spy case was my most important possession. Unfortunately, I didn't think to stash the James Bond album among its secret contents. When Uncle Jim Hunter saw this book he promptly confiscated it. One photo, from *You Only Live Twice,* among a series of full-page movie stills of 007 in action, showed Bond being bathed by several bikini-clad Japanese maidens. (Honestly, a picture of smirking older women stupidly posing in their underwear didn't exactly hold my interest.)

Uncle Jim couldn't confiscate my imagination, though, and I quickly set about organizing a network of secret agents. Being ahead of my time, I saw no reason why girls shouldn't be included in the ring, since they could spy without being suspected. And Elaine Roub, the principal's daughter, was the obvious first choice. Elaine and I had played together before my family had gone on furlough. She was a great story-teller and together we acted out complicated sagas, usually about an orphaned brother and sister, long separated, who are finally reunited (we just pretended to hug, though, feeling too self-conscious to do more than mime the gestures of a joyful embrace).

My first message to Elaine went like this:

> CODE: 14850 CROSSFILE: AN03 SUBJECT: RECRUITING AGENTS. CLASSIFIED: = TOP SECRET = MESSAGE: THIS IS TO INFORM YOU THAT YOU HAVE BEEN ACCEPTED AS A PRIMARY-LEVEL AGENT IN THE SERVICE OF "TOPS" (THE ORGANIZATION FOR PHANTOM SPIES). REPORT FOR DUTY AT 4:30 PM BEHIND THE HOSTEL. ENDIT. SIGNED: 005.

Soon after activating my new spy ring, I had a running "cold war" going with the fifth graders. I had three agents among the sixth grade boys, two counter-agents from the fifth grade, and two seventh grade girls. (Elaine had picked 00X as her code name because of her own fascination with the fictional French spy, "M'amselle X.") There were no sixth grade girls in the ring because there were no sixth grade girls that year.

One day I arrived back at the dorm to discover that my spy case was missing. This was a major security breach, maybe even a national crisis. I had hidden the case in our sixth grade bedroom, in a spot where I was sure the fifth graders would never find it, but a hasty investigation located it in their room. I quickly noted with relief that it was still locked—but with an added dimension: it was also locked to the bedpost. A truce conference was held and I discovered that all my agents, except the two seventh grade girls, were traitors. The fifth grade ring leader had been one hour's step ahead of me in getting recruits. And now, alas, the only course that remained to me was to acknowledge defeat—under the condition that I get my attache case back.

The hurt I felt from this humiliation was far from imaginary. I had been so glad to have the guys play my game for a change, only to find that they were just mocking me. I didn't understand why. Times like this were also a painful reminder of the almost total lack of privacy in boarding. Since it wasn't nearly bedtime, I couldn't even retreat to my own bunk without it being obvious that I was "feeling sorry for myself." No one would actually have to call me a sissy.

A few of us knew about a crawl-space between the ceiling and the next floor that could be accessed by a loose insulation panel at the top of the linen closet in the hall. This is where I went, and my tears fell in puffy plops onto the dusty pipes. The dinner bell rang, but I ignored it till I was sure that everyone had left and then waited a little longer. The meal was well underway when I entered the dining hall and, in response to Uncle Jim's query, I explained that I had been playing way over on the other side of the school building and didn't hear the bell.

I think my dusty clothes must have given me away, or perhaps someone had seen me enter the linen closet, for later that evening Mr. Hunter summoned me to his room and confronted me again. He deemed my lie warranted three whacks with the leather slipper.

"Hand!" he demanded, with that bug-eyed look of moral intimidation that only the British can affect.

I meekly put out my right hand, palm up, and winced at the stinging clap of the first two strokes. On the third one I lost my nerve and jerked my hand away. With so much force behind the downward swing, Mr. Hunter nearly lost his balance. It was the first and only time I saw Jim Hunter lose his composure—and only for a moment. He warned me that if I did that again I'd get five more. It would have been worth it. I now had a story to tell and gained the special status of being the only boy to spurn Uncle Jim's discipline.

We clashed again soon after that.

On Friday morning several of us woke up early and were horsing around before breakfast. Our grand revelry apparently roused Uncle Jim a wee bit before he had intended to get up, and he was not amused. As punishment, the culprits were assigned to write 500 times: *Consideration for others is a virtue to be highly commended at all times.* And, further, if we didn't have them done by the following morning, we couldn't go on the bus trip to Pindi planned for that Saturday.

This amounted to a double punishment: There was no way we could get that many lines done before the next morning—and even to try would require skipping Friday night games. We wrote furtively during class and through recess and lunch time, but it was hopeless. So after school, Tim Old and I decided to pay a visit to the principal's house. The assignment itself seemed pretty severe, we told Mr. Roub, given that we hadn't broken any rules; but the time requirement, with its likely consequences, was really unfair.

"Well, boys," Mr. Roub said, "I can understand how you feel but, as principal, I can't sit here and tell you that you don't have to do something that one of my staff members told you to do. Maybe I can help make it a little easier for you, though."

And the school principal then proceeded to show us how to hold two pens at a time so that we could write two lines at once. We, of course, were delighted at this creative and slightly devious solution. And, with the help of one of my faithful fifth grade buddies whose handwriting was similar to mine, we got the job done.

We sat at a table in the empty dining hall while the rest of the elementary school was out playing "Kick the Can." We were gleefully finishing up the last twenty lines when one of the seventh grade boys came through the room.

"Did you hear about David Hover's father?" he asked.

No, we hadn't.

"He got killed in a traffic accident yesterday. His car was hit head-on by a truck."

It was too horrible to be a joke. David was the same age as me, but was now in junior high—like some of my other friends from Auntie Inger's department, because I had repeated second grade. "Hover," being from England, was the source of the *Adventures of Tin Tin* books that we all relished (translated from the French hardback comic series). And in fourth grade he had included me in scuba-diving adventures in one of the hostel's bathtubs, with his new British Action Man toys. He let me play with him because the other American boys thought it was sissy to play with dolls. I knew David's sister, Meg, a fifth grader, and he had another one in my sister Miriam's first grade class.

By now the other kids were starting to come in for Friday night snacks. Some of them had already heard; soon everyone knew. No one knew what to say—except the slightly scandalous quest to get the details.

Dr. Hover and his wife, also a medical doctor, worked in the Sind. The truck that hit him was trying to pass a bus on the narrow highway, and, in the big cloud of dust that had been thrown up by a previous vehicle, didn't see Dr. Hover's car coming the other way. The sudden tragedy shook the missionary community in Pakistan, but its implications were too big for my little-boy heart. I could hold vast imaginary worlds in my mind, but the finality of this was too much.

For the first time I thought about whether I loved my parents or not. The truth was, I didn't seem to feel much either way. Was it a sin not to miss my parents when I was in boarding? Was there something wrong with me? I felt terribly guilty about this for a day or so. But the attentions of my heart soon began to focus elsewhere.

It began with the consolidation of the remnants of my spy club—namely, me, Elaine, and her friend, "006." This arrangement developed quite nicely for awhile with very official and very secret messages being relayed back and forth—none of which had anything to do, of course, with boys and girls sending notes to each other.

Then one day a message arrived, via one of our secret couriers, that wasn't from them. It was a desperate, unfamiliar scrawl. "Beware. Agents 006 and 00X are on your trail!" it said and was cryptically signed, "a friend." This note troubled me terribly. Why would my own agents be trailing me? And who would know if they were? The new organization was supposedly not known to anyone outside it. Could the note have been forged—by one of the girls themselves? Was it a joke? This seemed the most plausible and I proceeded, surreptitiously, to check out 006's handwriting. I never thought to suspect 00X/Elaine. The results of my investigation proved inconclusive, but missions started going unacknowledged. In response to a message of inquiry I received a curt note, informing me that neither girl was interested in playing my games anymore. Goodbye. With a heavy heart, I dutifully retired their numbers and went back to designing moonships.

A few weeks later I was sitting on a wall watching 00X playing freeze tag on the basketball court. Suddenly I realized that the way I felt towards her was no longer that of a spy ring director. I was old enough to know what "falling in love" was, but not old enough to

know what to do about it. Elaine's older sister Becky, one of the
sweetest senior girls, happened to be sitting next to me at the time; I
turned to her and said, "You know, I think I like your sister."

Becky thought that was funny! But she agreed to instruct me
on the birds and the bees, at least in so far as concerned a sixth-grade
boy. Of course, I couldn't just go up to Elaine and *talk* to her, so I
had to write a note. Fine. I certainly knew how to do that. But it
couldn't be one of those serious, dramatic kind, or the equally silly I-
love-you-do-you-love-me? type. So I composed a short note stating
my opinions and inquiring of hers.

A few days later I got my reply: Yes, she thought I was nice; in
fact, maybe even the nicest boy in the sixth grade. I was thrilled!
After that we started writing short but frequent letters back and forth
—all delivered *very discreetly.* We asked each other about immaterial
things, just to have something to write about; and one day I became
daring enough to start with *Dear* Elaine and end with *Love,* Paul.

It didn't take long for people to catch on though, and one day I
was sitting by the basketball court minding my own business when
one of the seventh grade boys, trying to be cool, shouted out, "Guess
who Seaman likes! Who? . . . Elaine Roub? . . . WHO?" Boy, was I
embarrassed. Not because I was ashamed, but I knew I would get
mocked to death for this little revelation. I called the kid aside and
pleaded with him to keep his fat mouth shut, and to please help deny
these false rumors. Little did I realize that nobody really gave two
hoots about my affairs.

Soon it all leaked out anyway, and Miss Cunningham kept to
herself why my grades suddenly started going down at the end of the
year. I passed, though, and boarding ended for the summer. The
first minute "home," my sisters had to tell Mom the big news—and
get a few giggles out of it. Mom said she could tell right away: she
could see the sparkle in my eye . . .

The new school year began, and even though I was still teased
occasionally, there was a special status in being the first boy in seventh grade to have a girlfriend. Things became easier for us fledgling
(and still unofficial) sweethearts now that we were both in junior
high. I could pass a note to Elaine across a study hall table. Or,
passing each other on the stairs between classes, I'd catch her eye for
a moment and find that something had been placed in my hand.

Elaine's sweet affirmations sent me into the clouds; and her
slightest hesitations ("Couldn't we just be friends?" she wrote once)
sent me into doldrums ("Your last note pierced my heart like a
bullet," I wrote back). But I had a new outlook on life; I was now

halfway to grown up. I had fallen in love for the first time. The world was full of possibilities, and I had a place in it.

Then Elaine's family left for furlough.

It was a hot July day and the heavy monsoon clouds had not yet dumped their daily torrent. Just before lunch the whole school was let out to see the Roubs off. I waved dutifully from amidst the assembled well-wishers, hoping to exchange a last glance with Elaine; but she was already in the car, looking straight ahead. When I could contain my tears no longer, I retreated to the safety of the now empty main hall and sat down on one of the chapel benches near the front. Just then Mr. Nygren, the high school English teacher and vice principal, came through the long alcove from the side door.

Seeing me sitting there, sobbing not very discreetly, he paused for a moment. "It's tough, isn't it," he said.

"Yeah," I replied. "It is."

5

Dancing Bears
and Cotton Candy

In the early nineteen-hundreds the British army built a large church three miles outside of Murree to serve their summer barracks located nearby. It was a startling sight. Coming around a bend on a winding back road, the forest opened suddenly into a large bare field with a white goal post at either end. Behind the far edge of the playing field, where the road dipped sharply to the left, the tops of pine trees stuck up from the hillside below; beyond them, the wispy blue outlines and sharp white accents of the Himalayas floated across the sky.

The church stood on the right, snug between the road and the slope of the hill behind it. Constructed of rough-hewn stone, it had a solid, Norman quality, made lighter by the double rows of long, narrow windows on either side. The building was cross-shaped, laid out on the compass points in traditional fashion, and a small bell frame capped the entrance in lieu of a steeple. An iron fence embedded in the low stone wall surrounding the property appeared to connect a row of old chestnut trees along the road in front.

When the British left in 1947, the Pakistan Army inherited the military station, but not the religious property. The church fell into disuse for several years until the Anglican bishop donated the estate for educational use, and it became Murree Christian School. To make classrooms, the interior of the church was walled up along the sides; two additional levels were built into the transepts, with a library on the top floor of one, a science lab in the other. This still left the main sanctuary open to serve as an assembly hall and indoor basketball court. It never struck me as incongruous, while sitting in Friday chapel services, to have a backboard and hoop right in the middle of the aisle between the pews.

The vicarage, sitting on a low rise behind the school, became the principal's house, and a few years later a modern three-story boarding hostel was built beside it. The former parade grounds across from the school now served as a hockey and soccer field—for both Pakistani soldiers and the children of missionaries.

Up in the woods above Jhika Gali, the nearby crossroads bazaar, another estate had been built as a convalescent center for British soldiers during World War II. Sandes Home was a wonderfully rambling two-story Victorian lodge with wide wooden verandas on both levels. After Independence, the American Presbyterian Mission bought the property and used it for missionaries coming to Murree for the summer. But during the spring and fall, Sandes Home became a dormitory for the junior and senior high boys attending MCS.

At the end of May our parents took us out of boarding and we lived with them in Murree for the first term of the new school year, which ran all summer, since we had the winter months off. The green and white MCS bus came wheezing over the hill each morning, crossed the town's tiny main street, and turned stiffly down the tightly twisting lane to Rosenheim, to Rock Edge, to Forest Dell. Now full, it climbed the long grade back past Sunnybank at a quicker pace. The bus squeezed through Jhika Gali—smoky, wood-framed country shops clinging to the narrow saddle between two mountains—then another mile out to the old British garrison church that was Murree Christian School.

The bus didn't come past our house; my sisters and I had to walk down to the lower road at seven-thirty a.m., to the bus stop for Bexley, a collection of cottages used by families from The Evangelical Alliance Mission (known as TEAM). To get there, we always cut through the Civil Hospital grounds, through a narrow alley between whitewashed buildings, heavy with the smell of disinfectant. (Who knew what incomprehensible agonies lay beyond those musty walls?) Then, we descended a long flight of stairs that connected several tiers of level ground behind the main wards. Here, staff quarters and outpatient offices were shelved into the hillside, but I almost never saw anyone around. The place often seemed deserted and had a spooky feel about it.

I didn't notice this when it was raining and all the scenery bled together like a cheaply-dyed Pakistani shirt; or when I was late, which happened a lot, too.

Then, I took the cement steps two, sometimes three, at a time. One morning, I slipped on the wet steps and had gone sprawling across the pavement. My elbows and knees, exposed by summer shorts, got painfully scraped and bruised. But of course I didn't think about that as I dashed down the stairs a few days later. I was watching the green and white school bus waiting on the other side of the road at the bottom of the last flight of steps, and prayed it wouldn't pull away before I got there.

I started yelling and waving my free arm as the bus rolled forward a few feet and then stopped. I ran around the front and banged on the closed door only to be answered with jeers. For a moment I felt eight years old again, not the mature eighth grader I was now. Through the window I saw the driver wave his arm impatiently and one of the kids opened the door. As I climbed in, breathless, Allahdad frowned at me from the driver's seat, but a smirk of gentle resignation curled the corners of his mouth.

With bushy gray eyebrows that mocked his trim moustache, Allahdad had the weary and wizened look of a fairy tale cobbler whose earnest eyes might sparkle suddenly with mirth. As the official school driver, he was as much a part of MCS as Auntie Inger or Mr. Roub, the principal. So were some of the other Pakistani staff: Deodar, the janitor, whose chief function seemed to be to ring the bell between classes; Mr. Lawrence, the more Westernized office clerk who taught us Urdu in third and fourth grades; the numerous ayahs who did housekeeping for the boarding department; and, of course, Khan Zaman, the chief cook.

During World War II Allahdad drove a jeep for a British general throughout the North African campaign and on into Italy. But his English was limited and most of his past was shrouded in mystery. He was an excellent driver—friendly, but capable of fearsome authority when rowdy kids warranted it. As I grew older I discovered that, between Allahdad's fatherly mischievousness and his Muslim curiosity, his interest in our romantic attachments could be quite lecherous.

Still gasping for breath, I found a window seat and tried to make myself as small as possible, hoping the other kids would soon forget my offense and go back to gabbing with their friends. I knew that even insults became boring after awhile; and I wasn't really worth that much of their attention. I stared at the window pane, watching the streaming water break into ripples at every bump in the road.

The monsoon season brought a nearly constant, chilly dampness, even when it wasn't raining. Mildew grew everywhere—on furniture, footlockers, books, and bedsheets. Shoes and suits were often ruined by mold; its pungent smell pervaded everything, even where there was no visible damage. The ground became waterlogged, loosening the earth. Landslides were common. One year, the entire hillside near Sunnybank, just below Murree, slid down the mountain, washing out a half mile section of *three* roads.

The summer's warm wetness encouraged the rapid increase of all kinds of tiny, multi-legged creatures. I knew that most varieties of beetles were harmless, but their large size and the loud clackety-buzz of their erratic flight always startled me. Scorpions required more serious respect, and provoked a nervous fascination in all of us boys. My father repeatedly admonished my sisters and me to check our shoes before putting them on in the morning, as shoes were known to be places scorpions favored for naps. Once, I was sitting on the toilet—the old-fashioned kind with a water tank overhead—and when I pulled the flush chain a scorpion fell on me. Fortunately, it bounced off my head and onto the floor, instead of down my shirt. But my heart jumped, as if I had almost stepped on a cobra, and a tingling sensation raced across my skin from my arms to my toes. By the time I thought to scream, the little black creature was already safely behind the bathtub.

At the bus stop one morning some of the older boys put a scorpion and a large centipede in a glass jar to see which one would kill the other first. Now, bouncing along toward the school at age thirteen, I thought about that glass jar. For countless mornings I had stood at that little roadside pull-over just above Bexley, waiting for the bus. Through the rainy window I recalled a group of us standing there in the rain, huddled together like ducklings, all dressed in those silly too-big yellow rubber raincoats with their yellow hoods. I remembered, too, the times my sisters and I got ridiculed for not being able to dress right. "Even Debbie Nygren has better clothes than you guys," someone said, getting in two insults for the price of one.

Once, when I was eight or nine, I broke under the scornful jabs of my classmates even before the bus arrived, and ran home in tears. For hours I could not control the great, shuddering sobs that hurt deep in my stomach. And long after I had forgotten what they teased me about, I still carried the memory of those tears.

❋

Sometimes my sisters and I were late getting ready and missed the bus by accident. On those days Dad hired horses to take us the three miles to school. There were always plenty of horse-*wallahs* on the road next to our house, catering to summer tourists. Dad charged us each a week's allowance for this arrangement, though the actual cost was probably closer to three.

The narrow, sharply winding lane of Bank Road rose from the big post office at the upper end of town, past our house, and up to Kashmir Point, so named for the panorama of mountains that could be viewed from there. Our route to school by horse took us this way, past St. Denys Anglican School for Girls, past the municipal water tanks, to the loop where all the embassies and rich Pakistanis had their holiday villas. Just before the President's Summer Home at Kashmir Point, a trail cut down through the forest to Jhika Gali. The horse-*wallahs* walked beside us, keeping a loose grip on the reins, in case the horses slipped on the wide but very rocky path. I would always argue with them till they let me hold the reins myself.

From Jhika, it was another mile to school on the main road. I could certainly think of worse punishments for missing the bus. The fun out of arriving by horseback easily outweighed the embarrassment of getting to school late.

Summers provided missionaries not only with a welcome reprieve from the heat of Pakistan's plains but also with the kind of social and cultural opportunities rarely possible during the rest of the year. Murree Christian School used these months to show off student talent and accomplishments with music recitals and student plays. Hobby shows offered stamp collections, sewing, art, and science projects, with butterflies and beetles displayed in shiny glass cases. PTA meetings gave parents a chance to get acquainted with our teachers. Bake sales and barter sales and Sunday services—in English—at Holy Trinity Church in Murree, were a real treat, especially for the missionaries who had few Western colleagues where they worked.

When I was eight I came home from the school's annual rummage sale with a toy bow-and-arrow set. I went immediately up to the small grassy field behind our house to try out my new purchase. A moment later one of the missionary *missahibas* living in the single ladies' bungalow behind the Big House heard screaming and hurried out to see me running off the field, blood streaming down my face.

I was put on a *charpai,* a Pakistani wood-framed rope bed, and carried down the few bends in the road to the Civil Hospital. There (as my father reported afterwards), after wiping the needle with his bare hand, the government doctor gave me an anesthetic injection in my *arm,* rather than at the site of the surgery. When he sewed up my nose, they had to hold me down.

Later, I explained that I had gone up to the field to practice with my new bow and arrow and, remembering Dad's admonitions, had been careful to shoot into the embankment, not out in the open area. Even so, some Pakistani kids nearby must have thought I was shooting at them and threw a rock back at me.

What really happened that day is this: I crossed the field to the big wooden bungalow where a middle-class Pakistani family lived whose children I had played with before. When there was no answer at their door I stepped back into the courtyard and yelled up at the shutters of the enclosed second-story veranda. I knew they were ignoring me. In frustration, I tossed a couple of rocks at the upper level shutters. I vaguely remember seeing faces above me, older Pakistani children, then POW! Something hard hit me square in the face, splitting my nose open—"like a book," my father later described it.

I never did 'fess up to the true sequence of events. And for years I told the story of that sad and tragic misunderstanding, complete with descriptions of the size of the large, pointy rock, which I never actually saw.

Until the British began developing the area as a hill resort, Murree had been a scattered collection of villages and farming hamlets. The town as we knew it was constructed in the 1860s, and ten years later Murree briefly became the summer capital for the British administrative jurisdiction in the Punjab. But cholera epidemics and water shortages plagued Murree throughout the 1800s, limiting its potential political importance. To counter Murree's poor reputation, British citizens were authorized to buy land at the near-give-away price of fifty rupees (about five dollars) per acre, even for residential plots near the town center. This effectively re-popularized Murree as a perennial vacation spot.

Hill stations were common to the colonial experience throughout Asia: India, Ceylon, Thailand, Vietnam, Indonesia, China, and the Philippines all had them. Fleeing the heat of the plains and tropical diseases, jungle isolation or the press of the native population, the English, French, and Dutch built European-style country towns where they could revive their spirits and bodies in the crisp mountain air. Beautiful bungalows, villas, and quaint chalets clustered around the obligatory promenade, or "mall," lined with tea rooms, libraries and churches. Almost all of these towns had boarding schools to which the European children were sent. When the colonists left, the upper class of new nations sent their children to these same schools.

Lawrence College was one such school. MCS had sports matches with its Pakistani students. Every year we beat them at basketball and every year they beat us at soccer, but we always enjoyed the games played on their campus. They were impeccable hosts and after the game we would be ushered into their dining room for "a bit of tea" that was invariably a feast. The oak-paneled hall was draped, Oxford-fashion, with school flags and banners hung in stately rows from the ceiling. The whole experience was far more British than Pakistani.

The town of Murree was built along a gently-sloping ridge where two hills merged. A single main street, looping the summits at either end, ran the four miles from Kashmir Point to Pindi Point, with the "Mall"—the main commercial area—roughly centered between them. The local tenements and villages of old Murree lay on the westerly slope of the ridge below the Mall, squeezed among the truck stations and terminals for buses to Rawalpindi. There was no road from here up the few hundred yards to the Mall, only a paved footpath. Bus passengers had to walk the last couple of miles to their place of lodging. Overeager coolies soon regretted insisting they could carry *two* of Dad's footlockers on their backs, not realizing they contained his summer's-worth of books. Grim, too, were the four men straining to pull the mountain "victorias" loaded with plump Muslim women in their best dress *burkahs* (the brown or black hoods that covered traditional Muslim women from head to toe whenever they went out in public).

The GPO, the General Post Office building, sat atop a wide triple tier of steps at one end of the Mall, and St. Margaret's Catholic Church, down toward Pindi Point, defined the other. Blocked to motor vehicle traffic, this shop-crowded lane served as a kind of commons. The sparsity of buses and cars, and the complete absence of bicycles, *tongas,* and rickshaws, made Murree unique among Pakistani towns; and the Mall was the only area that ever seemed crowded.

All the restaurants, souvenir stands, shoe shops, billiard clubs, and book stores were crammed into this one-mile stretch, along with several hotels and even a modern drug store. The shops built on the precipitous eastern side of the road clung impossibly to the edge of the hillside so that, of necessity, their back side was built out on scaffolding, as if on a high wharf. Behind the brightly painted signs and gleaming windows on the Mall, the sublevels of these same buildings became the dilapidated tenements of the Lower Bazaar. Almost literally beneath the more Westernized and tourist-oriented shop fronts, a narrow cobblestone street descended steeply into a timeless past, a storybook version of the Middle East. Here, local merchants were organized by commodity: several cloth dealers in a row, then jewelers, grain sellers, cobblers, and butchers.

The few establishments on the other side of the Mall included a modern cinema (out of sight, up a steep, well-shaded knoll) and the great stone building of Holy Trinity Church, which rose behind the green-painted latticework of a high wooden fence. This centerpiece of British architecture in Murree seemed like a cathedral compared to the building MCS had converted into a school. MCS held its annual high school graduation ceremonies at Holy Trinity Church. And every Sunday during the summer we worshipped here with our families, just like back home. The addition of three to four hundred foreigners added significantly—and conspicuously—to Murree's local population.

The church grounds were also home to the Murree Language School where new missionaries spent most of their first three summers in Pakistan. When it wasn't raining, folding chairs could be seen scattered across the large parish lawn in pairs, missionary and tutor, or in groups of five or six clustered beneath a shady tree. The Pakistani language teachers were a familiar presence in our homes, often staying for supper after a long tutoring session. One young teacher, who was like an uncle to me when I was little, took me to the back porch of our house in Raiwind, down on the plains. After making sure no one else was around, he lit a whole box of wooden matches for me. The sulfur ends flamed up with an impressive *PHOOOSH!* He blew the tiny fire out immediately, then presented me with a safe box of "matches" to play with.

The bell tower of "Murree Union Church" (as the interdenominational administration of Holy Trinity was known) could be accessed by a steep wooden staircase that angled up around the inside walls of the steeple. A trap door in the ceiling opened onto a dusty platform that revealed another flight of rickety stairs. Even with three of these levels to reduce the vertical drop—and the sensation of being inside a well—the open-slat steps were so steep it felt like being on a high, flimsy scaffolding. I was in seventh grade before I could even pretend not to be scared. But the view from the roof—and the sense of importance of being somewhere most girls wouldn't even try to go—made the heart-pounding climb worth it.

Sam's Restaurant, directly across the street from Holy Trinity Church, was shunned by all the missionaries—more for the supposed unsavory clientele of its "nightclub" than anything immoral in its Muslim-muted entertainment. My family regularly ate dinner after church at Lintott's Cafe, the other, more wholesome, Western-style restaurant a block further up the Mall. I ordered cream-of-tomato soup and fried eggs and chips; or sometimes, fish and chips.

The Methodist mission compound where my family lived was called "Ospring." Besides the servants quarters further up the hill in back, the estate included four houses: the Duplex, the Triplex, the Big House, and the Single Ladies' House—each in a different style of stone or painted brick with wooden trim, but all with corrugated tin roofs.

We lived in the new Triplex, an impressively-modern building made of lilac-colored cement bricks. It had a wide overhanging roof and wall-to-wall windows on two sides. From the dining room of our second-floor apartment, we could look out over the front yard to the road below. A stone retaining wall held the yard in place, topped by a chain-link fence that kept children from falling off the edge. The road ran along the bottom of this wall the length of our compound then folded back in a hairpin turn and climbed out of sight around another curve.

For most of my years at MCS, the Seamans were the only Methodist family at the school. And the summer residents of Ospring were mostly single ladies, young couples from other missions, or doctors from United Christian Hospital in Lahore. I didn't know their children, who were usually girls or not my age, anyway.

Still, I relished this "in-between season." I had my own bedroom and much greater freedom than boarding school afforded. Every day I took a homemade lunch to school, and every night our cook prepared delicious dinners for just our family. As I got older, I could walk almost anywhere by myself or with a friend. Murree's modest scale gave me access to its many layers and infinite details. I grew up rich with both outdoor experience and urban savvy, in ways that would not have been possible in a larger—or smaller—place.

I knew where to get a watch repaired, barter for scarves, or buy a switchblade knife. Going from the roller skating hall to the old movie house required walking through "Tikka Alley" where quick-order chefs peddled Pakistani shish kebabs from a dozen smoky tea shops. Rarely could I resist the rich aroma of chicken or beef *tikkas* being grilled after soaking in spices for hours.

Though it might not feel like it when you were soaking wet and shivering miserably from a monsoon downpour, Murree was a holiday town. And during the summer, Mall Road from one end to the other was like a carnival midway. On any given afternoon, walking home from the bus stop, I could buy fresh roasted corn from a dozen sidewalk vendors squatting over their charcoal grills and blowing earnestly. Or try my luck with a BB gun aimed at a balloon-filled backboard; it always frustrated and puzzled me how many times I could miss completely from less than ten feet away. Up the block, the grinding whir of a cotton candy machine called me to witness again the magic transformation of its pink sugar into puffy, balloon-like clouds on a stick.

Portable pastry shops offered delectable edibles: cream horns and candy sculptures and sticky buns; rows of brown squares and round, yellow-frosted things—all laid out for display in a single aluminum trunk, which the pastry-*wallahs* carried from place to place on their heads. The fragrant baskets of humble fruit-sellers contained an astonishing wealth of seasonal produce: apricots, apples, and oranges; guavas, peaches, plums, blackberries, and bananas. Traveling salesmen might wear traditional garb, but plied their wares with modern slickness: silver ornaments, jewels, brightly woven Kashmir coats, and soft, circular hats made from yak's wool; gaudy Peshawar vests—red velvet embroidered with mirrors and golden thread—dangled from long wooden poles across their backs. Gypsy minstrels vied with snake charmers and monkey trainers, visiting each estate to demonstrate their skills, hoping to entice bored vacationers into paying for the "free" demonstration. Or they simply set up on the street, working the crowd that inevitably gathered. And always the haggling with the horse guides, bargaining a "fair rate" for an excursion around Kashmir Point or down a forest trail.

Sometimes our parents would arrange special shows for all the families at Ospring. The only one I didn't enjoy was the dancing bears. They always looked so sad: trapped, muzzled, expected to perform.

My classmates from MCS and I often laughed at the "teddy boys" who were another ever-present part of summers in Murree, in spite of our being several years their junior. These Pakistani college boys on holiday, emboldened by camaraderie and the safety of a town where no one knew them, would strut up and down the Mall in their tight pants and dark sunglasses, swinging recently purchased walking sticks. Like Pakistani film stars, their sense of Western "cool" was invariably fifteen years out-of-date.

Ours was only ten.

One of these teddy boys tried to get the horse he rode to rear up so his friends could take a picture of him posed like a cowboy hero, like the Lone Ranger. As I watched, he kept whipping and whipping the horse and yanking hard on the bit, but the horse's iron shoes skidded on the paved street and both horse and rider took a hard fall. I felt sorry for the horse.

Another time I visited the stables and watched a blacksmith shoeing a horse. In a kiln beside him a few horseshoes were being heated for fitting and glowed red hot; several more lay on the ground nearby, as if cut from a flat metal stencil. Hoping to buy a souvenir, I picked one up from the stack of extras. With a startled scream I flung the metal bar down too late as tears involuntarily filled my eyes. The horsemen were sympathetic, but some of them couldn't help laughing at my stupidity.

Things were not always as they appeared.

6

Stumbling Toward Pentecost

One evening at Sandes Home, toward the end of the spring term just before I started eighth grade, some of the high school boys were discussing a recent trend in schools back in the States. In imitation of a fierce American Indian tribe, some football players had been shaving their heads, leaving a shock of hair on top in a thin line from front to back. The guys laughed and kidded each other about getting a "Mohawk," but I had read *The Last of the Mohicans* years before. In my young adventures I had penned a tortoise "tattoo" on my chest, leaving the warrior haircut to the privacy of my imagination.

"I'll do it," I said, always ready to barter my way into acceptance, or at least notoriety.

"Shut up, Seaman," came the usual reply.

"Really, I will."

"I bet you wouldn't dare," Tom Ketcham said.

"How much you wanna bet?"

Tom carefully examined the contents of his jeans pocket. "I'll give you eighteen rupees" (about two dollars), he said, "—if you let me do it."

And that is how I came to be sporting a Mohawk the day I met the girl who would love me forever.

The deed was performed in Dudley "Moz" Chelchowski's room, and for the privilege of witnessing me getting sheared by Tom, Dudley charged the guys a rupee each—which he was *supposed* to have split with me. My suddenly exposed skull proved to be quite unattractively lumpy, especially with the numerous nicks and abrasions on skin unaccustomed to a razor. A lot of the girls at school found this repulsive, but it did get me some attention—more than I wanted.

"Pink bellies" were a traditional form of hazing and harassing underclassmen: a couple of guys would pin the victim down on the floor, lift his shirt, and slap his stomach vigorously until in turned bright pink—or the boy's cries of pain persuaded them to let up. My bare skull provided a novel variation on this practice which I had not foreseen. One of the high school boys—often Tom Ketcham himself—would grab my head in a wrestling lock with one arm and attack my scalp with his free hand.

"Ow!" I cried. "Cut it out!" But the fast little slaps usually produced the desired results before I could wriggle out of the hold. And after my head stopped stinging it still tingled strangely, like a foot that's half asleep.

I couldn't really blame Tom, though, for his extra "enthusiasm." I had been grounded for two weeks for this unauthorized personal hair sculpture. But Uncle Paul Davidson's punishment for Tom and Dudley was a severe haircut of their own, and he sent them to the barber in Jhika Gali for a *ganja*—a crew-cut. Both of them had long hair—an important symbol of "cool" (not to mention that the girls adored it, especially Dudley's curls), so Tom and Moz were terribly humiliated by this involuntary scalping. Fortunately, as my hair—and theirs—began to grow back, "pink-topping" my head became a less interesting pastime.

When I came home from boarding for the summer, however, my Mohawk was still very much in evidence, much to my mother's shock. A week later a new missionary family from Canada came over for dinner. The Corcorans were "Pentecostals," something I had never heard of before. I was familiar with Methodists and Presbyterians and Conservative Baptists; I had met some nice Catholic priests and nuns (though the formality and mysteriousness of their rituals made me uncomfortable); but here was an expression of Christianity, I soon learned, far different from any of these.

The parents were dressed nicely enough but had a plain, Appalachian look, like in photographs of farmers during the Great Depression. Mrs. Corcoran carried this appearance more strongly because of her long hair which was tied up in a bun. Most missionary women, while old-fashioned in other respects, either permed or bobbed their hair. The Corcorans had two girls, Esther who was ten, and Ardith who was thirteen—the same age as me. Like their mother, both of them wore thick horn-rimmed glasses and long hair.

Ardith and I quickly became friends. Her family had arrived in Pakistan only a month ago and she was dazed from culture shock. Her parents were so conservative that they wouldn't send their children even to Murree Christian School, but instead taught them at home through correspondence courses. Ardith was glad to have someone her own age to talk to.

So was I.

When I first visited the basement "flat" near Kashmir Point which the Corcorans had rented for the summer I was stunned. I knew that the Methodists were better off than many of the "faith missions" working in Pakistan, but these quarters were exceptionally sparse by Western standards. The four of them lived, along with another single lady missionary, in a tiny two-bedroom apartment with no kitchen. They cooked on a little camp stove on the porch. The only toilets were the Pakistani kind that required squatting on a little cement platform over a hole, flushed with a bucket of water. Ardith said that at night big rats ran back and forth across her bedroom floor.

Ardith's parents, though enrolled in the Murree Language School, wouldn't attend services at Holy Trinity Church because they didn't believe in the Trinity, and the preachers there "didn't have the Spirit." The Corcorans held their own services on Sunday mornings. Sometimes I would go to their house for variety and, of course, to be with Ardith. Rev. Corcoran conducted the worship for the six or seven of us, both preaching and playing guitar. They were a musical family and made up in enthusiasm what they lacked in numbers.

It was not the singing, however, that truly distinguished these meetings as much as the prayer time, when everyone prayed out loud—all at once. And spoke "in tongues," too. Some months later, when I visited the church Ardith's parents had established in Lahore and heard an entire congregation carrying on this way, groaning loudly and praising Jesus, it still . . . um, took some getting used to.

The girls studied in the mornings. A couple times a week I came up to their place after I got home from school and was allowed to take Ardith for a walk—as long as we took Esther with us. That seemed a more than fair trade-off for getting out of the house, especially given that Esther was enough years younger not to seriously inhibit the interaction between Ardith and me. Even more isolated than I sometimes felt, Ardith relished the freedom and the company, while I treasured the privacy. (At MCS, any time spent with girls had to be in a group, and the only privacy possible in boarding was in a bathroom stall.) And it felt wonderful just having someone eager to spend time with me.

Ardith's natural free-spiritedness, in contrast to her family's Pentecostalism (which she seemed to embrace wholeheartedly, if not as solemnly) repeatedly challenged my assumptions. Our public discretion had less to do with her religion than with respect for the local Muslim culture. In private—on a secluded trail, or when her parents were out of the house—Ardith was glad to hold hands with me. On one occasion, I casually ran my fingers through Ardith's luxuriously long hair; Esther gasped righteously and said: "He's *petting* you—I'm telling Dad!" And that was the end of that. Another time, Ardith told me they didn't believe in co-ed swimming—but when they did go swimming, they swam in the nude. "Why not?" she said. "There's no boys around to see us."

The Forest Trail below Hill Lodge and Marsden seemed to have been built specifically for romantic strolls; from here, several smaller paths offered even greater privacy for more adventurous souls. One afternoon, far down in the woods, we got caught in a monsoon downpour and the three of us sought shelter in an isolated gazebo. Under the roofed porch, a long bench curved around the inside like a circular church pew.

Soaking wet, we huddled together for warmth. I put my arm around Ardith's shoulders and she shifted slightly, welcomingly, both of us secretly aware of the deeper meaning of this perfectly natural gesture. The shower ended abruptly, leaving an expectant hush till the forest soon filled with the soft *plat, platy-tap-plat* of water dripping from leaf to leaf. Coaxed out by the rain, the pungent scent of sap and bark and moss filled the air. Somewhere in the distance, Esther's irrepressible chatter had taken on a complaining, impatient tone. I could smell Ardith's hair, smell the wooden planks of the gazebo, different than the wood of the trees. I felt Ardith's thigh pressed against mine through her wet dress, felt her body breathing beside me. A strange warmth pulsed through my blood; and in my stomach where guilt usually tied knots I felt a different kind of tightness.

It was a far more intimate moment than our first clumsy kiss several months later. And probably not what Rev. Corcoran had in mind when he prayed that I would be filled with the Spirit. But the way he described the "Baptism of the Holy Spirit" sure sounded like the joyful-scary rush I experienced that day in the woods, even if I hadn't spoken in tongues.

❁

I quickly learned that what most distinguished Pentecostals from other Christians was their belief in and emphasis on a "second baptism." At Rev. Corcoran's urging, I earnestly tried to receive the Baptism of the Holy Ghost. I raised my hands and praised the Lord and praised Jesus, trying to get it right and waiting for the supernatural faucet to turn on inside of me and unknown languages to come flowing out.

Unfortunately, nothing quite that exciting happened in my spiritual life that summer. I did feel ready, though, to be baptized in the more conventional sense—something my parents were much more approving of. They made arrangements with the Anglican chapel at St. Denys School for Girls, and one Sunday morning both my sister Martha and I were sprinkled symbolically in a proper cere-mony—despite Rev. Corcoran's earnest admonishments that obedi-ence to God's Word required nothing less than full immersion. My parents, like many Methodists, believed that the particular method didn't matter. The important thing was the public confession of faith. Therefore, baptism should be done not at infancy but when a child reaches the "age of reason"—old enough to be accountable for personal choices.

It seemed significant that this important rite of passage was held away from Murree Christian School. And because of the odd blend of my parents' conviction about believer baptism with the Anglican tradition in which the sacrament was performed, I was able to choose my own godparents.

I did not, however, choose another baptism of sorts that happened to me soon after that.

One afternoon I needed to get some materials for a science project I was working on. I had barely left the Methodist compound when the local crazy man suddenly appeared next to me. "BABY, BABY DON'T YOU CRY: MAMA FOR YOU SUGAR FRY!" the crazy man exclaimed, while bobbing along beside me.

He repeated this rhyme every time he saw me and I never could figure out if he was trying to show off what little English he knew or whether the phrase was the random pronouncement of an unhinged mind. Some said that his family had been slaughtered in the Hindu-Muslim riots during the Partition of India in 1947. My mother always seemed disturbed by this man. Though he never did anything improper toward her, she viewed him more as depraved than deserv-ing of pity; and her anxiety produced a contagious sense of dread.

It was this oppressive feeling, more than his loud, insistent company, that I found annoying. It may also have motivated the vehement slurs my classmates made about him, talking with suspiciously exaggerated earnestness about how, on such-and-such occasion, they had narrowly escaped his crude sexual advances: "Pervert!" they decried, "Homo!" In our pubescent nervousness, however, we applied those labels to all the Pakistani boys who held hands with each other—a common Eastern custom.

One afternoon, the student body was treated to a special show put on by a traveling magician, who turned out to be pretty wild and crazy himself. Like most Pakistanis, he spoke "chi-chi" English: exaggerating his enunciation and using a sing-song manner that sounded perfectly natural in his own language but silly in ours. The magician's favorite prop, which he held up like a puppet, was a monkey's skull, and between tricks he carried on loud conversations with it. *"Hello, Mr. Monkey Skull!"* he would say in his thick accent, made even funnier by his dramatic showman's style.

From that day on, the crazy man in Murree was referred to as Mr. Monkey Skull.

After a few minutes, trying my best to ignore him, I turned, feigning to go back home; but he turned in step with me, as if the matching movement had been choreographed. Just then I spotted one of the language school teachers coming down the road.

"Hello, Mr. Paul," he said, using the respectful form in the Pakistani manner. When he realized what was going on, he spoke harshly to the crazy man—more than I thought necessary—and gestured threateningly. The old man gave no indication that he had even noticed the rebuke, but he did not follow us when we proceeded to walk again.

"Where are you going?" the language teacher asked, and almost before I could explain, added: "I will go with you."

I happily accepted his offer—grateful to be rescued and, since I spoke only street-passable Urdu, delighted to have someone along to help translate the particulars of what I was looking for.

While most language teachers tended to favor Western-style suits, the younger ones showed a fondness for what they perceived to be modern fashions, such as turtlenecks or those English-style silk cravats. When they weren't working, some even wore jeans. The older generation treated the missionaries' children politely or affec- tionately, but clearly as children. The younger teachers, however, enjoyed chatting with the teenage boys, hoping to pick up American- isms. Unlike most of the Pakistani college students who tried to be our friends, they weren't clingy or pushy, and we found their eagerness amusing.

My turtleneck-and-jean-clad companion proved to be invaluable, with a remarkable knowledge of where to find things in Murree, even if he didn't quite understand what it was all for. Our search for the specified dyes and wax and metal joints I required took us far down into the Lower Bazaar, farther than I usually had any reason to go. Creaky balconies and colorful storefront canopies reached out from either side of the passageway till they almost touched, creating the appearance of a long, descending tunnel. Near the bottom, this closely-hemmed marketplace extended seamlessly into a little village of blacksmiths and lumber yards.

After securing the items I needed, we began the steep climb back up to the Mall and home. My friend wanted to make one more stop, promising me I would find it interesting. We ducked under the awning of a dry goods shop and general store, unremarkable except for its cleanliness and the superior security provided by its cement walls. The inside smelled faintly antiseptic, like a pharmaceutical store. My friend extended his hand over the display case to greet the proprietor, and let their hands remain linked for a couple of minutes while they chatted in Punjabi, which I knew even less of than Urdu. Beneath the glass-topped counter lay an assortment of imported items: watches, cameras, cassette players, lipstick, cologne, and English cigarettes; even a couple of American baseball cards! I guessed that this was a black market shop and wondered if the older boys from MCS knew about it. Either way, it was a secret I now shared!

The owner disappeared into the back room and returned carrying a brown paper sack which the language teacher immediately tucked into the cloth shopping bag he had been carrying. As he did so, I heard the clink of glass. Then the other man reached into a drawer below the counter and pulled out a deck of cards. He shook the cards out of the box and, with a grin and a wink, handed the pack to my friend. The language teacher smiled slightly then fanned the cards out face down on the counter.

"Pick a card," he said to me.

We did not have playing cards at home, at least not real poker-playing ones, and they were forbidden at boarding school. I had seen the language teachers playing cards and smoking cigarettes at their quarters down behind St. Margaret's Church at the far end of the Mall, which confirmed my impression of how worldly these guys were. I felt a little guilty—and immensely grateful that he was going to show me a trick, not asking me to play.

I drew a card and turned it over. On the other side was a color photograph, making it hard to identify the suit or number. Then I saw the naked man and woman, with only parts of their bodies showing because the picture had been taken up close. My heart pounded. These must be from Sweden, I thought.

"Look at another one," the language teacher said, studying my face eagerly.

I slowly scooped up a few more, keeping my eyes down. I had never seen photographs of a woman's private parts before. In the States, a friend had once shown me some *Playboys* (damp and dog-eared after being rescued from a garbage dump)—they only showed bare buttocks and breasts. Here were close-ups of men, too; and couples *doing it!* One card showed a woman's head arched back, with her mouth open and her eyes closed. There were drops of white stuff splashed on her face. I knew what that was.

"Have you ever seen pictures like this before?"

"No," I managed to get out in a hoarse whisper, my heart pounding in my throat, my stomach sucked inside out.

"Do you like them?" the language teacher asked me. "I'll buy them for you—for a Christmas present, okay?"

Later, I didn't remember the walk home. I went to my room early that evening and lay on my bed for a long time, staring at the ceiling, or sometimes curling up very small. I wanted to grow up fast, but not this fast. I hadn't even kissed a girl yet! And hearing the word "masturbation" out loud still made me blush. I badly wanted to talk to someone, but couldn't think of anyone. Confusion and guilt mingled with an unnerving sense of the huge world out there beyond the one familiar to me. Instinctively, I knew that something violent had happened—and something raw and forbidden inside of me had been exposed.

Lying on my bed that evening, I thought about the time the previous summer when I stumbled onto some kind of religious ritual going on in the middle of the Mall. (Afterwards, I learned that this Shiah Muslim ceremony, "Muharram," mourned the assassination of one of Mohammed's grandsons.) A crowd of young men were chanting and thrashing themselves with ropes knotted with nails or sharp pieces of glass; others simply slapped their bare chests with the same rhythmic repetition, so hard that blood flowed without the use of any implement. Until this moment Pakistan had seemed a civilized country—poor, backward, but woven through with modern Western structures in transportation, education, entertainment, and fashion. Now suddenly, here was this barbaric rite being acted out—right on

Main Street. I was frightened by the force of it more than by the sight of bodies drenched in blood—by something I had no reference for.

I thought too about what happened when I was eight years old. Left to myself during much of the winter break at our home on the plains, I delighted in the amount of time another Pakistani language teacher made available to spend playing with me. One day, we both happened to be in the staff restrooms behind the church office and he asked me to do some things to his private parts. Nervous—and, yes, curious—I complied, because it seemed important to him. Sometimes I went along with things I didn't understand because some form of attention was better than none at all.

I knew that I must have been doing something wrong, but I wasn't quite sure what, since nobody ever talked about sex. Two years later, during a Bible study class in fourth grade, we were reading the passage about Sodom and Gomorrah, the two cities God destroyed by fire after Lot visited them, and Lot's wife was turned into a pillar of salt because she looked back when they were fleeing. The teacher said how wicked these cities had been, to deserve God's wrath, but wouldn't say what exactly their sin was. "Something so terrible, such an abomination to God, that I can't even talk about it," she said. But I knew, as my body got suddenly hot all over, that she was referring to what I had done.

I wondered then, as I did again now in eighth grade, how much people knew that they weren't telling.

My mid-term report card that summer revealed I was failing almost all my classes. My mother decided that a lack of adult male role models accounted for this, as well as for my increasing sullenness at home. I certainly wasn't going to pour my heart out to my father —not that he was exactly available, anyway. (Even for the few short weeks he was in Murree for "vacation," he served as resident manager of Ospring. He spent most of his time at his desk in my parents' bedroom and the family saw him only at meals, on public outings, or in brief allotments of time on Sunday afternoons for individual games of ping pong or chess.) So Mom arranged for me to spend a weekend with a priest I liked who worked at the Catholic Girls' School at Pindi Point.

Father Daniel Dubos understood what it was to be an outsider, and knew firsthand about the struggle to fit in. He had been born in Ceylon to a French father who did not want to take a native wife and son home with him; so Daniel was sent to England to be educated.

There, after a boarding-school childhood much more miserable than mine, he found a sense of belonging in the Church. As in England, Catholics were a tiny minority in British India, where the young Father Dubos was sent at the end of World War II. No sooner had he begun adjusting to a new country when his adopted homeland itself became another nation. The new Pakistani Roman Catholic officials didn't know what to do with him, and, after four agonizing years of limbo, "Father Dan" ended up here: the resident priest to a group of Italian nuns running a school for wealthy Muslim girls. He had remained for more than twenty years now. Apparently, he found his niche.

Father Dan's face was round and deceptively boyish, with shiny-smooth brown skin like that of South Pacific islanders. His dark eyes were somehow piercing and gentle at the same time; I can't explain it, but when he looked at me, I always felt both safe and a little self-conscious.

One Saturday evening we climbed to the top of the hill at Pindi Point to watch the sunset. This spot offered an impressive view of Rawalpindi on the plains in the distance. From here, we could also see the silvery glint of Rawal Lake, where we used to go swimming. We sat on the grassy slope just outside the high chain-link fence surrounding the television transmission station.

"Okay, Paul," the priest said. "When the sun goes down and before it gets dark, I want you to watch and notice which shiny spots are water and which are electric lights."

Father Dan spoke in slow, measured phrases that gave weight to his words—and contradicted the high tone of his voice that made him sound like a woman if he talked rapidly. This only happened rarely, when he was irritated; then he sounded silly and he knew it, irritating him even further. Father Dan was the first person I heard use the word "meditation," referring to something other than a part of the familiar religious ritual—as in, "We will now have a moment of silent meditation." For him, meditation described a spiritual practice intended to actually change a person's perspective and emotional health through stillness. This apparently ancient Christian method of steering the soul toward truth was the polar opposite of how Pentecostals sought holiness—and equally strange to me, used to very structured religion.

Unlike most people I knew, Father Dan didn't mind contradictions. He didn't even seem intrigued by them as an intellectual or spiritual challenge. He took them so much for granted, in fact, that only when apparent opposites managed to achieve a kind of symmetry did he find it worth remarking on. That is why he loved the shrine to Mary across the meadow from where we sat below the microwave communications tower. In the twilight we could still just make out the crude, whitewashed monument, a small tower of a different sort. Above it, a faded green flag hung limply from the long wooden pole wedged at an odd angle into the ancient pile of stones.

Father Dan had told me this was a sacred place to Hindus, Muslims, Sikhs, and Christians alike, a symbol of tolerance and "transcendence"—another big, spiritual-sounding word, but one I hadn't heard at MCS.

"Some people say that Murree was named after the mother of Jesus and that she is buried over there," I said skeptically.

"My local friends tell me that an elderly woman named *Marrhi* is said to have lived on this spot," Father Dubos answered after a pause that might have made me think he was distracted by something else, if I hadn't been used to his slow replies. "Perhaps Murree is named after her. But the reasons for her sainthood remain a mystery. The Mary story is probably an imaginative version of this legend, adapted to ingratiate Western visitors."

After a moment he added, "People invent history to explain the mysterious; and they invent mysteries to make history less . . . disappointing."

In eighth grade we studied Pakistan history under the creative tutelage of Miss Ellen Brell, who was also our algebra teacher. Miss Brell managed to keep our attention (the boys, anyway) with choice descriptions of how the Moghul emperors dispatched their enemies —such as flaying them alive, or having an elephant stomp on their heads.

Nobody is quite sure when the Murree Hills were first inhabited, but their proximity to Taxila and to Kashmir indicates that permanent settlements here, as outposts and trade routes for both of those kingdoms, existed more than two thousand years ago. Buddhist stupas found in the area date back almost half that far. However, the few remains of forts and towers, indicating Murree's military importance as a border area, date only from the seventeenth and eighteenth centuries. The Sikh rulers of Kashmir built a large fort at Pindi Point in the 1800s, right here where the television tower now stood. There was no trace of the previous structure except the wide, flat perimeter of its foundation.

The nearest visible "historic" ruins in the area lay six miles below Pindi Point—the crumbling stone walls of the Murree Brewery, built during the colonial period. It was burned down after Independence by temperance-conscious Muslims.

The English first used Murree as a summer training camp for British soldiers—conveniently close to their military headquarters at Rawalpindi. Murree, in fact, bordered the still wild and unsubdued North-West Frontier Province and establishing an army cantonment here, they reasoned, would also help keep the local people in line. Instead, the British presence in Murree served as a lightning rod during the Indian Mutiny—the first war of independence—in 1857. Local tribal leaders planned a raid on the English settlements, but were betrayed by an informant. In spite of the fact that the raid never took place, British reprisals were swift and harsh. Eleven villages suspected of participating in the plan were burned to the ground. Several local leaders were executed. This was done in the manner favored by the British at the time: the rebels were strapped to the front of canons and blasted apart at point-blank range.

I once saw this depicted in a comic book history of the British in India and I had stared at the illustration with the same mixture of fascination and horror that the Swedish playing cards had provoked in me.

Neither Father Dan nor I had spoken for some time and I began to notice the hunger pulling at my stomach—the same way guilt did. I wanted to tell Father Dan about the playing cards, but I couldn't. What could he say, anyway? The thing had happened. And somehow it seemed like it was my fault for knowing more than I should. He would probably laugh at me for taking myself too seriously. He did that sometimes. But Father Dubos was one of the few adults who also didn't take himself too seriously, and I knew he took a sincere interest in me. Finally, it was enough just to be sitting beside him, knowing he would understand.

The hillside had grown dark, and in the unusually clear night air the city lights of Rawalpindi, together with those of Pakistan's new capital, Islamabad, gleamed and twinkled like fairy dust strewn across the greater length of the horizon. And in the sky, the stars burned softly like the scattered lamps of nomads in the desert.

Miss Brell said that strange rock drawings found on the Potwar Plateau, at the foot of the Murree Hills, indicated that prehistoric tribes had been studying the stars in this area two thousand years before Stonehenge. Artifacts had been found here from human communities more than 500,000 years old.

And then there was Mohenjo-Daro, the City of the Dead, Pakistan's most famous ruins, out in the desert two hundred miles northeast of Karachi. Five hundred years before the Pharaohs built the Great Pyramids along the Nile, Mohenjo-Daro had flush toilets, an underground sewage system, and the first known ritual burial grounds. More than a thousand years before the Babylonian Empire began to spread out from the Tigris and Euphrates, the Indus Valley Civilization had a standardized system of weights and measures and a network of cities that specialized in the mass production of glazed pottery, stoneware, woolen cloth, or other handicrafts. Then, after flourishing for over a thousand years, this great society vanished.

Miss Brell said that it was a mystery to archaeologists. Some thought a great flood had wiped out the whole civilization, or that a great drought had caused people to leave the area suddenly. But Tim Old and I thought it had something to do with flying saucers. We had just read Erich von Däniken's *Chariots of the Gods?*, which proved that extra-terrestrial beings had helped to build the Great Pyramids and the Ark of the Covenant and other things in the Bible. That could explain the advanced technology in such ancient ruins, too.

"What happened to Mohenjo-Daro?" I asked Father Dubos.

"No one knows," he replied, pausing, it seemed, on each word. "But perhaps we would have more clues if the British had not been so hasty in bringing their own civilization to this land." And then he proceeded to tell me a story about two English brothers, both engineers, who became engaged in a competition. Starting from opposite directions, like the Union Pacific Railroad in America, they would complete a rail link from Lahore to Karachi on the coast.

Construction on the line between these two cities began in the early 1850s. With the vast deserts along much of the route, the British engineers had difficulty finding stone to fill the track bed. What they did find were a series of mounds filled with layers of crumbling brick, the long-abandoned ruins of some earlier inhabitants. The debris from these sites was carted away and used as ballast for the railway. A few decades later the discovery of Mohenjo-Daro brought the realization that some of the world's most ancient cities had been turned into road gravel.

The excavation of Mohenjo-Daro in 1920 proved to be one of the greatest archeological discoveries of all time. Here was the missing evidence for the existence of a stable nation state far earlier than had been previously thought to exist in this area. But these ruins only hinted at the work of artists, scientists, architects, and philosophers in that region 5,000 years ago. "Who knows what further secrets might have been revealed about the Indus Valley Civilization if the other ancient sites had not been destroyed to serve the needs of the present," Father Dubos said.

"So next time you go home for Christmas," he added, "remember that the mighty locomotive that carries you knows nothing about history."

He leaned back on his hands and looked up at the night. No stars were visible in the western part of the sky where clouds had begun to gather—just a great, black expanse of unfathomable emptiness. Yet, in front of us, the city lights still twinkled below. Looking out into the darkness, itself divided by shadows, I felt that this moment was somehow important, that every day, in fact, was shaping me for a larger destiny. When I was younger, I sometimes pretended that I was really a prince and that all my suffering was to teach me wisdom; one day my real parents would come to reclaim me—and reveal my true identity. I felt like that now, except that I was missing some key piece of information that would make everything suddenly clear, and things would turn out all right.

Visiting Father Daniel Dubos did not change my life; but in some small, quiet way he had given me a glimpse that the wider world could be faced without fear. I could embrace the uncertainty, claim the confusion as my birthright, as the price for finding my own truth. But this new confidence did not leave me content; it made me reckless. And I did not comprehend then that although I had changed, the community I lived in had not. And this divergence would soon lead to disaster.

7

Different Trains

When the British left India in 1947, the subcontinent was divided into predominantly-Hindu India and majority-Muslim Pakistan. To accommodate this religion-based division, two major states, the Punjab and Bengal—located on opposite sides of India—were "partitioned" into Hindu and Muslim halves. Those of one faith who found themselves on the wrong side of the border when the maps were drawn fled to the other side, only to meet refugees coming the other way. And each time, in the frenzy of confusion and fear and loss, there was slaughter. In the Punjab the Sikhs, who had gotten short shrift in the deal—seeing their homeland split and apportioned to others—went on an indiscriminate rampage of killing, looting, and burning. "Ghost trains" would pull into Lahore Station from the other side of the new border, their silent carriages filled with the blood and bodies of those trying to escape the carnage—hacked to pieces on the road to freedom.

Pakistan was a state unique in world political history, with two separate "wings" on either side of India: the four provinces of Punjab, Sind, Baluchistan, and the tribal areas of the North-West Frontier made up West Pakistan; the single, divided state of East Bengal became the other "wing," or East Pakistan. In between lay a thousand miles of hostile India. Although East Pakistan contained over half the nation's population, most of the administrative, industrial, and military centers were in West Pakistan. While the eastern province produced ninety per cent of the country's export earnings, from its jute crop, most of the government's expenditures were invested in the west. Culturally and historically the two wings had little in common except the Islamic faith. And given the often callous aloofness of the central government, this proved to be not enough. The election results of March 1971 gave East Pakistan its first majority in the National Assembly, but the military rulers in West Pakistan refused to recognize the Bengali victory. This led to nine months of civil war even more bloody than Partition, twenty-four years earlier. And this time it was Muslim killing Muslim. When the Indian armed forces intervened in December, it was largely in response to the economic drain and social turmoil from ten million Bengali refugees now camped on India's side of the border.

During all this time, the media in West Pakistan made only occasional reference to "miscreants" and "Indian provocateurs" over in East Pakistan. There was no mention of the Bengali uprising and the subsequent military crackdown. Or the fact that the Pakistan Army's "police action" had quickly become bogged down in a guerrilla campaign not unlike the one being waged in Vietnam, just on the other side of the Burmese hills. Superior fire power and the most modern military equipment—supplied by the United States— were no match for the tenacity of the Bengalis' desire for freedom. Pakistan's tall and more fair-skinned troops from the West felt like foreigners. Bigotry and propaganda could justify slaughter, but it could not sustain the will to fight.

Astoundingly, the government of Pakistan complained to the world of Indian aggression. It was easier to blame their debacle on the interference of a big foreign power than to acknowledge their own failed policies. As the secession of "Bangladesh" became inevitable, Pakistani radio and newspapers hysterically embellished the steadily increasing tensions with India—so that there would be a plausible explanation when the country was suddenly dismembered. By October, most of the automobiles in West Pakistan sported bumper stickers, in English, with the rather incongruous slogan, *Crush India.*

Even with such a carefully-orchestrated disinformation campaign, the missionary community knew what was really happening. The parents of some of my classmates worked in East Pakistan and often came to Murree for the summer, like the rest of our parents. Only this time they were refugees, not vacationers. Uncensored copies of *Time* or *Newsweek* smuggled into Pakistan by folks returning from home leave provided a fuller context to the personal horror stories. In nine months of unrestrained pillaging and rape, government troops massacred more than two million Bengali civilians. Conservative missionaries had something of a political identity crisis as they confronted the fact that the United States was taking the wrong side in one of the most clearly defined and morally compelling conflicts of the twentieth century.

In spite of the atrocities—well-documented by the world press —the Nixon Administration continued to ship arms to Pakistan throughout the war. Bigger things were at stake than a few million peasants in a place most people couldn't even find on a map. Richard Nixon was about to play "the China card," undoubtedly his greatest foreign policy achievement; but the re-opening of diplomatic and trade relations between the United States and the People's Republic of China came at a terrible price.

Both countries had long-standing trade and security agreements with Pakistan. India's recent "mutual defense pact" with the Soviet Union gave these ties even greater strategic importance. And in the summer of 1971, Pakistan played host to the secret negotiations between the U.S. and Communist China. Henry Kissinger met with an official Chinese delegation for the first time in Nathiagali, an isolated summer estate only a few miles from Murree Christian School.

We didn't know about that meeting, of course, but my friend Becky Ketcham—Tom's younger sister—had told me about what was happening on the other side of India. (Their father was a doctor in East Pakistan.) Right now—during the summer of 1971—Pakistani soldiers were killing thousands and thousands of Bengalis— most of them civilians. There was a revolution going on, but here in West Pakistan they were acting like nothing was happening. Once, under the cover of darkness and behind Ospring's compound walls, I joined Tom Ketcham in a couple of defiant shouts of "Joi Bangla!"— the rallying cry of the rebel forces seeking independence for "Bangladesh." I enjoyed the scandalous thrill of verbalizing something taboo, even if none of the Pakistanis around could understand Bengali.

Military personnel and vehicles were part of the daily scenery around MCS, our school being located in the middle of a cantonment area. Sometimes the older boys would sneak a ride to school in the back of an army truck. I couldn't imagine these friendly soldiers shooting women and stabbing babies.

I turned fourteen just before Pakistan and India went to war. Our three-month holiday got an early start that winter, when all of us were sent home to be with our parents in case an evacuation became necessary. I learned then what it was to be a refugee, to wonder if I would ever see my home again. As it happened, my family did not have to leave the country; however, because our mission station was very near the border with India, we spent December in a vacant house at Forman Christian College in Lahore. One evening the air-raid klaxons sounded while my parents were out visiting friends. I quickly shepherded my three sisters into the L-shaped trench that had been dug for us in the back yard, grabbing a card table to put over our heads, as Dad had done before. Listening to bombs going off nearby, my chest tightened with fear, and with a self-conscious sense of importance.

That spring, my younger sister, Miriam, rode the train party to boarding school for the first time. By then I had been going to boarding for more years than she had been alive; MCS was more home to me than my parents' house. Even knowing what she was in for, I participated in the charade of how exciting boarding was going to be. I should have felt protective of Miriam, but after we got to Murree we rarely saw each other, and I became caught up in my own projects and problems.

Miriam always got the most attention in our family, anyway. Dad and I were hardly speaking to each other. If he said goodbye to me at the station that year, I didn't notice. But since that first train party eight years earlier, I could hardly remember any of the times I had had to say goodbye to my parents. Perhaps the awkwardness of these moments was simply lost in the hustle of boarding the train and the excitement of seeing old friends. Perhaps there were other reasons.

When I was fourteen, Dad did not trot up to the end of the platform and wave his hat—because I was wearing it. I also wore, with equal pride, both "hippy" bell-bottoms and the official Boy Scout knapsack my parents had bought for me when we were on furlough in the States a couple of years before. Dad never wore his formal businessman's hat anymore. (He now had a genuine colonial-style missionary "pith helmet," to wear in the summer sun—though I never saw him use it.) So I convinced him to let me borrow his black felt hat, still practically new. By tapping out the creases and flattening the brim, I discovered that this hat could be shaped into a fairly good imitation of the one Arlo Guthrie wore on the cover of the album, *Alice's Restaurant*. Whether or not it impressed my classmates I couldn't say, but it impressed me.

I looked at things with a new eye that spring. I had confronted new responsibilities, and proved myself in the trenches—literally. I was more confident and also *less* sure of myself than ever before. Like Bangladesh, I felt a swell of independence, but at what cost? My need for ownership in the choices available to me pushed dangerously against the dictatorship of Dad's "preferences" in almost every matter, from dinner conversation to family devotions. The boundary disputes between my father and me were erupting with greater and greater frequency. I did not anticipate, however, that these border skirmishes with Dad might lead to another great power being drawn into the conflict. It was the school that would make a preemptive strike, not to liberate me but to crush my rebellious spirit. Carried out with the complicity of my parents, the damage sustained by this betrayal—only a few short months away—would last for many years. Of course, I had no clue to any of this as I returned to boarding school in the spring of 1972, for the second semester of eighth grade. I was glad to be going back, glad to be away from my father.

The shadow of the train rippled across the salt dust, jumping gullies, shrinking below a bridge, and stretching with the afternoon. I watched it change shape as the sun went down, making the cars look more boxy—bigger, but more like toys. Drowsy with heat and the confines of travel, it always seemed to me that the last few miles took forever. By now, travel grime and cinder grit covered every exposed inch of skin and hair. But when the train pulled into Rawalpindi Station, the already cooler air promised our destination was near, awakening sharper memories of Murree.

Our luggage was transferred onto a hired truck or to the top of the old green-and-white school bus. From experience, I fervently hoped—as did everyone else—to get on the other bus, rented from the commercial Pindi-Murree Transport Company, because it was much newer and roomier. *All right!* This time I drew the rented bus, though even it was crowded with thirty kids and their carry-on luggage—shoulder bags and knapsacks and extra blankets for the trip into the still-wintry mountains. A two-hour ride remained and we were anxious to be done with it.

Beyond the halfway bridge, we passed through a Christmas-card scene of silent villages and bazaars covered by recent snowfall. Half-hidden fires flickered beneath the shadows of thick timber roofs, casting a soft yellow light into the darkness. I could just see the outlines of rough stone dwellings embedded in the hillside. Here and there, a tin roof gleamed in the shifting moonlight like a signal flash.

When the bus broke down just five miles short of Murree, our jubilant anticipation of the rare opportunity to play in fresh snow came to an abrupt halt. We had to get out and walk through ankle-deep snow on the road, around the hill past Sunny Bank and up to Jhika Gali. Some of the kids were only wearing their sandals from the plains and would not soon forget their foolishness. A few of the boys were wearing shorts. My oldest sister Ruth and I took turns carrying Miriam piggy-back. I didn't help that much, really wasn't very manly at all. I wanted to help, felt that I should, but it was so painfully cold; it was all I could do just to keep myself walking.

How could such a beautiful place be so miserable?

When we finally reached Jhika Gali, we older boys turned up the steep hill to Sandes Home; for the rest of the group, it was still another mile to the school. As we dragged ourselves into the dormitory, thoroughly wet, aching, and shivering uncontrollably, those who had the "misfortune" of having to ride in the old school bus kidded us mercilessly. *They'd been there for hours.* And of course there was no hot water.

On the bright side, I had been assigned to the coveted small bedroom that slept only two people—no double bunks; but my roommate was the most religious and intellectual twerp in our class. It was going to be difficult to sleep through "Quiet Time," the pre-breakfast personal prayer and Bible reading that we were all expected to practice; and there certainly would be no quarter when it came to keeping the room tidy. Wanting to start the term out right, Darryl and I said our evening prayers together, somewhat awkwardly, with the obligatory earnestness that MCS elicited. But I knew he was no more thrilled than I about our involuntary partnership.

I didn't hate Darryl, but he represented everything I was coming to hate, and "involuntary" summed it up pretty well. In our rigidly regulated environment there weren't a lot of options for expressing individuality. I desperately wanted to be accepted. But I wasn't good at any of the things for which MCS offered recognition: excelling in school or sports, displaying musical talent or spiritual traits, and—most mystical of all—*being cool.*

My mother had always encouraged my creativity, and imagination was the one thing that served me well—even if it sometimes reinforced my solitude. People were impressed with my "Moon Base" version of Monopoly and they actually played the "Sea Chess" game I invented. But "creativity" didn't provide me friends or improve my academic standing. One day, I was working on some creation during study hall in the library when Miss Brell said, "If you would just put half as much energy into your studies as you do into those silly games, Paul, you'd make straight A's."

I didn't care about A's. I just wanted to be liked.

The message from the Sixties was "do your own thing," and rock and roll comforted me with an imagined connection to a much wider community. But I still felt cheated somehow. I also had a growing sense that many adults were not worthy of the respect they claimed. Yet, what the school perceived as contempt—refusing to study, cutting up in class—was really mostly boredom.

The kind of Christianity practiced at MCS put a premium on conformity, beyond the practical necessity of order and efficiency—it was a sacrament. There wasn't room for anyone who expected more out of life than packaged answers from authorities whose primary credibility was based on God's ordained hierarchy. To question the system was to rebel against God. And, as even my mother reminded me, the Scriptures say rebellion is "as the sin of witchcraft." How's a kid, earnestly trying to follow the faith—and find himself, too—supposed to deal with that? If I wasn't angry before, such heavy-handed reprimands certainly made me so.

By the middle of eighth grade I was failing in every subject, even English, which I liked. Perhaps, like the Bengalis with their nationwide strikes, to work or not to work was the one thing in my life I had some control over—even if I were the one to suffer the consequences. All of us at MCS were uprooted from our home country, uprooted again from our families, but woe to the outcasts among the orphans.

I found little comfort in prayer that first night of the spring term; and not much more under the blankets: I felt smothered by their protective covering—and too cold without them. Even the soothing continuity of the train had turned against me. I was no longer content with the familiar scenery, the familiar routine, and though I still trusted the Engineer, even he seemed confined to a path laid down by others. *Clickity-clack, clickity-clack,* why did we stay on the same old track? I was going someplace else, and though I didn't know where, I was impatient to get started. The jackals were circling inside me now, in a ritual as old as blood; and I was caught—between the rhythm of the cradle and the call of the universe.

8

The Legendary
Screamin' Seaman

And How He Was
Temporarily Tamed

The highlight of that spring term, at the end of eighth grade, was a bicycle trip the junior high boys took from Jhika Gali to Kohala. The 25-mile ride, downhill all the way, ended beside a rushing mountain river at the border with Kashmir. We left early on a Saturday morning in April, just those who wanted to go, and most of us made an all-day arrangement with one of the bike shops in Jhika. Uncle Mark Jones followed in the school's '57 Chevy pick-up. The squeaky wooden frame mounted over the truck bed swayed and jolted with every curve, but nevertheless provided hand holds and some measure of safety for the thrill-seekers who sat on the side panels behind the cab. We loved that little green Chevy with its bubbled hood, running boards, and wide sun visor that hung low over the windshield. On trips like this one, any cycler who had problems could just toss his bike in the back when the truck came along. When we got to Kohala, all fourteen of us would somehow cram our bikes and ourselves into the old Chevy for the trip back up the mountain.

About half way to Kohala, we passed through a village as school was letting out for lunch and a mob of exuberant young Pakistani boys filled the street. I rang my bicycle bell furiously, impatient with this hindrance to the exhilarating free-fall of my flight down the mountain. I had just successfully negotiated my way to the far side of the village when I heard the clink of a rock bouncing off my bicycle fender. Turning to see who had thrown it, I crashed into a stone guardwall and went flying over the handlebars.

Several yards further down the road, my mind caught up with what had happened and I stiffly picked myself up off the pavement. Except for some painful scrapes and bruises, I seemed to be okay. The bike was another story: its front end was totally mangled. Waiting for Uncle Mark to come by, I began to realize—with a wave of goose-bumps—how narrowly I had missed a more deadly accident. Had I been thrown slightly to the right instead of to the left, I would have gone over the edge of a steep, rocky slope. It was a sobering, cautionary moment, which I soon forgot—except when opportunities arose to recount my close brush with destiny.

The school's Chevy pick-up served as rescuing angel on another dramatic occasion—and this time I was doing nothing but trying to sleep. The junior high boys and girls had taken the bus down to Rawal Lake for a camping trip; the school truck carried tents, food and cooking supplies. Weekend camp-outs were the highlight of each boarding term, a time not only to get away from the schedules and rules of school, but when the unofficial but equally rigid peer dynamics seemed to relax too. We swam, played games, and washed our own dishes after meals, enjoying a welcome variety of food, including pancakes for breakfast and hamburgers for lunch. The break in routine also brought the possibility of new friendships, born from the kind of casual camaraderie I seemed shut out of most of the time in boarding.

For several years, Pindi Lake (as we called it) had been a popular spot for MCS camp-outs. Day trips from here into Rawalpindi, only a short bus drive away, offered the excitement of big-city shopping and eating dinner at a fancy restaurant. Near the shore where we camped, the old road went straight into the lake and disappeared. From here, the lip of the dam was just barely visible between two hills of rolling savanna. The combination of cold mountain water and hot grasslands made great swimming. The school bus used to drive out up over its axles to a point where a now-submerged retaining wall made the water deep enough on one side that we could dive off the roof of the bus.

As the lake level rose, however, the blacktop receded more and more, and the bus couldn't get out as far. The once-grassy shoreline was now full of brambles. Commercial truckers had begun using "our" spot to wash their vehicles and the water became fouled with industrial grime and trash. This weekend would likely be the last time we camped at Pindi Lake.

I was wading in the muddy water beside where the road ended, testing the depth to establish a perimeter for the non-swimmers, when I felt a sharp pang in my left foot. It took me a moment to realize, from the curiously warm and cold sensation between my toes, that I'd cut myself on something concealed by the murky surface of the lake. The wound didn't really hurt much—until I climbed out of the chilly water: YEEOUHH! With a little first aid by tall Uncle Paul Davidson from New Zealand the bleeding stopped and the pain in my foot soon receded to a dull throbbing. But I wouldn't be doing any more running around for awhile.

Early that evening it began to rain and continued raining. There weren't enough tents for everyone, as most of us boys had planned to sleep out on the grass, under the stars. Some of the popular boys claimed the last dry spot—underneath the school truck, while the rest of us huddled together under the makeshift protection of wind-breakers or canvas tarps. Around two a.m., when the rain hadn't let up, word came down that we were breaking camp; Uncle Paul was concerned that the lake might overflow. All the girls and the younger children were directed onto the bus, where most of them had already taken shelter. It turned out that Suzy Pietsch's parents lived in Rawalpindi and the bus went to their house, where Auntie Rosie Stewart explained what had happened. The rest of us followed, crammed into the back of the old pickup. Our clothes already soaking wet, quickly turned freezing cold as the whipping wind pasted them tightly around us. I hugged myself to control the shivering and clenched my teeth till they hurt, but there was no shelter. I couldn't remember ever being so miserable. The half-hour ride seemed endless.

At last—a warm, dry living room floor. Despite the hour and masses of wet clothing, Mr. and Mrs. Pietsch welcomed all thirty-two of us into their home and even served us breakfast the next morning.

Whether you were popular or not, boarding was inescapably a group experience, grounded in the public routines of school and meals, of religious ritual and daily chores. The three-mile run around the hill, a PE requirement each spring, was loathed by everyone. But it was an individual decision that led me to slice my left foot with an Exacto razor-blade knife to get out of this twice-weekly torture. I discovered that scar tissue had fewer nerves in it than regular flesh and simply opened up the old cut between my toes that I had gotten in Pindi Lake the term before. I made sure that my roommate was around that evening to see me earnestly carving something clamped between my feet—and could thus authenticate my "hobby accident" claim when blood streamed over my ankle moments later.

Faking sick—from boredom, laziness, or depression—was a popular pastime at MCS; I had just taken it a step farther. I used to listen carefully to other boys describing their real ailments to our boarding father so I could later mimic them convincingly. But Roy Montgomery held the record, feigning illness for ten consecutive days—just to see if he could get away with it.

The uneasy parallel of inner and outer worlds expressed itself most strongly in the religious realm. As a group, we were shaped by the earnest sense of mission that motivated our parents; we couldn't help feeling important for "having the privilege of knowing Christ." We might criticize specific school regulations or staff actions, but for the most part, we accepted as a given the view of the world taught to us by the school.

This still left plenty of room for private anguish over the state of our souls. And though we publicly expressed essentially the same beliefs, we experienced our individual relationships with God quite differently. At least mine seemed to lack the certainty and vividness that others professed. Then again, there was a certain status in having a powerful "testimony." There was nothing like a conversion to win the approval and acceptance—at least temporarily—of both peers and staff. And presumably not everyone felt the spiritual perfection and contentment we all sought, or there wouldn't have been any response to the "altar calls" that periodically ended our weekly chapel services, especially when there was a guest speaker or designated revival emphasis.

The pressure to "go forward" at these times always seemed to come from an undefinable sense of guilt, but the reward was to be treated like somebody special. Similarly, when visiting evangelists scheduled private appointments in the school library or one of the music rooms, many of us were always able to find some spiritual difficulty that needed attending to. This was the only way we could get private attention from adults. An elderly Englishman, Mr. Cecil Johnston, who used slides and tiger stories to illustrate Christian parables, was a highlight of my elementary years at MCS. Perhaps I found in his exuberant indulgence the grandparent that we, as missionary kids, were deprived of overseas.

High school was a more difficult time. Some of us felt a natural teenage instinct to seek our own answers, but were inhibited by a religious perspective that equated doubt with unbelief. Those who showed too much interest in "worldly" ideas got labeled pompous by their peers and spiritually degenerate, or "backslidden," by the staff. But these outer judgments bothered me far less than the uneasy sense of being disloyal to God that always lurked behind my curiosity. The school saw no need for us to have any real knowledge of other viewpoints when Christian truths were self-evident and sufficient for our complete sanctification. Our education about other religions and Christian "cults" was limited to a "biblical" explanation of why they were false—so we could better *witness* to the unsaved or to those who had been led astray.

When I once expressed my opinion that the newly-popular "situation ethics" might have some validity, I was ridiculed by my dorm parent. He asked me if I knew who Hugh Hefner was, which I didn't. "If you don't even know who the editor of *Playboy* magazine is, how do you think you can be capable of deciding your own values?" he asked. I never did understand the connection.

1972 was the height of the "Jesus Movement" then sweeping America and Europe. As part of the corridor to the hippie Meccas of India and Nepal (with easy access to drugs in all the surrounding countries), Pakistan saw a lot of counter-culture traffic. And inevitably, the Jesus Movement finally found its way to our obscure paradise. The more clean-cut fringes of it had come to Murree Christian School the previous summer in the form of young mission teams who left us with fresh "youth hymns" that revived the high school's Sunday evening singspirations.

I went forward after one of these special presentations—to get the guitarist to write down for me the lyrics to Peter, Paul and Mary's "I Dig Rock and Roll Music," which he had sung earlier to loosen things up.

The summer I started ninth grade we were visited by some ex-hippies living at a Jesus People commune in Kabul, Afghanistan—the Haight-Ashbury of the East—and their lingo quickly permeated our social lives. We would raise our index fingers heavenward and say "One way" in greeting to each other. It was great: we could keep our hair long and still feel pious. One way, man; praise the Lord. Imitating some of the high school boys, I wrote JESUS ONLY in big, black psychedelic letters on the back of my tan waistcoat. The staff rejoiced at these signs of another school revival, and for some of us it was an important part of finding ourselves, if not God. For others, it was just another one of the trends that swept through the school every couple of seasons, like silly handshakes, or the constant verbal evolutions in our vernacular. The staff didn't seem to notice that the kids who tearfully responded to this week's altar call were mostly the same ones that had come forward at the last revival.

But the contrast between these pious rituals and the way we actually treated each other was painfully obvious to me. The first poem I ever wrote—in seventh grade—was called "Prayer for Care" and included these lines:

> Father, I don't try to be the most popular guy
> or to have the crowd on my side.
> That's the problem,
> Lord, the crowd is on the other side.
>   We're supposed to need only You
>   but I need HUMAN companionship . . .
> And Christ, I'm sick of all the violence
>   the bullies, the snobs, the fakes
>   and the HATE!
> God, there must be a solution
>   there must be a better way
>   or is there?
> Lord, the people—the people You created
>   the people that YOU care so much about . . .
>   make them care.

As I began defining myself more clearly apart from the adult world, I thought I would find more commonality with at least some of my peers. By condemning the hypocrisy of adults we could feel both righteous and a little rebellious at the same time. Both the staff and other students said it was important to "be yourself"—but in reality this meant only if your "individuality" conformed to some pretty narrow expectations.

In junior high, as these contradictions increased, I drifted more and more into a separate world. I never decided to be a loner, I just got tired of the effort to fit in. I couldn't seem to please anybody anyway, so I just gave up. And my low grades certainly showed it—except in Science: In Mr. Murray's class, you didn't dare not do your homework.

Ian Murray, a short, bearded Scot, also served as the boys' PE instructor and justified his brutal regimens by personally leading us in every exercise he ordered us to do. I had heard there was a heart of gold underneath his frequently explosive temper, and that he practically pampered the seniors. But in junior high, we lived in fearful awe of him, cringing against his disciplinary projectiles of chalk, blackboard erasers, and shouted rebukes.

Despite my poor grades, I somehow graduated into senior high. Just before eighth grade ended, I surprised everyone—including myself—by taking first place in the school's annual creative writing contest (Poetry, Junior High Division). My winning entry was a properly religious give-your-life-to-God-or-else poem called "Passed Time." The last verse went like this:

> Time had been only a passing flicker.
> But it had decided the fate of Man
> for Eternity.
> All those who had taken the time they had,
> For Him, God gave them Eternity
> with Him.
> And all those who just couldn't find time
> for Him, God gave them Eternity too, but
> without Him.

I had somehow got it right that time and, more importantly, after receiving this award, I began to realize for the first time that perhaps I had a talent for writing. Feeling more confident about my artistic potential, when the new semester began, I signed up for senior high choir.

This was a new extracurricular venture for me. Upperclassman Glen Hamm patiently took me under his wing. I'd never been taught anything about music, and could sing only by imitation and memorization. Glen encouraged me and showed me how to read notes; I was actually learning something—and enjoying myself. Then, during one practice, a couple of the guys in the back were cutting up. Mr. Huffaker stopped everything and yelled at them. As I happened to be standing near them, we all got to stay after class to get a lecture about disrupting the sessions.

"But I wasn't talking," I protested.

This set off a blistering tirade about talking back to your elders that widened to raise ominous concerns about my character and ended by telling me that choir was a privilege that I clearly didn't deserve. I would not be welcome back.

When I asked why, he said, "For insubordination."

This seemed to be a handy label for teachers' general mistrust of any student who had the impertinence not to fit the mold; and it was easier than admitting that they might have made a mistake.

Mr. Huffaker was the boarding superintendent, and I couldn't understand why he took the job. He didn't seem to like kids. I never did learn how to sing, or to play an instrument. Instead, I immersed myself even further in my growing record collection. I liked the catchy guitar melodies by Lobo and America, and memorized the same songs by Simon & Garfunkel and Bread that appealed to everyone else. But privately I connected with the spacey chaos of Pink Floyd and the raw energy of Iron Butterfly.

The fifteen-minute jams typical of these two groups came in handy for an English assignment once when we were asked to pick and interpret a song. Between the two of us, Tim Old and I managed to use up the entire period with our lengthy presentations.

Another day in English class I had the impertinence to ask a procedural question about what we were studying. This resulted in a loud and essentially one-sided argument. The lecture ended with the usual ". . . and that's the way it is." And tacked on to that was the clincher, "And if you don't like it, you can just leave."

So I did.

I liked English. I liked Miss Brown. In fact, she had recently lent me her copy of *The Godfather*, saying that she thought I was the only one in our class mature enough to appreciate it—a rare vote of confidence in me from an adult.

But this kind of tirade was too much. So I stood up and walked out in the middle of class. After all, she had given me that option. I walked down the stairs and into the silent, cavernous auditorium. I wondered if I was demon-possessed for daring to defy the authority that God, in his infinite wisdom and love, had placed over me. I wondered if the earth would split open and swallow me up into its volcanic depths. Not knowing what else to do, I went out to the boys' restroom behind the school and sat down in one of the stalls to ponder my fate.

After a short while I heard footsteps, then: "Paul? Are you in there?" It was the voice of Mr. Nygren, the vice principal.

"Yes," I replied gloomily from the stinky cubicle where I was holed up like a fugitive—still not really understanding what crime I had committed to deserve the overpowering sense of guilt I felt. My righteous indignation had initially led me, impulsively, to take Miss Brown's summation as a challenge, but I didn't feel like a martyr now. I just felt alone and confused.

"What are you doing?" Mr. Nygren asked. And then, with typical self-effacing logic, added: "I guess what people usually do in the bathroom." I was relieved by this lighter touch and began to relax a little, so grateful that Mr. Nygren had been the one to come looking for me. Then he asked me if I was going back to class soon.

"Yeah," I said again; and he left.

That was it.

Mr. Nygren was my hero after that. By his matter-of-fact way of defusing the situation, rather than making some profound crisis out of it the way a lot of the other staff always seemed to do, he had treated me like a real person.

Just a week later I had a run-in with another teacher. Posture was a very important lesson in typing class and Mrs. Roub was vigilant against any laxness in this area. "You're slouching, Paul," she said in the middle of a practice drill. "Sit up straight."

"I am sitting up," I said, and was promptly rebuked for contradicting her. It was the same old trap. There was no more room between my tail bone and the back of the chair.

Mrs. Roub warned me that if I didn't straighten up by the time she counted to three I would have to leave (*this was ninth grade, for godsake*). "And you won't be coming back," she added. "You're going to have to learn that you can't always do just as you please, and if you choose to continue being defiant there will be consequences." And so on.

So the countdown began. Perhaps I could have made some deferential gesture by adjusting my position, but I resented her accusations and her assumptions about my attitude. Some of my classmates, who could see plainly that I *was* sitting up straight, exchanged looks of bewilderment and sympathy (*for me, even!*), as I sat there helplessly till she finished and then ordered me to the principal's office.

In the midst of all this, I decided to run for student council president. David Addleton, a senior, had been the only declared candidate at the beginning of the term and I felt that his campaign should at least be dignified by some competition. I had no illusions about my chances, but I intended to give him a run for his money. And it would be the first time a freshman had run for president of the senior high student council. I wrote tracts on my positions and created eye-catching psychedelic campaign posters, modeled after rock album covers.

Tom Ketcham got into the fray, miffed that his roommate's only opponent was a ninth grader, and engaged Stan Brown as his campaign manager. But Tom treated the whole thing as a joke. His sole campaign slogan, magic-markered onto typing paper, was "Tippy canoe and Ketcham too."

I didn't win the election. But I collected a dignified fifteen per cent of the vote (never mind that there were only 49 students voting)—a very respectable return for a maverick with a lot of name recognition, but no previous campaign experience. I had made my dent.

That summer I bought my own redemption through another means. I cashed in my life savings, mostly accumulated by my parents as birthday contributions, and purchased a bicycle. It was a beauty, too—a silver, lightweight Raleigh ten-speed, sold to me by one of the high school boys who was returning to the States. Thrills and liberty were now mine to command; power, prestige, and—most important—a place in the informal fraternity of cycling. My limited skills at regular sports left me with little interest in basketball or soccer; but here was something I did well—and now had some of the best gear on the hill to do it with.

During the long winter holidays I rode my family's old Pakistani bike all the time. When our cook's son, Javed, came with me I could go for much longer rides. The weather was always perfect— sunny and cool; but the dirt roads were rough and dusty. We usually rode on the hard-packed trail along the irrigation canals and dogs chased us every time we passed a settlement. Their vicious barking and snapping motivated us to pump the pedals with greater purpose, our hearts pounding in terror, until we passed some invisible territorial boundary. Another favorite route took us along the railroad tracks. This was tricky riding, trying not to slip off the narrow, often bumpy path between the tracks and the steep slope of the raised gravel bed. When a train came we had to dismount and scramble down the dirt embankment till it passed. So I had spent years developing leg strength and a keen sense of balance.

I complemented my new racing bike with an old-fashioned brass bus horn—the kind that, when you squeeze the big rubber bulb, honked like a goose pretending to be a donkey. I attached the horn to the handlebars of my ten-speed. Thus, on the narrow curves between Jhika Gali and the school, when I got behind a slow-moving truck taking up the whole road, I'd pump the rubber bulb a couple of times. Hearing this huge *bah-WONK, bah-WONK* behind them, the trucks would pull way over to make room for the expected bus —only to see the slim streak of my bicycle zoom past.

Having a bicycle in Murree increased my options just like having a car; that it was an expensive imported one didn't hurt my status, either. While the older boys predictably pretended not to notice, wherever I went, the Pakistanis were openly admiring of this elegant, aerodynamic machine such as they'd never seen before. I rode my bike to school almost every morning—*what freedom*—and could go directly to see Ardith in the afternoon.

During Social Studies class about a week after the student council elections, a messenger came to the door and I was mysteriously summoned to the principal's office. I couldn't think of any reason why. I had returned to Miss Brown's English class without further incident or animosity; and Typing was an elective anyway. Everything had been resolved, right?

When I got to the office, I found my parents, Mr. Nygren, and four of my teachers there waiting for me, as well as the principal. Before I had time to comprehend this strange gathering, Mr. Roub informed me that I was being suspended from school and that my parents were here to take me home. Each of my teachers then cited a litany of my offenses to justify the decision: Mr. Huffaker, Miss Brown, Mrs. Roub, Mrs. Calderwood.

I was stunned. Some of the things they said weren't true. And choir wasn't even a real subject—why were they using that against me? The only one who could offer anything close to specific was Mrs. Calderwood, who said that I disrupted Algebra by cutting up and eating my lunch during class, and that I had scribbled swear words on the blackboard with her name after it. It was true I didn't like Algebra, or Mrs. Calderwood, and one day in a reckless mood before class started, I had scribbled comic book symbols for cussing (#@&*!#) on the board, writing her name after them. In fact, I had immediately regretted that graffiti—because Mrs. Calderwood's son, Doug, was in our class, and I belatedly realized the unkindness to him. I knew I had crossed over the line of acceptable mischief with that one, but it hardly qualified as a suspendable offense. And why all the secrecy?

Everyone was clearly uncomfortable. Mr. Nygren tried to say something reasonable, to help me understand their position, but it felt like an empty formality.

My heart was pounding. A hot salty wetness filled my eyes, stinging them. I couldn't believe this was happening. And the humiliation made the tears spill over. I started to leave, but was stopped by my father's voice:

"Just a minute, young man. I didn't hear the principal dismiss you, yet."

It was incredible.

"May I please leave?" I blurted out, angry and pleading, while tears streamed uncontrollably down my face. When Mr. Roub assented, I fled the room.

I waited for my parents in the driveway, sobbing in great, trembling heaves. There had been no warning; no counsel; no "If you don't straighten up, then . . ." I was devastated. To my mind, being suspended was the same as being expelled, and had the connotations of juvenile delinquency, the wretched of the earth, the spiritually lost.

Was this supposed to teach me a lesson? Was this the kind of discipline and instructive consequences they thought would cure my "rebellious spirit"? Instead, it confirmed with a vengeance my growing sense that most adults were arbitrary, heavy-handed with authority, and, when challenged, would fight dirty to maintain their control. They hid behind their power rather than earning the respect they thought was their due.

And there were other students who had certainly done worse. I knew of scandals involving drugs or sex. One of the high school boys would be gone for awhile and then come back more settled, apparently as a result of spending some extended time with his parents.

But *my* parents . . . Far worse than the surprise or the excessive weight of the action was the complete lack of support from my parents. I didn't expect them to take my side, but I couldn't believe they had automatically sided with the school against me.

The worst thing was the sense of total helplessness. I learned the meaning of betrayal that day, and I would never be the same. For a long time afterwards, I wished repeatedly that I had made them all confront the depth of my feeling—the consequences of *their* action. I had nothing left to lose. I wish I had yelled and screamed and sworn, and turned over the principal's desk or something. I wanted so badly for them to share the pain they caused. All of us were at fault, but I'm the only one who paid the price.

That summer, the Addleton family lived above us at Ospring. My former rival for student council president was supportive and suitably dismayed at the school's handling of my situation. David assured me that the day after I was suspended a lot of the students were upset; they knew I had been treated unfairly. Though my fantasies about organized protest and David's intervention on my behalf were short-lived, it was comforting to know that I had stirred up some rumblings of indignation and sympathy.

For the rest of the summer, my teachers sent assignments home to me. The agreement was that if I kept my grades up and indicated an improved attitude I might be allowed back into school for the fall boarding term.

Auntie Inger's son, Paul Gardner, who had graduated from MCS in 1965, was in Pakistan that summer to visit his mother. His life had been turbulent, too. After a stint in the Navy, he had gotten mixed up in drugs and had just drifted for awhile. He found salvation again at a Jesus People commune in Chicago and had the zeal of those with a revitalized faith. My parents thought it would be great if he could be a big brother to me, maybe take me camping somewhere, and help me "find myself." Paul agreed to the idea— and I certainly wasn't going to complain about getting away from my parents and school work for a week.

So we took off for the rugged back country of Kaghan, an un- developed tribal region high in the mountains beyond Murree. The game of Polo originated in this valley—not the gentlemen's sport refined by the British, but a kind of rugby-on-horseback, played in the old days with an enemy's head as often as with a goat-skin ball.

After two days of scary rides in World War II jeeps and a long hike on the third, we reached Lake Saifil Muluk, at ten thousand feet. This natural reservoir, more than a mile wide, was the highest glacial lake in the world; bare, marbled peaks swept skyward from its shores on every side, cupping the lake in a raw, timeless silence. But our first night there it rained heavily. Soon water began flowing through our pup tent. Our sleeping bags were soaked. We finally fled to the porch of the government rest house on the rise above us, where we spent the rest of that long, cold night. The next morning we bought eggs and *chapatis* (local bread) from the caretaker who lived nearby.

Later, when the sun finally came out, I found some driftwood and whittled it into a sailboat with an outrigger. With a ballpoint pen, I wrote *S. S. Ardith* on its prow and proudly put it into the lake.

That day a couple of high school boys from MCS arrived for the weekend. When they saw my little boat they pelted it with stones, laughing. At first they threw pebbles at it, just to see if they could hit it—to "guide it along." Then they tossed bigger rocks at it, pretending it was a war—"just having fun"—until it broke and capsized. I don't think they saw my tears, they had already moved on; but if they had—well, you know the story: *Awh, come on—what's the big deal? Can't take a joke? What a baby!*

When I was in second grade we played in the sand box at every recess and lunch time. We built roads and "dinky towns" and "wild animal traps"—deep holes which we covered over with twigs and leaves and a thin layer of sand. One day I was in the middle of digging an elaborate tunnel beneath one of our "roads" when a couple of older boys offered to help. With feigned enthusiasm for my project they dug the tunnel wider and wider until the whole thing collapsed, and then they went away laughing.

Even in Shangri-la there were sandbox bullies. These two boys were popular; they had friends, they were both good at sports—why did they need to pick on someone? Just like Lucy Carter the year before. The scene came back to me clearly: *One day during recess, a small group of us are standing on the sidewalk at the side of the school, right at the corner between the sandbox and the picnic table where the staff took their coffee break. Lucy knocks my prized Arlo Guthrie-style hat into a puddle left from an earlier rain. Before I have a chance to recover it, she takes a quick step forward and casually stomps it flat. The other girls all laugh. I silently bend down, pick up the black felt hat— the one my dad had let me borrow—and straighten it back out. But the message is clear, and at some level I wonder if that really is all I'm worth.* I didn't feel sorry for myself. I wasn't even that angry, just bewildered.

Later that night in Kaghan, as I watched the full moon come up over ancient, snow-capped mountains, their severe majesty bathed in a ghostly glow, these things seemed very far away.

One afternoon, Paul Gardner impressed me with a complete recitation of Johnny Cash's "A Boy Named Sue," but my companion lost some credibility when, after a proud lunch of fish we had caught and cooked ourselves, he gave me an unexpected lecture on the evils of rock music. "Just look at the names of some of these groups," Paul said. "Like Santana—it even sounds like Satan." I may have lived a sheltered life, but I knew that Santana was simply the Mexican-American surname of the group's leader. It was disappointing to discover that even youth-oriented Jesus People weren't infallible.

Overall, I had a good time in Kaghan, but it didn't change my life. However, I thought the wisest thing to do was to convince my parents that it had. That's what they wanted. The day I returned home I called my mother into my room and told her—honestly— that I intended to make a fresh start, and to re-dedicate my life to the Lord (which, practically speaking, meant trying harder to do what *they*—my parents and teachers—thought I ought to). I accompanied this little speech with visible signs, giving her my switchblade and toy hookah. The switchblade was broken anyway (it was the kind easily purchased in Murree's Lower Bazaar that many of us carried just to feel cool); the hookah was a tourist trinket that had struck my fancy once. It actually worked and I had experimented with it a couple of times using pipe tobacco, filtered through a miniature water bowl.

When I gave my mother the pouch of Captain Black she looked at it closely and said, "It says 'tobacco.' Is that really what's in it?" I assured her solemnly that it was, while inwardly rolling my eyes.

I didn't know if I despised my mother more in that moment for being so ignorant, or for the assumption that I might be doing drugs. My parents seemed to know so well what all the experts said about teenagers and what we were doing, instead of taking the time to get to know me.

I stuck to my earnest, repentant posture, though—with only a few setbacks. Like when my mother smashed one of my records. I was playing Jefferson Airplane's "Don't You Need Somebody to Love" one evening when Mom burst through the closed door of my room, grabbed the forty-five off the portable phonograph with a fearful *zzzzzhhrrk* of the needle, shouting something about how could I possibly be doing my homework with this awful noise blaring. She threw the record down on the table and it broke into tiny pieces.

"HOW DO YOU EXPECT ME TO RESPECT YOU, WHEN YOU DON'T RESPECT ME OR MY PROPERTY?" I yelled. There wasn't any place I felt safe anymore.

Much to my relief, however, by the time the fall term started, I was allowed back into school. In spite of the marked improvement in my attitude and academic work, the day before I left for boarding my father told me that I had better behave this time. If I got kicked out of school again, he warned, he wouldn't take me back. He'd put me to work on a road gang or something. I was too much trouble to handle at home and he couldn't afford the distraction from his work—the work that God had called him to do.

He could have saved his breath. I was no more enthusiastic about being stuck at home with him than he was. Boarding school, with all its rules and obligations, was a welcome relief from him, and I couldn't wait to get back.

I once happened to see, on the desk in my mother's bedroom in Murree, a letter my father had written to her from the sweltering plains. It began, "My most precious, beloved wife," and continued on to declare poignantly, tenderly how much he missed her. The man writing this letter to my mother was a complete stranger to me.

The second term started out well enough. Even if my name did become a swear word that fall. One Friday morning in chapel the sermon was on the second commandment and the evils of cussing (*Thou shalt not take the name of the Lord thy God in vain*). "How would you like it," the guest speaker said, "if every time people were upset they used your name in a disgusted way?"

From then on, whenever someone missed a basket or a billiard shot they would hiss, "Oh, Seaman!" And if they were really disgusted or amazed they'd say, "SCREAMIN' Seaman." Or sometimes just for fun, they would sing out, "Screamin' Seaman from *RYE-wind*" (after the village near Lahore where my parents worked).

I was not offended by this new fad at my expense. After all, when the guys farted they said "Tewksbury!" instead of "excuse me"—and Ray Tewksbury was one of the most popular boys in the school. And I had always wanted a nickname—a badge of belonging. (At MCS we had the peculiar habit of calling each other by our last names.) "Screamin' Seaman" soon evolved into "Screa-Rai" when applied directly to me.

The "mouth guitar" and drumming noises that I was becoming known for got dubbed "Screa-raiing," as they began to be recognized as . . . well, as recognizable. I still got ridiculed for this habit of imitating rock and roll instruments, instead of just humming like normal people. It was not the peculiarity of the sounds that annoyed others as much as my insistence on entertaining myself in public places. Unable to appreciate the finer points of a fuzz bass guitar (by way of *Grand Funk LIVE* and Black Sabbath), Uncle Mark Jones once responded "Please save those noises for the bathroom."

Eventually, I did get some acknowledgement for my unique talent. One day, Nate Irwin heard me doing my version of a trumpet between classes and actually paused to look at me, as if for the first time. "That's pretty good," he said. "That really sounded like a trumpet."

"Thank you," I replied casually, while inside, my heart leapt with pride and a sense of vindication.

For my electric guitar to be properly appreciated, however, I needed electricity. In the true spirit of rock 'n' roll, I needed *amplification*. The opportunity came one Friday night at a junior high party in the school gym. The music that accompanied our rolling skating—tapes by the Four Seasons, the Carpenters, maybe some early Beatles—was run through the sound system for the stage. (Only the really "in" guys got to pick the music and operate the P.A.) During a break, one of the guys offered me a microphone and said, "Go on. Now's your big chance. Show us what you can do." I tentatively took the mike and walked out onto the stage, my heart pounding. I blubbered a few chords and did some experimental drum rolls, clicking my tongue and teeth, but I was just too nervous to get my mouth to work right and after a couple of minutes I gave up.

But nobody had laughed. A few kids even clapped.

For months—for years—after that I would lie awake and think about the missed opportunity. I could have done it better. I could have really showed them.

I could afford no such regrets about the more general situation, though—I was already giving it my best effort; and this was proving not to be good enough. Gradually, things began to deteriorate. My renewed efforts to fit in, to study hard, were more the result of repressing my natural inclinations than a genuine conversion, and this became increasingly difficult. Both my grades and my attitude started to slide again. I really *wanted* to succeed, to be a good Christian. I became obsessed with the fear that I would slip back into unacceptable behavior, that I would be thrown out of school again, and that my family would reject me. I prayed earnestly, but there seemed to be no power in it.

My need to express myself as an individual created an unresolvable tension in an environment that equated conformity with spiritual maturity. The most popular kids, those who excelled in school and sports, were generally the most pious Christians, too—reinforcing this equation. And the converse assumption weighed heavily on me. My spirit, though confused, rebelled against these unspoken but powerful judgments. Inside, I knew that I was a good person. At least I wanted to be. I sought the Lord in anguished prayer; I sought God's guidance through the Bible; I strained to hear his voice as I contemplated my dilemma. I wasn't making it in school, and ending up at home was definitely not an acceptable option. My dad had made that clear. It seemed that the only alternative was to run away.

Like a good Christian, I sought the counsel of a couple of others whose faith was strong—and whose confidence I trusted. One of these was David Hover. I trusted his spiritual wisdom because, with his father's tragic death, he had struggled more than most, and more authentically, with questions about God's goodness—or even existence—and the meaning of Providence.

David did not believe it was God's will for me to run away, but he did believe that God would honor the sincerity of my search and make his will clear to me. David's trust in God's faithfulness was so strong that he suggested we "put out a fleece" like Gideon did in the book of Judges and ask God for a sign—one that was *against* the odds of occurring. David suggested the name of one of the Jesus people from Kabul who had visited MCS earlier that fall. Our agreement was that if I did *not* receive a letter from this person by my birthday—November 5—then we would both accept that it was God's will for me to run away. And if that indeed was the case, he added, putting his money behind his faith in a way that I would never forget, then *he* would pay my airfare out of the country.

I believed in divine guidance, but my faith in divine interference was not as strong as David's. So I began making preparations for what seemed the more likely outcome. Then my sisters and I went home for the mid-term long weekend. One night after I was sure the rest of the family were asleep I snuck into the pantry. This was a narrow room off the kitchen, lined with shelves from floor to ceiling. After pulling the door firmly shut behind me, I felt for the switch in the dark, moving the plastic lever by tiniest degrees till the light came on—a single bare bulb hanging down on a long chord. I scanned the shelves quickly, selecting cans of stewed peaches, Spam, sweetened condensed milk, and placing them ever-so-gently into the pillow case I had brought with me. I grimaced when the light clicked off again and waited for a few moments, listening. My pulse throbbed, like a bunch of little fists squeezing in unison. Back in my room, I carefully hid these items in my suitcase, along with other supplies I thought would help me survive across Asia with almost no money. My intention was to fly from Rawalpindi to Tehran and from there to hitchhike across Europe.

My fifteenth birthday came and at noon I checked my mailbox, as I had every day, hundreds of times before. A stack of wooden slots had been built into the wall right next to the little office window where Mr. Lawrence, the Pakistani clerk, sold us notebooks and pencils. Leaning down to see into the bottom row, I felt the weight of the moment, felt a sense of disbelief; perhaps there had been a mistake. Maybe the letter from Kabul had gotten misplaced in another box. But finally, I knew that now there was no turning back. The constant *clackity-slap* of the old mimeograph machine stopped while someone re-inked it; Mr. Lawrence suddenly sounded louder as he yelled "Hello! Hello!" into an office telephone, like he always did. In a moment, the Gestetner started its endless racket again and I walked slowly across the gym, out the big front door, and down the sidewalk by the old sandbox.

I told David the results, and the next weekend I rode my bike in to Murree. From the public telephone exchange I called the office of Pakistan International Airlines in Pindi. The plan was that the

Sunday of Thanksgiving weekend, David and I would go to Murree for dinner right after church, I would get a bus to Pindi, and be out of the country before they noticed my absence at supper time.

When a "mono" epidemic broke out and the school decided to shut down two weeks early it seemed that God was paving the way for my departure: The passports were all kept in the boarding superintendent's safe and would be distributed back to the students in preparation for the journey home. I could now simply walk up to Mr. Huffaker and, with complete credulity, request my passport— "to pack in my trunk." Mr. Huffaker always sounded like he was reading from a handbook of regulations and made you feel like you had done something wrong, even if you hadn't. He said that passports would not be distributed until the day before school closed, and that he would be giving mine to my older sister for safekeeping.

I was dumbfounded. This was the first real snag in my carefully laid plans. The simple reality was that I could not get out of the country—certainly not through an airport, anyway—without a passport. I didn't know what to do. In desperation, a couple of days later in PE class I confided my plans to John Huffaker (a tenth grader) and pleaded with him to get my passport for me. I assured him that this scenario had been all properly checked out and was definitely God's will. Naturally, he had serious reservations, but he also claimed that he didn't know the safe combination anyway.

The next day was Saturday—what should have been the night before my big departure. But everything had come unraveled because of this one stupid thing. I paced the upstairs veranda outside my bedroom at Sandes and listened to a senior high party breaking up below. Couples or groups of friends were drifting out of the recreation room, calling to each other. A group was sitting on the porch directly below me. It was a cold night and their laughter crackled like a blazing fire, and the warmth of their conversation floated up to me. I had never felt so alone in all my life.

I found myself holding the long, military green silk rope that belonged to Tim Old, my roommate that term. I stood by the corner railing and looked at the big metal bracket fastened there years earlier for someone's meteorology project. A good place to fasten a noose, I thought. I was famous for swinging out on that rod, suspended over nothing but air, like that goofy silent film star hanging from the clock in Times Square. Wouldn't that break up the party, if a body with a broken neck dropped down into their happy group. That would show 'em.

I contemplated this temptation for some time, then wandered downstairs with no destination in mind. Walking along the lower veranda, I heard Tom Ketcham, just as he was coming out of the rec room, make a comment about his dad to someone inside. I mumbled something and Tom said, "What'd you say?"

"I said, I wish I had a Dad like that."

"Why do you say that?"

I mumbled something again. Then Tom sat down with me on the edge of the veranda, leaned against a pillar, and proceeded to tell me about his recent conversion experience, about his reconciliation with his father, and how he had come to appreciate his father's unconditional love for him and, through that, came to understand God's love.

My dad's love was far from unconditional, but something in what Tom was saying stirred hope in me for the first time in years. Although he mostly talked about his dad, he related it to our being teenagers here at MCS. He talked about how he had hurt his dad by letting him down, by getting involved in drugs and sex, and then letting it happen again. In spite of this, his dad bought him a new stereo system.

So that's where his fancy stereo had come from. Earlier in the term I had gotten into trouble for breaking Tom's tape recorder. One day I had snuck into his and David's room—a forbidden lair of the senior boys— to practice *screa-raiing*. On a previous visit, Tom had showed me how the tape recorder could be used as a public address system by plugging a microphone in and running it through the speakers. What I didn't know was that there has to be a tape in the machine in order to physically be able to depress the record button. I just thought it was stiff . . . and it broke off.

Uh-oh.

But like David Hover, Tom had been swept up in the hip, youth-oriented Christianity that had recently re-vitalized MCS. While David's conversion had left his philosophical arrogance more or less intact, Tom had visibly mellowed. This impressive change had a very practical benefit to me when I broke his tape recorder, and I escaped the expected wrath. I had to pay Mr. Murray a few rupees "technical services fee" for repairing the damaged switch, and got off with being grounded a few days for getting into another boy's belongings without permission.

As Tom continued to talk that night, he seemed to know too much about my situation and I began to fear that I had been betrayed, that David Addleton, one of my few confidantes, who happened to be Tom's roommate, must have told him about my plans. But when he started talking about fathers and sons he seemed to know things about my home situation he couldn't possibly know.

And I realized then, with a long, slow shiver, that *God* was talking to me. Tom said something about how the connection between my dad and I had been broken and we couldn't fix it. But we had another connection—he sketched a triangle in the air—through God. Yes, I could see it; the image gave me hope. And there on the front porch of Sandes Home, on Thanksgiving weekend, 1972, I encountered God in a way that had never happened before. For the first time in my life, I felt God's concern and wisdom directed specifically to me. This is what I had been looking for all along— just to know, just to be assured that God really was there, that I wasn't alone.

With a geyser of joy slowly permeating up through me, I finally stopped Tom and told him what was happening. I told him everything, interspersed with several Praise-the-Lords, and laughing with the giddy high of spiritual ecstasy. God had finally come to *me*. I had heard his voice myself.

That same night I rushed over to the hostel to tell Becky Ketcham, the one girl I had confided in. There was little time to tell anyone else, besides David Hover and David Addleton. A few days later the school closed down and we all went home. I couldn't wait to tell my parents. After the long train party to Lahore, we had an hour's drive to Raiwind. (Our big cream-colored Land-Rover was still painted with red crosses from the war a year before). I spent the entire trip telling Mom and Dad what had happened, and that I wanted this experience to also affect our relationship, and that I intended to submit to them in every way, because that was God's will.

My mother was deeply moved that God would honor one of her children by intervening so directly. Dad didn't say anything. It wasn't the first time I had made such resolutions. Mom said it also saddened her, though, that I had felt so disheartened, and so isolated, that I had felt driven to consider such extremes. Indeed, on that long ride home her mind must have raced through the tragic possibilities and the terrible grief she herself narrowly escaped. Committed to dividing her love and attention equally, she was aware, too, of her other three children who had sat quietly in the dark all the way home. It would not be the only time my new convert's zeal steamrolled over social tact or consideration for the needs of others.

In February of 1973, while still on winter break, my sisters and I joined other MCS students aged ten and over for a week of "Kids Kamp" at Taxila Christian Hospital. Designed to give missionary kids a Christian camp experience once a year, Kids Kamp activities included team competitions in Bible knowledge and sports—touch football, softball (the only time we got to play those sports in Pakistan) volleyball, and fling-ding, as well as field trips to the Taxila ruins, Muslim shrines, and a nearby cement factory.

But the highlight of Kamp was the daily Klubhouse time, which always began with everybody enthusiastically singing its theme song:

> Kids Kamp Klubhouse time:
> This is our Kids Kamp Klubhouse time.
> We run to meet it, we run to greet it
> It's Kids Kamp Klubhouse ti-IME!
> Happy hearts have we,
> Using our talents all for Thee;
> We come not sadly but singing gladly
> To KIDS KAMP KLUBHOUSE TIME.

Then followed more singing, debates, Bible quizzes, and skits led by Paul "Uncle Freddy" Lundgren or Russ "Uncle Rope" Irwin, the camp directors. Some of the memorable skits included "The Spitball Pitcher and Catcher," "The Burping Coke Quartet," and the always-popular "Short People," dancing or feeding themselves (using one person's arms for the legs with an unseen second person providing the arm movements). Debates ranged from the relative merits of the Pakistani and Western dating systems (a hilarious release for culturally-repressed teenagers) to the uniqueness of Jesus in a non-Christian world (a more thought-provoking challenge designed to help us better articulate our faith).

We had been divided into three teams which competed against each other throughout the week, and during the first day's Klubhouse there was a contest to see which team could come up with the best team cheer. We were all named after prehistoric animals that year, and my team was the "Do-dos." Suzy Pietsch suggested that we could simply chant the name itself, ending with a short *screa-rai* performance by me.

We won hands down.

Still lazy even after my "Damascus Road" experience, I resisted one of the more pious preoccupations of Kid's Kamp—memorizing Scripture. I earnestly explained to my camp roommate Bruce Rasmussen (a fellow Do-do) that I thought team competition was a poor motivation for memorizing Bible verses. He didn't share my view, but said he admired my integrity.

My big moment came toward the end of the week, when we all gathered for the traditional testimonial bonfire. After waiting politely through the warm-up remarks and a couple of short confessions (always with a virtuous resolution), I launched into my story—sparing no detail. By the time I finished, the bonfire had died down to almost embers and the counselors were probably torn between the inspiration of this truly monumental testimony and being conscious that very few others had gotten to share that night.

My real testimony, however, the living-in-victory part, began the following spring. While my relationship with Dad had remained unsteady over the winter break, a funny thing happened when I returned to boarding for the last term of the year. Without my having to put a noticeably greater effort into it, things at school—both socially and academically—seemed to get easier. I became one of the regular leaders for group devotions and was elected *captain* of the team for a Capture the Flag day. Female classmates, who previously disdained me, now sometimes came to me, especially during more informal occasions like camping weekends, for counsel about *their* problems—and not for religious advice, but because they thought I could understand. It was an unaccustomed role but one that felt natural. Here, finally, was the acceptance, the recognition, the belonging, that I had wanted for so long. I was happier than I'd ever been in my life.

Almost every day I wrote a poem—about the meaning of life, the suffering in Bangladesh, the beauty of nature, the mysteries of love; about Elaine Roub, about suicide, and about MCS.

FOR THE GOOD TIMES

Outside, a great white blanket flutters to the ground
And the old stove heater calls many boys around.
A couple of guitars appear in the gathered mob
And brother Tim starts his usual fantastic job,
With occasionally someone else joining in.
And I sit, listening, and writing this poem
To remember the good times.

I don't like being away from home so much
And often the school work seems like too much.
I don't like all the rules that come with it,
But there's no reason I'd want to miss it
Because with the bullies, the boredom, the loneliness and
        heartache
Comes talking after lights out, camp-outs, and April Fool's
And lots of other good times.

Sometimes the teachers are hard to bear
They always seem to be in your hair
But it does something to see one of them in tears,
Behind their back only jeers—
All the time they've been wasting, trying to help
A rebel kid make it; and I wonder how far
They are from the good times.

I think about the mountains, the forests, the snow,
Classroom parties, and chapel services, and quietly I know
There's not a feeling anywhere, I'm clear,
Like not wanting to be anywhere but here.
There's so much to say, I could write a book
And maybe some day I will . . .
To tell about the good times.

That spring I won first place in both the prose and poetry categories of the annual Creative Writing contest—this time as a ninth grader competing in the Senior High Division.

But it was my yearbook, the 1973 *Kahani,* that provided the final testimony to the change that took place that year. Page after page of autographs bore witness to the glorious mystery of those days. The congratulatory tone of their words amazed me, for it was not with a sense of accomplishment that I had changed, but from inner peace.

Dale "Mr. conformity-priority" Huffaker wrote, *"Thank you for being yourself and progressing in many ways. We will miss you."* (In my glory of spiritual contentment, I didn't hold the irony against him.) Wilma Wilson, the Scottish French teacher whose poor luck it was to teach the most boring subject, and thus endure our most relentless cut-ups, wrote, *"You are a person who is a walking example of someone who has let God do something in him. May He do great things in you. Keep writing good poetry."* Evelyn Calderwood said: *"Even though you may not have learned much Algebra this year, you have learned many important lessons which will be more useful to you. We are proud of you."* And Irv Nygren, in his inimitable way, wrote simply: *"Paul—It's an experience knowing you."*

Leslie Christy said, *"You really have changed millions and millions this last year. And its really helped me to see it happen. Thank you for all you said at Kamp—you don't know how much that affected me (and probably lots of others)."* Another senior, Scott Kennedy, wrote: *"Man, you've grown this last year like it was Joe's Pizza Parlor!"* And added, *"Now that I'm splitting, I give you permission to bang ALL you want on the stove or plates!"* Tom Ketcham inscribed this: *"Dear Brother Paul, I'm praising our Lord for all that He's done for you. He's just too beautiful to be true. I've just discovered Him myself."*

Many people commented on my *screa-rai* "noises," mostly positively. Lucy Carter wrote, *"Keep on 'singing,' who knows? You might make it—pop gets weirder all the time!"*

Twenty years later I finally got a few minutes in the limelight. I had never forgotten that night in the school gym and the discovery of how amplification could demonstrate the potential of my strange gift. When the seminary where I now work held its spring talent show, I gave a performance of my "invisible instruments"— uninhibited this time—and had a hundred and fifty people clapping along to Iron Butterfly's "In-A-Gadda-Da-Vida." And after the climactic drum solo they gave me a thundering ovation. Not to be bested—or, perhaps because he now had permission—one of the professors got up and did "Laura's Theme" from *Doctor Zhivago* on *his* mouth version of a balalaika! Then he did an impressive "trombone" rendition of "Moonlight Serenade," to everyone's delight.

I felt like an orphan who had just found his long lost older brother.

9

The Year of
Snakes and Ladders

(excerpts from a diary)

June 1973
        Tuesday—26th. Well, here I am—on a train to Lahore
again. This time by myself. Today I left Murree, the
school, and my girlfriend, Elaine, for the last time before my family
leaves for a year's furlough. I've decided to keep a diary every day
while we're in the States, and now seems like a good time to start.
The Roubs had invited me up for the weekend so Elaine and I could
spend some time together, and it was really beautiful. It was cool
staying in the principal's house and eating with his family, but
especially, having Elaine mostly to myself for two days!
        Last night Raindrop (Elaine) and I went to our special spot
behind the school. We sat on the steps outside the first grade
classroom and joked again about why there were steps going up to a
window! In front of us, just inside the iron fence, was the big tree
the Juniors used for their "Tarzan Swing" during the fall carnival,
which the eleventh graders put on every year to pay for the Senior
Banquet in the spring.
        The "swing" is more like a chair lift, suspended from a heavy
rope on a pulley; you sit on a board and zoom through the air, way
down the hill almost into the woods. The carnival includes bobbing
for apples, "science" experiments with electricity (group shocks), and
a spook house. But this ride always has the longest line. When I get
back from the States, it will be my class's turn to put on the carnival
and I'll be out there pulling the rope for little kids. And the next

year, I'll be a senior! Elaine will be gone, then, but I don't want to think about that right now.

This spring I got to go to the banquet for the first time. Most of the other ninth graders weren't that excited about it since they're not interested in girls, except Tim, but Kathy is in eighth grade so he didn't go. Elaine and I have been going steady since Kids Kamp, but I still asked her to be my date months before the banquet, just in case any of the boys in her class got any ideas. I heard she was kind of hoping Jonathan Addleton would ask her. As it turned out, Jonathan asked my sister, Martha! I don't think he's really interested in girls, but I guess he heard that she really liked him and wanted to be nice.

The banquet was at the American Club in Islamabad, but I still got K.Z.'s disease real bad right after dinner. Oh, *man,* I was in pain! Tom Ketcham (bless you, brother) found me in the restroom, sitting on the commode doubled over with stomach cramps. This wasn't my idea of a romantic evening. But Tom instructed me on how to get the gas out of my system and, sure enough, within two or three days I was ready to go back out and attend to my date.

That night something happened during the movies that probably shouldn't have. It was the first time Elaine and I had been together for such a long time—two full hours "alone" in the privacy of a darkened recreation room. When I finally got my courage up, she didn't say anything and she didn't pull away. Later, on the long bus ride back up the mountain way past midnight, Elaine said she thought we had lost something innocent. I cried when she said that, and held her hand tightly against my face (partly so she would know I was crying real tears).

I first kissed Elaine just three months ago, during a skating party one Friday night—in this very same spot behind the school. She said, "I've never kissed a boy before," and I said, "I could teach you." I didn't close my eyes then, like I did the first time with Ardith Corcoran and accidentally kissed her on the nose; and afterwards Elaine said, "You're a good teacher."

Last night things were pretty equal—except that I was leaving. We prayed together one last time; then, before we went back to the house, I sang "Leavin' on a Jet Plane" to her: *"Now the time has come to leave you. One more time, let me kiss you. . . . Tell me that you'll wait for me, Hold me like you'll never let me go."*

One of the best things about a girlfriend is that they're the only one who will indulge your really serious and sentimental sides. The staff is so afraid of what might happen if couples are left alone together, but most of us just want a chance to have a private conversation with the opposite sex, and be with someone who treats you gently. And I don't know when the staff think we're going to do all this hanky-panky, they keep us so busy with scheduled activities. Besides, most of the guys are so scared, it takes them almost a whole hour—the length of a Sunday night walk to Jhika and back to the school—just to get up the nerve to hold hands.

Wednesday—27th. Yesterday on the train I talked with a Pakistani Army major who wanted me to pimp a Western girl for him. That was a new experience, but I stood by my beliefs—and told him so. I don't know any American girls in Lahore, anyway. Last night I stayed with the Corcorans, my old girlfriend's family, before coming on to Raiwind this morning. It was hard to tell Rev. Corcoran my answer. After all he had talked to me about and "convinced" me of, and then for me to admit my "compromising" theology, he was quite sternly disappointed. But his anger and disappointment don't really bother me. I know the peace I have and what Christ has done and is doing for me, and I'm not going to get re-baptized in the United Pentecostal way.

Got home just before lunch and spent the afternoon carrying boxes of family stuff to the farm storeroom. Heavy, hot work! We had supper at Doris Edwards' house. Doris is a single missionary from Wales who works in the next village over. I read my poem, "Something Beautiful," and she was quite impressed, as people usually are.

Thursday—28th. Went to Lahore today; swimming at the InterCon Hotel. Some rich Muslim businessman was cussing out the bartender as if the guy had raped his daughter. Later I found out he had just written her a friendly letter, which had been censored at the private boarding school she attended. I bought some beautiful new space stamps for my collection, which leaves me with no money through Europe. Had another stupid argument with Dad about calling things stupid. He said I was being unreasonable. Then he said calling things stupid was an indirect cut at *God*, who made things good. How unreasonable can you get!

Saturday—30th. We leave for Karachi tomorrow. Took our trunks to the station with Dad, then helped him oil the guns. It was a good evening because with all the last-minute packing Mom and Dad where too busy to argue.

July

Wednesday—4th. We are on a Lufthansa plane somewhere between Frankfurt and Zurich. We took a PIA plane from Karachi to Frankfurt and the Pakistani captain invited me up into the cockpit. What an experience! I was amazed by all the buttons and switches and asked him how he kept them all straight. He said, "You get used to it with practice," and he pointed to my shirt. "Look at all the buttons you have to button each morning; you have to buckle your belt, zip up your pants, tie your shoes—but it comes naturally to you now." He thought the movie "Airport" was unrealistic. Later he let me come back up and watch the landing. That was really cool!

Frankfurt airport was HUGE, and beautiful except for all the short skirts and the pornography being sold openly, which was sick.

I should be excited about this trip, but instead I'm busy catching up on my diary and what I have to report isn't much fun. On Monday night there was an incident with Dad, stemming from his unnecessary support of Mom. We were staying at the Wilmot's house in Karachi; Mom had told us to get to bed and we were half an hour late. Then Dad came up and gave us the old line about having to crack down; he said he'd have to start requiring strict attention from us, get us to repeat instructions back to him, and respond with a proper "Yes, sir" to every order. Martha resented his interfering and told him so. That did it. The tension mounted. Dad said something. Martha snapped back. Dad sent her to the living room. She spit in his face and screamed like the devil was in her. One thing I had to admire about Dad was his self-control beyond human expectations.

Everybody was really uptight, but Dad very matter-of-factly said, "We're in a city, so you have to use some self-control or we'll have to control you."

Martha spit again and stomped into the living room. As Dad followed I said, "See what you've done to your daughter!"

After he had quieted Martha, he came back and said to me, "It'd be wise not to make comments. I still have some strength."

"So do I," I replied.

"Be careful. I'm using a lot of self-restraint."

"So am I—a lot more than you," I added.

I desperately wanted to let out the flood of words I felt had to be said, but I knew the consequences. Dad went into his bedroom, allowing Miriam to come with him. I went into the living room where Martha lay in a heap sobbing. I put my hand on her and asked God to give her peace. I don't know what happened but she stopped crying. I went back to my bed and could hear Dad in the next room talking to Mom about whether "the cross or the switchblade" was first in my life.

"Based on his behavior tonight, we don't know how subversive Paul is," he went on. "We should probably get customs to check through all his luggage for hidden switchblades and drugs." He wondered whether I should be allowed to have my belt, which was wide leather with a steel buckle: "the kind they use in gang fights." That was a laugh, but it wasn't funny. The thing that infuriated me most was spoiled eight-year-old Miriam being allowed to listen to all that, and Dad, in effect, telling her how bad I was. Fortunately, I managed to get to sleep without nightmares.

The next morning Dad had left early to go see some agriculture project, so I didn't see him till night. I went out to spend the day doing research at the American Center library. I'm writing a book called *Stolen from the Stars* about a secret international organization trying to capture a UFO. I didn't get much done, though, because I had so much on my mind.

I went to a nice Western-style restaurant for an expensive lunch. When I came out, a world traveler offered to sell me some hash. I asked him why he pushed drugs. He said "I don't push drugs. A dealer gives me a commission and I need the money." I told him he shouldn't be getting his bread at the expense of other people's freedom. Then we had a discussion about harmless "grass" and hash—stimulating like coffee, but doesn't blow your mind like H or LSD. I think he's right, but that's one opinion I would never even try to discuss with my parents. I'm not interested in drugs for myself, anyway. I get high on Jesus. And in spite of what my dad might think, I've never even tried pot.

Before I left, the guy asked me if I could spare five rupees—he didn't have enough money for a meal. I was kind of ashamed after coming out of a posh hotel and a big lunch. He was my brother and he was hungry, so I gave him the bread. Later I found out it was my mother's money and she wasn't too impressed with my generosity. I think she would have been proud of the way I witnessed to the guy, but it didn't seem worth trying to explain. I will do nothing that is against my parents' will until I am no longer under their authority—in most things, at least.

So that night I asked Dad if he and I could rap for a few minutes. I apologized for "interfering" and acknowledged that as his son I needed to obey my parents, no matter what I think of his procedures. Well, we had a good man-to-man talk and I went away with that feeling I get when I see things clearly: even though I hate so many things about my father, there is also a strange, unexplainable admiration, even love, for him.

Thursday—5th. We are staying at "Bienenheim," a rustic chalet in the Swiss Alps that is used by local vacationers. We are the only Americans here, which is cool. I have my own little room on the third floor, with a steeply sloped ceiling, a tiny window, and a big, fluffy comforter on the bed. The mountains are huge! Maybe not as high as the Himalayas, but the valleys are deeper, more spectacular than around Murree—and less intimate. We arrived late last night, and when we got up this morning the view was startling, like happened at Yosemite during our first furlough in 1968; except that this is a lot bigger! I spent most of the day working on *Stolen from the Stars* and got quite absorbed in it. I more and more favor my chances of getting it published so I want to really settle down and get into it. I'll have to revise my notes again, but I shouldn't waste too much time on that. Got to get started on chapter two!

Friday—6th. This morning I climbed a mountain with a couple of Swiss men who are also guests here. Spent the afternoon organizing my notes for *S.F.T.S.* and then writing to Elaine. After supper I tried to make friends with the Swiss waitress who is eighteen. I showed her my *Kahani* from MCS and helped with the two kids she was taking care of.

Sunday—8th. Got all dressed up this morning for what we thought was an ordinary outdoor service, but turned out to be a six-mile hike to some once-a-year event. I walked up with Christine and the two little ones. We sat together on the grass and neither of us was interested in the service, which was in Swiss. Coming back, she didn't have the kids and we held hands. (To my relief and her delight, she returned my squeeze.) We walked with a friend of hers who spoke a little English and seemed amused at Christine and I being together. We stopped at a cafe for drinks. Her friend had a car (with a chauffeur!) and drove us the rest of the way home. My family packed up and left for Zurich after lunch. Christina seemed sad to see me go, but not heartbroken; Praise the Lord!

Monday—9th. Up early to catch a Swiss Air flight from Zurich to Frankfurt. We were booked to Hannover, where we are going to see one of Mom's cousins; but there was an air traffic controllers' strike so we took the train. The airline put us in first class on an express train. That was neat and I slept most of the way. When we got off at Hannover I was tired and my guard wasn't up. So when Dad got disgruntled with the porter because he said he didn't know the rates, I tried to explain, but then realized it wouldn't do any good.

"You don't understand," I said, adding "hardly anything" under my breath; but he caught it and I caught it. He wouldn't let me help carry the suitcases—since I was "obviously uncooperative" anyway. This was really awkward when Mom's cousin's husband unexpectedly met us at the station.

Wednesday—11th. We are in Amsterdam now. This morning Ruth and I took a walk along the canals. In the afternoon Ruth went with the rest of the family on a boat tour of the city. I stayed home and worked on my book. Tonight we went to the ballet at a fancy European theater. I actually enjoyed it, even though we got off to a bad start, as usual. While waiting for parents to finish getting ready I started talking to this guy in the hotel dining room. He asked me to share his food with him, he couldn't eat it all. And I agreed—as a sign of friendship. Then Dad came in.

"I don't understand what's going on here," he said in his army sergeant's voice, pretending to be puzzled. I was really embarrassed. He told me I might have to pay for my portion and that it was not good stewardship (since we would be eating together later).

Yesterday at the airport I met a Methodist pastor and his family from Liberia. They were surprised that I recognized them, but I had overheard them talking. They were so happy that I had said something. I introduced them to Mom, who introduced them to Dad, who recognized the wife from Asbury College; and that finished my place in the conversation.

Friday—13th. Yesterday morning we went out to see windmills and the dike. Didn't get to the dike, but actually had a good time together as a family. On the way back we went into a "Penny Arcade" for the first time in my life. But when Mom saw all the pinball machines and video games, she said this was a very evil place and we hurried back out. But not before I had seen a flying saucer game and, like a little boy, just had to have a chance at "shooting down the UFOs." I finally convinced them (Dad didn't seem quite as concerned as Mom) to let me have one turn—with my own money.

Later, Ruth and I went to the new Van Gogh museum where a guy tried to sell me hash again (maybe it's my long hair). A simple "no" seemed so inadequate, but I didn't know what to say. I tried to witness to him about Jesus, but he just said, "Hey, man, just do your own thing."

Today we took a train to Brussels in Belgium (another country!) and a bus to Calais where we got a hovercraft across the English Channel. Dad had planned our trip to "take advantage of this rare opportunity," but maybe he thought it would be cool, too. It was a "beaut" experience, except that our new suitcase got damaged by careless handling and Dad was mad about it. Instead of just writing a complaint for compensation, he took it out on the poor stewardess, telling her how disappointing it was to travel by hovercraft for the first time and have this happen, and how "bad" the company was.

We're staying at a missionary guest house outside of London called Foxbury. After a quick dinner, I went into the lounge to watch "Star Trek." Then Ruth and I played table tennis for awhile. Later I got acquainted with two German girls who are working here and a Norwegian girl who's a guest. We went into the drawing room and talked about stuff. I read some of my poems and we talked some more, till one a.m. They couldn't believe I'm only fifteen. I'm going to like it here.

Sunday-15th. We had family devotions this evening. Nobody prayed except Dad, who prayed an unusually long one. After we finished, I started reading and so did Martha. Then Dad started a lecture about our rudeness and how we weren't going to get any privileges if we don't show courtesy. Then he asked me: "What do you think you should do now that I've told you this?"

"I think I should keep reading until you ask me to do something specific," I answered honestly, confused by the whole thing.

Of course, he thought this was "negative and rebellious," so he called off the discussion about me going to see my godfather while we are in England, and said that as long as I'm acting like this, as far as he's concerned, he's not going to help pay for my trip.

"So much for the fancy prayers," I said as I left the room.

Five minutes later he called me back in and gave me the usual about what he thought of my remark and my behavior. "As far as I'm concerned, you're in the rebel camp, and anything I do for you will be along the lines of loving your enemy, as God instructs us to do."

So he told me, in effect, that I was his enemy. That struck me pretty hard for some reason, but on the outside I returned his cold stare before silently walking out. I felt crazy after that, wandering around the hotel lounge, screaming a couple of times then putting on an amnesia act. Luckily there was no one in the room except this girl I had met the day before. I told her what had happened, but felt sort of stupid because I sounded like I felt sorry for myself, which I didn't want to do.

Tuesday—17th. This is a cool place. The library here has a secret door, made to look like a bookcase, so if you're not paying attention when you come in you might not be able to find the door to get out! I've been working on my notes for *S.F.T.S.,* outlining the main jobs of the major characters at the base. Talked some more with the German girl who works here, Hannah-Lora. I tried to talk to her about God without turning her off. She needs him.

This evening Mom and Dad came back from London and told me that they hadn't been able to get much done; but they did get tickets to "Jesus Christ Superstar" (for everyone except Dad) and bus tickets for Ruth and I to go see Mike Proctor, my godfather, in Northumberland. Dad was very helpful with maps and an expense allowance. I sure have mixed feelings about him. If he's doing this out of love for his enemy, he must really love his enemy a lot.

Monday—23rd. Flew to New York today, on one of the new 747s. Wow! Even after all we'd heard, the plane was incredibly huge: The cabin was like an auditorium and first class even had a second floor lounge. We got to watch a *movie* on the airplane, but the headsets cost $2.50 each!

I talked to Hannah-Lora for a long time in the library last night—about losing friends, searching for truth, and not finding any answers. I tried to explain Christ and we prayed together. I don't know what will happen. In five days she has come to mean so much to me. When we said goodbye this morning, the farewell was surprisingly strong.

So, here we are in the good ol' U.S.A. Actually, it's not very exciting. I realized today that I don't feel that I'm coming home— especially if home is where the heart is. All that I love I've had to leave behind.

Sunday—29th. We're staying in Trenton, New Jersey for a few days with my Aunt Nancy (Dad's sister). She goes to an Assembly of God church, which is Pentecostal like the Corcorans, but not quite as weird. We went to a really square church this morning and to a youth cook-out this afternoon. It was actually nice to be among United Methodists for a change, except that they only had *hamburgers* and I had been really anticipating getting some real

American hot dogs. I tried tossing an American football for the first time. The guys were pretty patient.

Last night I sat in the kitchen with Aunt Nancy and my cousin Barbara till four a.m., talking about sex and God and family stuff. Nancy doesn't believe in petting but she sure talks frankly about the birds and the bees! Uncle Joe, Dad's younger brother, tried to commit suicide because he thought he got a girl pregnant. Jim and Nancy got married because they had to. Aunt Nancy thinks Jim didn't really want to marry her, like he led her to believe—just wanted the kids, but he's never around to be a father to them. When he is here I guess it gets pretty rough. He used to beat her, till she threatened to have him put in jail. He can be very nice but then gets *real* mad—tears up the furniture, threw a casserole at the wall. He doesn't get drunk (thank God); Aunt Nancy thinks maybe its mental, like schizophrenic. Once when she didn't iron *one* shirt of his, he destroyed her favorite dress; another disappeared. She had to take him to court to get money for food. (She said she felt dirty, like a criminal, going to court.) She still has to work as a maid to support the kids.

I knew from Dad the part about Aunt Nancy having to scrub floors for a living—he used that story to make me feel guilty. But I didn't know the other stuff. It made me feel ashamed of the way I had talked about Dad the other night. I guess I'm pretty lucky.

August

Thursday—2nd. Yesterday we arrived at Bob Little's farm in Pennsylvania. He met us at the Greyhound station and all seven of us, including him, piled into his small Ford, with all our suitcases and a dozen bags. Last night Dad spoke about Pakistan at the church the Littles go to. I met some girls, but Mom sent me back to sit with Dad when I kept explaining her slides to them. I didn't care—she just made herself look uptight. Bob Little is short and balding, he looks more like a shoe salesman than a farmer, but he seems like an unusually nice guy. Turns out he hadn't heard about "my" plans to work on his farm for the rest of the summer—Dad hadn't told him yet! He's going to talk it over with his wife and understands that I also want to do a lot of writing while I'm here.

Got up early today—but late by their standards! Went out to "help milk the cows." Dad was already in the barn, not doing much, but feeling quite at home, telling me things I already knew or that Bob had told me. After lunch the rest of the family left and I slept gratefully till evening. Bob got me up to help feed the cows. I learned how to wash cow teats in preparation for milking. It was kind of embarrassing at first.

Saturday—4th. Up early to milk the cows before breakfast. I know how to put the automatic milkers on myself now, but still didn't get to help much. John, the farm manager, has his routine down, and I felt like a "fifth wheel on the wagon," like Bob warned me might happen.

This afternoon we went shopping. Now I'm all fixed up. I bought underwear, socks, jeans, and a really nice pair of cowboy-style work boots. I couldn't find any fountain pens, but I got *Jonathan Livingston Seagull.* We got home late and had to rush to feed and milk the cows. Plenty of work to do then! Watched "Mission Impossible" before bed.

Friday—10th. This morning I put up two full wagons of straw mostly by myself. (170 bales, fifty pounds each—wow!) Then I helped shovel corn out of a silo into a truck. That was the worst job I've ever done! You get all hot and sweaty and then the corn dust sticks to your skin and itches like crazy. After lunch Bob and I went up for a swim at the church camp where Mrs. Little is working. I was glad for a little "idleness"! Later, when I met the girls my age, I had my first experience being swooned over. They all wanted to sit by me at dinner, which created problems. It turned out that I was the special guest of honor—a new experience for me. I gave my testimony around the campfire while freckle-faced Tracy sat at my feet and Jolene on the other side. She's okay, except she keeps asking me why I'm the way I am.

Wednesday—August 22. After the milking this morning, Bob asked me to load a big pile of rocks from his other farm for a wall he is building here. I got to drive the truck there and back alone! This afternoon I finished all my notes and outline for *Stolen From the Stars.* I celebrated by watching TV all evening: "Archie Bunker," "Bridget Loves Bernie," "Bonanza," and "Gunsmoke." Saw Nixon's press conference on Watergate.

Thursday—30th. Our "home" in Ithaca is small, but I have my own room—along with all the luggage. We're staying on the third floor of the Presbyterian missionary apartments in Collegetown, right next to Cornell.

Last night I had another "disagreement" with Dad at the family conference. I made some remark, quite innocently, and when Dad asked me to explain it I told him it wasn't worth it. Then I got the usual line about subversion and trying to get attention. Of course, he had to bring God into it and said he'd pray that God would show me my sin. Then he walked out (his way of getting attention) with the calculated intention of making me feel guilty about causing the whole family to be in a bad mood.

I've pretty much decided to split, but I'm torn about leaving Ithaca and about not being able to see Pakistan again.

Tonight we went to a get-acquainted party for everyone in the building (there are four apartments here). I talked with Dr. Anderson, a former college president, about UFOs. He said he'd read *Chariots of the Gods,* but I think he was just being friendly. Later I sang a song to the whole group that I just wrote today. It's called "Family Man."

> He'd like to be a real family man
> And I know he's doin' the best he can
> He even helps with the pots and pans.
> The things he teaches are so high
> Made to help us reach the sky
> But they only seem to make me cry.
>
> I know he's not tryin' to be unkind
> But he really needs to unwind
> To give us all some peace of mind.
> I've tried so hard to make him see
> That it's best just to let us be
> Because I know I have to be me.
>
> We can no longer get along
> He doesn't know when he's doin' wrong
> And it's his only son singin' this song.
> Oh, God you know I just can't stay
> But why does it have to be this way
> Maybe I can come back some day.

October

Wow! I've missed more than a whole month. So much has happened—I'll never forget the agony I've gone through. Yet, looking back from a Christ-centered view, it all seems so empty. One night after spending the evening in Collegetown, I called Mom and Dad and told them I wasn't coming home. I stayed with a friend I met from Cornell in her dorm room. We didn't do anything—I wasn't even interested in her like that; she was just being nice. I showed up the next day and Mom and Dad were pretty upset. But I didn't run away. I did renounce Christianity for awhile. I told my parents that if being a Christian meant being like them I didn't want anything to do with it.

I found out last week that you can legally leave home at sixteen—and my birthday's in three weeks. But God showed me that He'll take care of me here.

Ithaca High School is huge. It has several buildings—like a college campus—and 2,000 students in just three grades. MCS has only 150 in twelve grades! I ran for student council, but don't really fit into any of the cliques here. That's okay, though, because I have friends from the musicians group, the theater people, *and* the "greasers." The jocks don't like me, but they're the most stuck up anyway. I've been frustrated with some of my classes, but two things happened this week that helped considerably. I got moved to a level four honors English class and Mr. Pullman agreed to be my advisor for an "Independent Study Course in Creative Writing." So, I'm using my five extra study halls to write my book for credit!

The Methodist church is boring and the youth group doesn't talk about God at all. Mom found out about a Jesus People church outside of town called the "Love Inn." It's built out of a barn and it's really cool, with guitars for worship and everything. They have a worship service/Bible study on Tuesday nights and Mom takes us out there sometimes.

Last night I got up at 11:30 p.m., dressed and went up to Collegetown. I saw Doc, a "hood" I know from school. He's a skinny guy with really intense eyes, hard muscles, and a weird nervous laugh. Doc calls me a "Jesus Freak," but he likes me—respects me for standing up for my beliefs. He's the PR man for Steve Watkins, a black guy who is number two in The Family, the largest gang in New York State. Doc asked me what a straight kid like me was doing out at that "evil" hour. I wondered, too. We just walked around awhile and talked. He would say something and then laugh, more like scoffing, at the end of every sentence. We met up with some of his friends and they warned me it wouldn't be safe to come home from downtown alone so I split.

I got back to bed without getting caught. I don't think I'm letting the Devil grab me by hanging out like that—I just wanted the experience. If it happens again, I'd begin to wonder, but I still love Jesus and follow Him.

November

Dear Elaine— It's Thanksgiving and I'm celebrating by writing you a letter, sort of. I've decided that writing to you is the only way I can start being faithful to my diary again. Last week I interviewed Carl Sagan up at Cornell University, about my book. I asked him if he believed in God and he asked me what I meant by God; I didn't really want to define it too narrowly, to see what he'd say, so I didn't really get an answer. I also got an appointment with Frank Drake who designed the *Pioneer 10* interstellar probe. He didn't have much time, though, and I was so amazed by the lab he has up there with models of the galaxy and stuff that I forgot to ask some of my important questions.

We are out-of-town this weekend, visiting another one of my parents' supporting churches. Last night I wrote a poem called "Gobble, Gobble, Gobble: Or, Thanksgiving at Light Street Methodist Church." I read it at the church potluck after Mom and Dad's presentation:

You sat in your central-heated homes
    or churches (it makes no difference)
And you say your graces and take your places
Around the naked turkeys without combs.

You stood in your sanctuary of bliss
    and chanted out your prayers (oh, such beautiful prayers!)
On pumpkin pie- and cookie-bloated stomachs
Satisfied with your $3,000 campaign
        for new carpets.

You lay in your bed, but to keep holy you made your sacrifice
    of the electric blanket
To kneel so beautifully by your bed
To thank God for your Thanksgiving
    and bless Him for your bliss.

God damn your mocking mayhem, you foul friends of the motherland
    —where is your fatherhood
To the starving babies you have abandoned
    who whimper humbly in their hunger
The result of your rape?

And the cold air shivers through the night
        but it is pure and sympathetic
    with me
As I wrap my cotton scarf around my bony blue neck
And hiss a loving little prayer for you.

Mom and Dad were shocked more than anyone else, I think, and of course they were mad about my profanity. I did feel inspired, though, and one of the Sunday school teachers said she admired my ability to express myself.

December

We drove to Louisville, Kentucky, for the Christmas holidays. That's where Grandma lives, and Mom's sister. Aunt Etta has two daughters about my age, so it hasn't been totally boring. Grandma came over Christmas Eve with her new husband, "Uncle" Ray. He seems very nice, reminds me of Mr. Little. Mom didn't want Grandma to re-marry, so it must have been awkward. She said that according to the Bible it was the same as adultery, even though Grandma left Grandpa Kunz more than thirty years ago because he beat the girls and had a mistress. But Mom still believes divorce is a sin.

I rode back from church with Aunt Etta's family. I sang some Simon and Garfunkel songs in the car, like "The Boxer," "Homeward Bound," and "The Dangling Conversation." They said I had a nice voice and kept asking me to sing another one. That was a new experience.

I've gotten kind of involved with the girl next door, Julie. The day after Christmas Aunt Etta took the three couples—Julie and me, and my cousins and their boyfriends—and Martha to the movies. We saw "American Graffiti." Afterwards, the couples went for a walk. Julie and I split off by ourselves and got back late. Even though we were just walking around the neighborhood, Mom was really mad and yelled at us both.

Tonight I went over to Julie's house to watch TV with her since she had been grounded. When I got back, Mom had my Bible open on my bed to some verse about "don't touch women." (I've been studying the *whole* passage, to see what it really means.) Dad just kids me about being a sailor "who leaves a broken heart in every port." That bothers me more.

May 1994

Dad graduated from Cornell today. Grandma and Uncle Ray came up from Louisville for the occasion. I was talking to Uncle Ray about my book and he offered to lend me $200 so I can hire someone to type it up for me! He said I could pay him back whenever I get it published. Wow. Praise the Lord. I've been concentrating very hard on my book, which is tricky along with trying to keep up passing grades in all the classes I'm taking, especially now that it's almost the end of the year. I really want to finish it before we go back to Pakistan next month. But Dad says my main job at this time in my life is education and that if writing my book keeps me from doing my best in school, then it's a sin.

June 1994

Pentecost Sunday. Last Friday afternoon we found out we're not going back to Pakistan. What a shock!

A couple months ago the mission board ordered psychological evaluations for all four of us children. I knew what it was about, but didn't think it could be *that* serious. Martha obviously has pretty serious emotional problems, but Dad said all of us "didn't pass," and that the Board thought we needed to be in the States where we could continue to get counseling and stay together as a family. Dad and I seem to be taking it the hardest.

Just a few nights ago, there was a movie on TV about *Apollo 13* called "Houston—We've Got a Problem." First, they didn't get to go to the moon after all that preparation; and then they weren't sure if they'd ever make it back home . . .

Tonight I went to the senior prom with an Indian girl, a senior, who asked me to take her. It was the first dance I've ever been to. The ballroom up at Ithaca College was really nice, but I was lonely— especially during the slow dancing, which I didn't do. I missed Elaine. On top of that, all the girls who might have come close this year to substituting some of what she meant to me had other dates. I wondered again if I could ever reestablish that blessed perfect relationship I knew one spring with a Raindrop . . .

Last week I got my book back from the bindery. I had a cover put on the typed manuscript, like a thesis. It's sky blue with *"Stolen From the Stars by Paul Asbury Seaman"* written on the front in gold lettering. I put it on the coffee table in the living room next to Dad's black-bound agricultural thesis. Today we had company and I overheard my dad say, "And this is a book my son wrote this year. Look: it's even thicker than my thesis."

I didn't say anything.

PART TV

Suspended Crossing

When I got back to the States, it took me several years to understand that I had no home in the world and that I had imagined a world, and that I was going to have to live in that imagined world and make it coexist with the real one. And the only people who can do that are writers or artists.

JON ROBIN BAITZ
acclaimed American playwright
("Three Hotels"), on growing up in
Brazil and South Africa

By necessity, I made my own private treaty with rootlessness and spent my whole life trying to fake or invent a sense of place. Home is a foreign word in my vocabulary and always will be. . . . I was always leaving behind what I was just about ready to become.

PAT CONROY
author of *The Great Santini*,
from his Introduction to *Military Brats: Life Inside the Fortress* by
Mary Edwards Wertsch

Some fell on rocky places . . . and they withered because they had no roots.

THE PARABLE OF THE SOWER
Matthew 13:5 (NIV)

The Seaman missionary family, 1969. Official United Methodist publicity photo: Ruth, Paul, Martha (standing), and Norma, Alan, Miriam (seated).

Chip Aldridge

Coming full circle: the author at age fifteen, just before returning to the United States in 1973; and twenty-three years later.

10

The Rattling Dream

. . . we speak the same memories;
dream ourselves in the same overloaded truck
rattling and bumping along in a cloud of dust
as we sing.

BETH RAMBO,
"Travelers"

My autobiography is a running debate in the nature/nurture controversy. Like everyone else, my life has been shaped by the hopes and explanations that defined the community of my upbringing, and also by experiences that often contradicted those expectations. But what qualities of character—and, consequently, the unfolding of my particular story—were predetermined by the imprint given to me at birth? Is there some holy intention to be discovered at the intersection of personality and circumstance? In the collision of chance and choice and providence, where do we find our identity and a sense of purpose for our lives?

I think some of the answer lies not in the big universe of cosmic questions, but the little one of our own life histories. Life's great truths are like musical chords that we recognize from their resonance, without ever hearing the notes being struck. We yearn to touch the tuning fork that first put its signature on our own peculiar melodies. But its pure measured tone is now dissonant, mingled with others. We strain to get closer to the source, hoping for clarity, for something that will sharpen the fading echo from that original moment.

My baby book—the photo album my mother kept of my earliest years—is one such source. It is both treasure and treasure map. There is a photo of me at age four sitting in my little red wagon that says *Radio Flyer* on the side. I have put a cardboard barrel in it to make a prairie wagon; my friends and I are playing Cowboys and

Indians. Two years later, another group of little boys are gathered on the front steps of our house in Murree. Every one of us has a black pirate patch cver one eye and is trying hard to look fierce for the camera. My sister Martha sits on the top step, just to be there.

Every year, the Methodist families would put on "the Ospring Circus." There are wonderful pictures of me, the master of ceremonies (in bathrobe cape and homemade top hat); me, the trapeze artist; and me, the lion tamer (in oversized rain boots). The toddler lions, the leopard (my little sister, Miriam), and the elephants can be seen in the background with shredded brown paper manes and huge, drooping cardboard ears.

In my favorite snapshot, taken when I was seven, I am standing alone on the side of a hill, dressed as Robin Hood. There is fog in the trees behind me and I am holding a full-size likeness of an English long sword. I had forgotten about that sword. It was wonderfully realistic: carved on a wood lathe, its handle was painted black, the blade silver. That was when my dad would still do things like that for me.

My father used to tell me stories about his cruel childhood—to illustrate, I think, how grateful I should be for my own privileged life. The lessons were lost on me, of course, but the stories were not. Dad grew up in southwestern Pennsylvania during the Depression, the second-oldest of eleven children. When I first heard the various installments of my father's early life I was much too young to keep straight the difference between tales of abusive foster homes, his coal-mining experience, and army training in preparation for the Korean War. Thus, for years I understood that his foster parents forced him to crawl through the mud beneath barbed-wire fences, dragging sacks of coal, while guards fired machine guns overhead to keep him working.

Imagination and emotion sometimes connect in creative ways that make memory—and, by extension, identity—an uncertain thing. Facts are but a rattling bone carriage suggesting the greater reality dancing within and beyond them. The ancient and universal ritual of retelling stories brings clarity and continuity to our understanding of who we are. But what about my private memories, or the ones that don't fit the cultural myths associated with my citizenship?

Twenty years after leaving Pakistan, the facts listed in my passport still seemed like an assumed identity. What did it mean for me to be an American, to be my father's son, when my roots were someplace else and in other relationships? Set apart both culturally and geographically in its mountain setting, the experience of community at MCS probably influenced my life even more deeply than growing up in an underdeveloped Asian country.

In many ways MCS was the ultimate small town. Although we represented fifteen different countries among us, we were a community all told of two hundred people (not counting the Pakistani servants). Besides the students, there were only forty or fifty teachers and boarding staff. My Scottish chemistry teacher was my PE teacher and my Sunday School teacher; my boarding father in junior high also taught biology. For ten years I attended class with essentially the same eight or nine kids. Every three years we moved from the charge of one houseparent to another, but continued to relate with the same core staff and peer group. Visitors were a big event and, in spite of the Christian values we so earnestly embraced, newcomers—both students and staff—often had difficulty fitting in.

What saved us from the parochialism that often plagues rural religious communities in Western countries was the very foreignness that caused our isolation in the first place. The global diversity within our small world made it difficult to make the kind of cultural presumptions often associated with evangelical or fundamentalist groups.

Still, we were taught a worldview at MCS that centered on a narrowly-defined Christianity as the only truth: The Bible was the literal Word of God, without error or ambiguity, and was the only resource necessary for all of life's questions and problems. Anyone could have a personal relationship with Jesus Christ, beginning with an intentional and specific moment of confession and conversion. Thus assured of salvation, we might face trials and temptations in the world, but supported by regular prayer, Bible study, and fellowship with other believers, we could be forever free of loneliness and doubt. And all "real Christians" believed just like this.

Long after this view became less vital to me, I acceded to its trappings: the deep spiritual yearning instilled in me at MCS was inseparable from the value of close community that I experienced there. Undeniably, we received a "firm foundation" from the love, commitment, and faith of those who watched over us and ran the school. But the maps MCS gave us were far from comprehensive.

The Bible taught that all had sinned and were equally unworthy, and that everyone had equal access to God's grace through the Lord Jesus. Yet, those who accepted this doctrine were the "elect," the chosen few—and vested with the sacred mission of "saving lost souls for Christ." Our being surrounded by a non-Christian culture that was poor and "backward" seemed to confirm the view that the West had prospered because of the influence of Christianity.

We proudly distinguished ourselves from the "ugly Americans" in the Foreign Service and international businesses, disdaining their lives of luxury and aloofness from the "real" Pakistan. But the essential characteristics of an expatriate lifestyle—practiced by almost all Westerners living in Third World countries—are the same: privilege, status, and an artificially high standard of living (in contrast to both the local population and what could have been afforded in one's home country). We were not immune to the attitudes inevitably bred in such a situation. It was hard not to feel superior.

Our circumstances gifted us with a certain cross-cultural broad-mindedness, yet we were ignorant of so many things. The Pakistanis with whom we had the most direct contact were servants—encouraging prejudicial stereotypes about the culture in which we were guests. We had even more misconceptions about our home countries. During the sixties and seventies there were almost no Pakistani students at MCS and one African-American boy, for only a couple of terms. Thus, we were unprepared for the racial and ethnic identifications that provide much of a person's sense of belonging—and community tensions—even in Western nations.

Similarly, the only professions considered worth pursuing were those that could be used in "God's work" on the mission field; we had no role models for lawyers, artists, or philosophers. We were sheltered, too, from both the diversity and the divisions that characterize the expressions of Christianity. The world we grew up in seemed like a cohesive, self-evident reality. Its multiple layers and uncertainties became more apparent when we returned "home" to an unfamiliar country. And the internal contradictions built into our background made the social displacement from this transition doubly isolating.

When we left the community of our upbringing not only were we uprooted, so was our family tree. So now, we cannot just turn to our grandparents and say, "Where did our family come from?" because, in fact, our family is not the same as theirs. Our family, our homeland, is the company of others with similar experience. Our heritage was not formed by a national tradition, but by a particular situation. And even there, the strong religious identity we were given proved, in the wider world, not to be enough of an explanation for who we were or where we belonged.

At MCS, we took it for granted that moral issues were of central importance in every aspect of life. But "back home" this seemed to be a rare perspective, and, except in the churches that supported

them, the fact that our parents were on a mission from God no
longer held any special status. The defining myths of our missionary
childhood lost some of their meaning when removed so completely
from the context that shaped them. While the resulting dis-ease
often went unacknowledged or unarticulated until much later, we
had, in fact, become cultural orphans.

We dreamed of the States like the Pakistanis dreamed of a
mythical America where everything was better, easier. But when it
happens, when you finally go "home," well—as a friend of mine
said—how long can you sit around eating Twinkies and watching
"Gilligan's Island"?

Some MKs (missionary kids) resented being so different when
they came back to the country that was supposed to be home; but I
was used to being an outsider at MCS, and my "adjustment problems" there probably made the transition back to the States easier.
When I was in eleventh grade, "Kung Fu" was a popular show on
television and I identified closely with the lead character, played by
David Carradine. Abandoned by his American father soon after
arriving in China, Kwai Chang Caine was raised in a monastery until
he returned to the States as an adult. Now, he wandered the Wild
West of the late 19th century, drawing upon the Oriental wisdom—
and the kung fu—learned in his youth to help him deal with a rough
and prejudiced world.

It wasn't long before I had shaved my head—like a Chinese
monk—ostensibly as a symbolic act of deeper spiritual commitment.
Of course, I couldn't see then the other posture it so obviously represented: my stubborn refusal to assimilate. Like many MKs, I was
proud of my ignorance of worldly ways—or pretended to be to cover
up my shame, as if my "innocence" were a badge of righteousness. "I
don't know how to play cards" became simply, "I don't play cards"
(said with a long jaw and arched eyebrows). Other times, I was deliberately vague about my background because of the blank reactions
it often elicited; I used to sometimes say that I was from India
because no one had heard of Pakistan.

Many years after my family returned to America I continued to
struggle with these same issues of identity and belonging. Contrary
to what I and others had assumed, it turned out not to be merely a
teenage "phase" that I would soon pass through. It is a legacy that
still haunts me. Like a ghost train chugging through my blood, it
goes unnoticed for long spells, imperceptibly pushing along my
pulse, only to clatter randomly through my dreams. I do not always
recognize the source of this restlessness inside me but there are things
that make its distant rhythm suddenly close—the smell of kerosene

or pine sap, a mango's slippery taste, the sight of a Land-Rover, the curve of a wooded hillside, a social embarrassment, or the loss of a friend.

The Lahore Railway Station, the transfer point for so many of my childhood memories, is a majestic blend of empire and adaptation. Yet, built into this quintessential monument of the British raj and its faded glory is a poignant longing for home. The station's oddly quaint spaciousness and the ornate ironwork of its lofty rafters are a nod to far-off London's Victoria Station. The empire has now gone home, but its legacy continues in the subcontinent's great railway systems—symbol of Western concepts of education, time, and organization. These ideals may have devolved into form over substance in Pakistan's tattered civil service, but they live on with pride through its trains.

Memories, too, can be more than vanished events and lingering emotions; they can be functional monuments. And like other monuments, they are neither meaningless nor omnipotent. By necessity or design, monuments simplify complex realities. They provide important reference points, but their claim to history is suspect if they have been constructed from denial or wishful thinking.

Gradually, the telling details that shaped us become obscured by the necessities of conscience, by cultural assumptions, and by the preoccupations of a different life. We can only manage generalizations, remembered through a few particulars that conveniently buttress our summarized feelings. But it is the particulars that have shaped us, not some notion of the whole.

We often speak of a mosaic when trying to reconcile the disparate shards of what we—or others—can recall of the past. Perhaps a prism is a more appropriate image. A mosaic takes meaningless pieces and makes them into a cohesive whole; a prism splits something seemingly transparent into meaningful pieces. "Only that which has been separated may be properly joined," Carl Jung observed about the subconscious mind.

At MCS we were firmly taught that there is only one truth; yet the process of exploring memories—especially discussing a shared experience with others—quickly demonstrates how one person's perception of a time and place can be true and yet contradict another's perceptions of the same time and place. Some choose to remember a near-perfect childhood and its obvious benefits. Others, like myself, may give unwarranted emotional weight to perceived injustices that happened a long time ago, trying to explain subsequent patterns that seem beyond our control well into adulthood.

While memories, like the Lahore Railway Station, may have been built to celebrate or lament the past, they can serve the present as places we pass through to uncouple old freight or choose a new direction. It is not enough just to revisit old memories, they need to be re-aligned. The uncomfortable divergence between our inner and outer journeys cannot be reconciled by a private pilgrimage. It requires the safe scaffolding of a re-connected community—even if in proxy—and the surveyor's stick of other people's stories. We yearn for the reassurance of a memory larger than our own.

The compelling shriek of a train whistle evokes for me something deeper than memories—a longing for a more reliable time when expectations were straight as the steel rails that offered us the comfort of a confined adventure. Trains were the safest way to travel in Pakistan; they provided the romantic thrill of moving rapidly through changing terrain, yet you always knew your destination.

For David Addleton, the memory of trains provokes an uneasy sense of life's painful uncertainties. He was six years old when his parents promised him he would be going on a "train party." He knew what trains were—and enjoyed riding on them; and he knew what a party was—and certainly liked them; so he was excited about the upcoming adventure. The big day came and he was bewildered when there were no balloons, or ice cream and cake, or games and presents. Then, on top of that, he suddenly realized that his parents weren't coming with him. Although over the next decade he would come to have many wonderful experiences at boarding—and on the trains in between—the shock of that moment has been deeply imprinted.

Marybeth Tewksbury remembers that in her house it seemed that, for some reason, the only time the record player was put on was the week before a train party, so for a long time after leaving Pakistan she associated classical music with goodbyes.

Don Calderwood, the principal of MCS during the early Sixties, once said goodbye too eagerly. One of the first train parties, shortly after the school had been established, was hastily scheduled when the school had to shut down because of a flu epidemic. Dr. Norval Christy, who was then chairman of the board of directors of MCS, agreed to help escort the party down country, along with Don and a couple of the teachers. It was a night train and the first children were let off at Jhelum, Gujrat, and Wazirabad. There were about fifteen students going to Gujranwala, the next stop after Wazirabad, and Don and Norval were carefully watching the stations. As the train came to a stop, the two men hurriedly ushered the children off and pushed all the luggage out onto the platform. The students were standing around the scattered piles of trunks and *bisters* looking for their parents. Don quickly decided that he had better stay with the kids until their parents arrived. As the train pulled out of the station Mary Louise Selby said, pointing to the sign on the station house, "But Uncle Don, this is not Gujranwala, this is Ghakkhar Mandi." So "Auntie" Joan Larsen had to tell the families, waiting for their children in Gujranwala, that the school principal and the chairman of the board had put them off at the wrong station. Further, there was no road from the Grand Trunk Road to the station where the children were waiting, so coolies had to be hired to carry the mass of luggage from the station to the vehicles on the road. It was a long night—but not half so long as Don Calderwood's lingering embarrassment.

I spent twenty years getting off at the wrong station. A patchwork career history, frayed faith communities, ambiguous friendships, and misplaced intimacy had brought me no closer to home. It seemed that most of the milestones in my life were monuments to disappointments. As I pursued my dreams, sought comfort and stability, I found the rug pulled out from under me again and again. I was bold, bitter, and bewildered all at once, until finally I just ran out of steam. Then I had to confront how totally lost I was.

11

Sirens

No one ever told me that grief felt so like fear.

C. S. LEWIS,
A Grief Observed

Twenty years after returning to the United States, one of my former classmates says he still thinks of Pakistan every morning when he takes a shower. After living with perennial water shortages, he continues to be grateful for this simple luxury that most people here take for granted. For me, the instruments of nostalgia are more capricious—like the phantom itch of an amputated limb. While the slightly dissonant twang of a sitar makes me smile, the distant whistle of a train passing in the night always reminds me how far I am from home. *Out of Africa,* the beautiful film version of Isak Dinesen's independent passions and failed dreams, ends with her boarding a train and saying final goodbyes, not only to friends but to her adopted homeland itself. As the credits rolled, I sat in the theater and wept inconsolably, even as people began coming in for the next show.

Sam Peckinpah's classic ultra-violent Western, *The Wild Bunch,* opens with a group of children trying to get a scorpion and a giant centipede to fight. That image yanked me back to the school bus stop in Murree and the emotions of an eight-year-old watching the same, long-forgotten scene. Not coincidentally, the movie's subject, like the memories it evoked, was cruelty, camaraderie, and social displacement in a changing world.

A more random intrusion is the sound of sirens—the particular kind factories use to signal a change of shifts. It terrorizes me. That slow rising pitch, dying in a long nasal whine, still signals an air raid, and brings back the edgy, intangible sense of danger that I experienced at fourteen.

Sirens always catch me off guard—frozen out in the open, as it were. They set off an air raid inside me, probing the painful ambivalence that has strained my attachments since leaving Pakistan. More recent memories have become entangled with the fear that sirens trigger, evoking the same dread and confused sense of guilt. The childhood source of these emotions has blended with other wars—with my father, with school teachers, with failed love, and with the many merchants of God who have preyed upon my desire for spiritual truth by bribing my hunger for community. And sirens never let me forget that I am still a refugee in my own country.

I remember sitting in a tenth grade history class in Ithaca, New York, the year my family returned to the States. The teacher was extolling the virtues of Charlemagne and the Magna Carta while my classmates whispered about who would be the captain of the football team this year, or whether Nancy the cheerleader was really going out with a "greaser." Then the siren on top of a nearby volunteer fire department building began its low, accelerating tone and endless, unwinding fall, starting up again just before it died out.

To my amazement, nobody moved; the other students continued writing earnestly or gazing out the window, lost in love scandals or dreams of sports glory. But my mind had been kicked into another world, banged like the side of an old TV set to switch channels. My heart raced. I clung to the edge of my desk, barely resisting the impulse to hide under it. Then I saw my mother's face during the war.

It happened three years earlier, in December 1971. The day had begun early, in a haste of last-minute packing at my parents' mission station in Raiwind. On the trip to Lahore, my sisters and I sat wedged between our most vital possessions. Mud had been smeared all over the outside of the Land-Rover for camouflage, and Dad had painted big red crosses on the hood and front doors. (The correct proportions for a medical red cross could be achieved by thinking of it as five squares fitted together, he had explained, and I had to admit, the results looked very official.)

As we approached the outskirts of the city, we heard air raid sirens and pulled over to the side of the road. Cramped from the rough trip, I was glad for the opportunity to stretch. Dad and I stood beside the Land-Rover waiting for the all-clear. Searching the dusty twilight, we could just see the soft orange glow from the tail jets of two planes as they circled twice over the city and then disappeared. There was no sound this far away—just two orange embers drifting across the sky. Right then, from the edge of town, the war was fascinating.

Unfortunately, a lot of other people thought so, too. Pakistan Air Force jets had scrambled to intercept the intruders, and, at a civilian airstrip in one of Lahore's suburbs, a crowd gathered on the runway to watch the dogfight. After dropping their bombs elsewhere the attacking planes had strafed the airport on their way out.

Half an hour later we pulled in the main gate of United Christian Hospital, all colored brick and glass-modern, and Mom went to offer her services as a nurse. While we waited, a busload of wounded drove up alongside us, packed with the results of the carnage at the airport. People clung to the hood of the bus, wailing fearfully.

I didn't see any more details; but Mom did, and when she came back to the car a few minutes later she had a look on her face that I'd never seen before: horror, sadness, bewilderment. "It's so awful," was all she said. And I knew it wasn't just the sight of so much blood that sickened her.

Until that moment, a vague awareness of death and destruction had barely tempered the excitement of being EVACUATED. It was a somber adventure, constrained by a premature nostalgia, an awareness that I might never again see the place I had come to know as home. Just three days earlier my sisters and I had left Murree, and for the first time in my life I was suddenly confronted by the impermanence of everything. I would never be the same.

At a special assembly Mr. Roub had announced that school would be closing two weeks early due to the national emergency. After we were dismissed to go pack, I started out for Sandes— walking by myself, as I often did, I guess by choice.

After a few steps, I turned around and looked deliberately at the big gray school building, at the stone wall that separated it from the road, and at the rusty cast-iron fence that topped the wall. Every vertical rod in the fence had a flat, pointed head, like a little spear, and we used to try and jiggle them out of their sockets so we could play with them. In third or fourth grade, I had sat on that wall with Mark Pegors, my best friend of the moment, eating smoked beef tongue that Mom had sent up in a care package.

I looked at the small cement courtyard inside the fence, where I always seemed to get picked last for Dodgeball or Red Rover. I glanced at the Army field across the road, where the girls played field hockey, the boys played soccer, and we all competed on Sports Day. When I was in sixth grade, one of the world's largest helicopters—a Russian MI-6—had been brought to this field after crash-landing on the road a couple of miles down from the school. One of the propellers broke off in the trees and a new one had to be hauled up from Rawalpindi by flatbed truck. How they ever got a thirty-foot metal blade up these mountain roads with their many hairpin turns, I couldn't imagine. But they did, and a couple of weeks later, when the giant helicopter was finally repaired, we all gathered at the edge of the lower field to watch it take off. The back wash was so strong it blew the tin roof off a nearby barracks!

Entering junior high had meant the dreaded three-mile runs for gym class every spring. The finish line was right there at the front gate, by the new metal sign with our school emblem enameled on it and the words "Murree Christian School."

As I walked on up the road I tried to drink it all in, savoring the snow-capped peaks along the horizon, knowing I might never see them again. I knew every curve and cliff of that wonderful windy road by heart: stone retaining walls on the outside, where wooded meadows fell away to valleys far out of sight; and on the inner slope, exposed earthen faces where the green flow of thick forest was suddenly cut off, scraped away to fit the road into the hillside. I remembered Sunday afternoon picnics in second and third grades, when Auntie Inger would take the Little Boys department down into the woods so we could build dams across the streams.

This mountainside held the memory of many fine adventures— Tarzan, Robin Hood, jungle commandos; and more recently, great games of Capture the Flag. The way we played it at MCS, each person wore a piece of colored yarn tied around their wrist, and if someone from the opposing team broke your yarn bracelet you had to go back to their fort as a prisoner. This version invited plenty of rough scuffles—a delight for the boys, but a surprising number of girls participated enthusiastically, too. Earlier that fall, the entire high school, including some of the staff, had played a night game all across the hillside above Sandes. I found myself wrestling with Cheri Longjohn as she struggled to break my life-thread.

"I'll kiss you, if you don't give up," she threatened in frustration.

But I was way beyond being intimidated by that prospect, and told her she could kiss me gladly. Disgusted, she had managed to get my bracelet anyway; and I was disappointed for another reason.

❖

The train party lacked its usual festiveness that year. Some parents had come to Murree to collect their children, leaving fewer of us to make the trip together. We traveled on a troop train, without the accustomed privacy of a separate coach for our group. Armed soldiers were everywhere. At one point, Roy Montgomery quietly called my attention to a man sitting across from us who I had assumed was a Pakistani. But while he had been transferring some papers from his briefcase, Roy noticed his passport, with the telltale emblem—a Gandhian spinning wheel—of the Indian flag. How isolated *he* must have felt!

In the days after arriving in Lahore, I began for the first time to see the oddity of our situation in Pakistan. The suburban college campus where my family had temporarily relocated was a real treat compared with the isolation of Raiwind. I enjoyed trading stamps and playing games with other American children who didn't go to MCS. But the manicured lawns, lush shady trees, and general serenity began to seem unnatural, given our reason for being there.

One Sunday morning at the American chapel, the air raid sirens went off during the service. The congregation elected to stay and continue with worship. At that point, the Indian Air Force was officially not bombing civilian targets and, more rationally, where were folks supposed to go? There were no bomb shelters, other than the L-shaped trenches that many families had dug—or had had their servants dig—in their backyards. Besides, Lahore was so close to the border that usually the Indian planes had already passed over by the time the sirens went off.

A few days later, the sirens started while Mom and Dad were at a meeting on the other side of campus. Then BANG! The loudest noise I had ever heard in my life. I was sure a bomb had fallen on the building that my parents were in. With a heavy lump in my stomach, I contemplated the finality of this separation. The war had temporarily improved my relationship with Dad, as both of us accepted my role as the other man in the family—a responsibility I took seriously, and one that made me more aware of those undefinable things that matter most in life, the things my mother gave me. Now they were gone.

We were soon reunited, however, and learned later that the bomb—indeed, a very large one—had in fact landed over a mile away. It had hit a railway station during rush hour, killing more than a hundred people.

Many years later, when I heard sirens, what I felt more than the lingering echo of fear was a wound of much greater impact. That slow, sorrowful whine voiced the rise and fall of my own spirit, the eagerness and despair with which I embraced my own legacy of separateness, as I continued sorting through the debris of choice and circumstance to rebuild a war-torn soul.

I used to be self-conscious about the affinity I felt with Vietnam veterans, as if I were trying to get some vicarious thrill from the association; or worse—affecting some pretense of having "been there." It was years before I understood that, in the absence of any similar community of my own, the bond I felt was a natural one: they, too, had returned to the States feeling like aliens in their own country. (By odd coincidence, my time in Pakistan almost exactly paralleled the years of the Vietnam war—1963 to 1973.) When I saw the movie, *Coming Home,* I connected strongly with a scene in which Jane Fonda visits her husband, a Marine captain on R-n-R in Bangkok. "What's it like over there?" she asks him at one point. And he replies: "I don't know what it's like, I only know what it is."

How do you explain to Americans accustomed to shopping malls and microwave dinners what it's like to see a beggar with no arms or legs face down on a crowded city sidewalk, with small change—*baksheesh*—scattered around him? Or, in our transient, TV-dominated society, the bond I feel to the tiny, evangelical community in which I grew up? Most Americans have no reference for these things.

In January 1993, I had lunch with an attractive woman from Pakistan. I eagerly anticipated the occasion, the chance to make a new friend, maybe something more. Here was someone with whom I could share my nostalgia without explanations or fear of perceived arrogance. Yet, while her Westernized manner made conversation easy, I was uncomfortable with the upper-class status indicated by this and by her fair-skinned appearance. Then she asked me about boarding school. Did I have any Pakistani friends there? Yes, but . . . well, actually, my school was just for missionaries' children; all the Pakistanis there were servants.

She was furious. "I can't believe it," she said. "I didn't know there were still any schools like that left in my country. I thought that only happened in South Africa."

My face burned, and my body stiffened in confusion. *But you don't understand . . . it wasn't like that.* Once again, I had sought an ally and found myself alone.

As I walked out into the snow, exhausted, I heard sirens.

That winter I entered one of the darkest periods of my life. Though outwardly I had been in worse circumstances—losing an important job, the breakup of my marriage—the accumulation of disappointments, longings, and isolation had eroded my internal reserves to the bone.

After leaving Murree Christian School, I spent twenty years trying to figure out where home might be now. I was a mountain man set adrift in harbor towns. I tried to create in relationships the roots I didn't have in a place. But all my efforts to find the right path or the right person rolled across the years like a loose cannon. The result was a line of sailing ships burning to the horizon. My marriage had managed to stay afloat for almost ten years before it, too, sank in a hiss of charred timbers.

When I lost the first woman I had loved after my divorce, I didn't have the energy to pick up the pieces again. It felt like someone had died. I had read such scenes in stories, seen them in movies —the awkward emptiness, the profound triviality of everything. I felt stupidly like a psychotherapy anecdote. But then, everything in my life seemed like an analogy, a re-enactment. I was never sure what I really felt anymore. Did I really love this woman that much —to be so bereft? I had plenty of things to be depressed about: a nowhere job, overdue bills, a best friend who I never saw anymore, ever since his first child had been born. I was getting on with my life pretty well, actually, with the exception of a few more shards in the heart. It didn't take me long to begin thinking in the old ways again —in terms of just myself, rather than as a couple. It had sometimes bothered me, how easily I adjusted to each new loss, how well I bounced back, but it was the one thing I knew how to do well: checking out. Only this time it didn't take. I was tired of being so good at saying goodbye. And when I touched that cold, slippery wall at the bottom of the darkness the only person left to say goodbye to was me.

I started writing suicide poems—a topic that hadn't compelled me since junior high. But the growing weight of shadows within me was no adolescent fascination with the mystique of death. I decided to buy a gun.

I had to look in the Yellow Pages. As a long-time opponent of the uncontrolled availability of personal firearms, it felt strange, walking into a gun store for the first time—like entering a porno shop, and I experienced the same guilty self-consciousness as when I bought my first *Playboy* in high school.

Late one afternoon, I tossed the .38 revolver, which still smelled oiled-metal new, into the yellow nylon saddle bag of my ten-speed bike and rode down to the Potomac River. The bare trees all had a sharp calendar-picture glow, even as the light began to fade. I stopped near the old railroad trestle that crosses a steep ravine above the C&O Canal, took the gun, and walked down through the thick underbrush. Just under the bridge, I sat down on a big rock at the edge of a secluded backwater. I breathed in deeply through my nose and smelled the earth and the dampness on the trees, and slowly breathed out, trying to relax. Holding the gun firmly, I pointed it at my head.

It occurred to me then that I had never fired a gun before. I found it grimly hilarious that I still wouldn't know what it was like, after I pulled the trigger. Looking around, I took aim at a spot on the opposite bank and fired. The gun jumped in my hand, making it seem heavier. Of course, I was prepared for the kick—I'd read about it in novels. I cupped my left hand under my right—like cops do on TV—and squeezed the trigger again. Another round exploded from the gun with a loud crack—just like in the movies—and buried itself harmlessly in the embankment. Swept up in it now, I fired again and again, spotting imaginary terrorists and predators in the undergrowth along the river's edge, then stopped, suddenly conscious of the racket I was making—and terrified that I might have aroused someone's attention.

I waited, listening with slow, measured breath; I felt my heart pumping. I could hear the water softly clattering over the rocks and around the ancient wooden struts of the railroad bridge. The long shadows had now merged with the thickening darkness. I felt my way back over to a grassy spot and sat down, leaning against a tree trunk. I shifted to get comfortable, knowing I was putting it off. I raised the gun and pressed the barrel against my right temple, not entirely sure if every bullet had been fired already; then flinched at the fearful-yet-impotent metal *click* as the hammer tripped against an empty chamber. My breath forced itself out again—like I'd just set down a heavy object—and my whole body slumped.

After a while I heard the water again. And then something else. The wind began to pick up, making a breathy, whistling sound under the bridge. Leaves rustled in the grass, only there were no dry leaves after the winter wetness. The high wooden trestle creaked and I heard the rails singing in the darkness, in that faint way they do, like telephone lines, at the approach of a train. Only this line had been abandoned for twenty years.

But unmistakably, I heard the muffled *puff-puffing*, the quiet *clackety-clack* rising, louder. I could smell the dust and debris beginning to shake off the pilings . . .

I heard in the distance the melancholy wind of a whistle—so absolutely lonely and completely consoling. I saw the bright beam of light flood the night, a hard looming shadow pushing behind it, piling up pillows of steam, stars flying underneath. I heard the muffled thunder moving closer, growing more urgent, then breaking off with a shriek of metal and the clatter of bumping carriages. A chain of glowing portals waited in the dusty void, like a whole train party momentarily hushed. Like a hundred breaths sucked in. Waiting for me to decide.

I did not hesitate; it was time to go home.

12

Communion and Shadows

Everybody loves the sound of a train in the distance
Everybody thinks it's true
What is the point of this story, what information pertains
The thought that life could be better is woven indelibly
Into our hearts and our brains.

PAUL SIMON,
"Train in the Distance"

Redemption is a process, of course; its beginnings often hard to define. My conversion away from despair involved many subtle moments, and the point of transformation is no less mystical for the deliberate choices required. I can identify several factors that brought me back from the brink of suicide: deciding to get therapy; falling in love again; starting to write this book; and reading William Styron's *Darkness Visible: A Memoir of Madness*, which recounts his own life-long struggle with depression.

Styron's short book emphasized two powerful truths that I readily identified with: first, depression is an *illness*, not laziness or self-indulgence, and second, most people who have not experienced depression will never comprehend the weight of it or understand the helplessness behind its symptoms. To have my own experience portrayed so precisely was a liberating acknowledgment; knowing that I struggled with an affliction common to many people, I could finally let go of the tremendous burden of guilt that always compounds the debilitating effects of depression. And this freed me to focus on those things that I could change.

The decision to seek counseling—admitting that I needed help —was an important step for me. This simple act of taking responsibility for my own fate was probably more significant than anything I learned in therapy. Dr. Gleason did give me a useful tool, however, with the concept of "emotional economics." I learned to look more consciously at what kind of emotional or spiritual payoff I was getting from the things in which I invested my time and energy. When I looked at what I most wanted out of life—an intimate relationship, a sense of community, and a clearly expressed vocation—I realized that my priorities in time and effort were exactly reversed in terms of what brought the greatest return. Writing was the one area that consistently gave me the strongest sense of accomplishment and the clearest affirmation of the best part of me. Yet this was the area in which I invested the least time.

The decision to write this book came, in part, from that realization, and from the growing suspicion that the disconnectedness in my life was related to a disconnected past. As I began to untangle the various emotional strands from my childhood, it quickly became clear that if I wanted to understand where I had come from, I needed to reconnect with the community that had shaped me. In fact, I had not been in contact with anyone from MCS for more than seventeen years.

So in March 1993, I sent a letter to all the alumni from Murree Christian School announcing my intention to write a book about growing up at MCS, and inviting them to share their memories. I thought it was a magnanimous project and had no idea then how deep a process I had set in motion within my own soul. I hoped to find some clues about my own identity in other people's stories; or, at least, a more objective understanding of where I had come from. I wondered how differently things might have turned out if my time at MCS had not been so unnaturally cut short. Just when I had finally found acceptance, we left; and I had had to start all over again trying to figure out where and how I fit in—under the debilitating constraints of my father's house and the anonymity of America. What would it have been like if I had been able to spend my last two years at Murree Christian School? And what of that special bond of friendships—often lasting a lifetime—of classmates who graduate together?

The interrupted momentum of a clearly defined childhood seems to have both crippled and liberated me. I am proud of the gifts my unusual heritage has given me—and repeatedly disoriented by how its assumptions have often blinded me. Does growing up anywhere result in similar contradictions? Always an outsider, I did not know how much the alienation I felt was inevitable given my background, and how much was, in fact, the consequence of personal choices. I did not expect to find simple answers, but perhaps a way to grapple more effectively with the questions, and to live more comfortably in the ambivalence.

More than a hundred people, including many former and current staff, responded to my invitation; a selection of these letters is included as a supplement to this book. The tremendous gift of such narrative contributions was that they allowed me to revisit some of these experiences vicariously, through others' eyes; to laugh and to grieve; and, ultimately, to properly say goodbye.

Beginning with the realization that my struggles were not unique, the fragments from a derailed identity at last began to come together. Over the next three years the pursuit of "research" took me from Chicago, Illinois, to Atlanta, Georgia; from Vancouver Island on one side of Canada to Prince Edward Island on the other. All the letters I received and countless hours on the telephone flooded me with a rich and soothing sense of community. At the same time, I struggled with the painful paradox that the connection was mostly an intangible one, based on long-distance memories of a place far away.

I phoned up Chuck Roub, the former principal of MCS, to solicit his participation in this project. As we talked, I occasionally heard an unfamiliar quake in his voice and realized how much older he had gotten in the twenty years since I had left MCS. Suddenly, it occurred to me that those adults who I felt had deeply wronged me back in eighth and ninth grade were no longer the same people. They must have changed a lot in twenty years—as I had. In that moment I began to understand how much the emotional weight I still carried from childhood was out-of-date.

One of the first responses I received to my mailing was from David Addleton. His letter opened with an early memory of his first year in boarding: It was a stormy night and the electricity had gone out; all the little boys were gathered close around the fireplace in their flannel pajamas and bathrobes, sipping hot Ovaltine that "Auntie" Catherine had made. With hot water bottles tucked between their knees, they listened quietly as she read aloud from *The Lion, the Witch, and the Wardrobe* in her soft Scottish voice.

When David described Catherine Nichols, he could just as well have been talking about Auntie Inger: *She mothered us and sheltered us, and when I think of her now, many years later, it is with a deep longing—and sadness, for the loss of that seven-year-old's uncomplicated adoration and sure sense of safety. The reality was not that simple, of course, even then, but the experience, however partial, has never since been duplicated.*

David's letter continued: *The confrontation between what we imagine the world offers to us and what it actually gives to us, and between who we are and what others imagine us to be, is the very stuff of conscious living. And we did not escape such confrontations at MCS. On a shoe-string budget and against great odds, our parents succeeded in giving us a remarkable education not only academically but uniquely for life itself.*

We're an odd, tiny group who passed through MCS—religiously and culturally distinct, but not, I think, emotionally or intellectually. We don't generally care much for the politics and disputes that divide American Protestantism, but we think the church in America could learn something from our parents' example! We ate the same bread, drank the same tea, acted out the same children's rituals, and camped in the same mountains that British boarding school students enjoyed a century earlier; but our parents didn't rule Pakistan. Our parents' peers in the West ran the Cold War and sent their children to Vietnam. When the Soviets shot down Gary Powers in the early 1960s, the U2 spy plane he flew had taken off from an American airbase in northern Pakistan (which shut down shortly after that from the resulting political fallout). We slept in U.S. Air Force bunkbeds, oblivious to the obscure circumstances that connected us to their meaning.

While our generation in the West looked eastward for spiritual and cultural guidance, we—who lived there—looked westward, to our parents' homelands, where they told us to look for our identities. Given our history, it is no wonder many of us feel a sense of cultural rootlessness. But our experience in Pakistan has bound us together in a hidden place somewhere within ourselves; even after years of absence and change, we still find a kinship and intimacy with each other that seems nearly impossible to find anywhere else. There were seven boys and four girls in my graduating class at Murree Christian School; thirty-five students in the entire senior high school. An isolated, ideologically-streamlined environment, MCS was surely among the smallest of sub-cultures. We were a tiny microcosm of Christian community thrown up on the shores of the Islamic Republic of Pakistan and then thrown back into the enormity of the modern, anonymous West to try to make sense of it all.

After twenty years in America, I am no closer to feeling fully American than when I arrived after my graduation from MCS in 1973. I also know it doesn't matter much. While I try not to give my cultural geography and history any more—or less—significance than it is due, neither do I deny the thousand ways it has shaped me. I have grown up to be other things—husband, father, lawyer, teacher—seemingly unrelated to that history. But at an interior level deeper than where cultural conflicts occur, and where emotions and intellect meet to create spirit, I can't imagine a life without MCS near its beginning.

In later telephone conversations, David told me about Tom Ketcham's apparent suicide just the year before. I remembered Tom as a mentor, the big brother who had inspired me and been so instrumental in my ninth grade conversion—one of the most cathartic moments of my life. Tom's death came as a shock to David but not a surprise. He knew something of the way Tom had lived his life and the demons he wrestled with. But I felt like one of my roots had been dug up and hacked off.

My subsequent efforts at some kind of spiritual journalism to understand what happened to Tom, and why, came up empty. His family didn't want to talk about it—beyond insisting that Tom's death was an accident. And they resented the way David had "romanticized" Tom's sometimes cruelly self-indulgent behavior in his uninvited eulogy (excerpted at the end of "Reunion" in the Supplement to this book). For another mutual friend who probably knew him best, Tom's memory elicited only harsh anger, an unwanted reminder of her own childhood horrors.

Tom could have that effect on people.

David wanted to know who else from MCS had responded to my invitation. He asked me about other alumni living in the Washington, DC, area.

"You know, Dudley Chelchowski lives up there. He's a police officer in Alexandria, Virginia," David said. "You should talk to him. He's got some stories to tell, not just about MCS—if you can get him to talk. He got shot real bad a few years ago, and his partner was killed, during a hostage rescue attempt that went bad. Didn't you read about it?"

No, I hadn't. But I didn't read the paper every day.

"The incident got a lot of publicity, all over the country," David continued, "because local TV cameras on the scene captured the shooting. You know, a cop getting killed live is pretty dramatic. I saw it on the news here in Atlanta."

Suddenly I remembered watching the evening news in the church parsonage; I was still married then. I recalled the brief images of a red-brick housing project, the rows of shabby wooden fences along a back alleyway, then the shots, and being stunned by the real death I had just witnessed—not a movie. *And right here, on the local news.* But it never occurred to me that there was a more personal connection. The incident had been dramatized in a *Reader's Digest* story (February 1990), David said, if I wanted to get the details.

This is what happened. On March 22, 1989, a thirty-three-year-old escapee from a Washington, DC, halfway house took four hostages in a drug-related dispute. Chelchowski was on the Special Operations Team that responded. Ninety minutes later three of the hostages had been released. By this time, over seventy police officers had descended on the Hopkins Court housing project. Snipers took up positions to support the ground team waiting for the outcome of final negotiations.

An hour later the gunman stumbled out the back door of the house, stoked on crack and PCP and holding a sawed-off shotgun to the head of the seventeen-year-old boy whose mother's drug debt had precipitated this deadly standoff. He turned and saw Chelchowski and his partner, Charlie Hill, waiting in the alley. Caught in a stand-off, the two officers finally agreed to put their guns down if he would do the same and release the boy. Chelchowski and Hill laid their weapons on the ground, knowing they were covered by the police snipers in a second floor window across the alley. But the convict continued to hold his shotgun against the boy's neck, swinging wildly from side to side as he looked for an escape. Then a sniper's bullet hit him in the back and he went down. As he fell, he turned toward the two officers frozen out in the open and fired.

"I looked him in the eyes and knew he was going to shoot me," Dudley would say later. "I felt the force of the first shot as it flew past my head. There's no question in my mind that it was intended for me."

Charlie Hill took the blast full in the face. Chelchowski took the next shot in his legs before a barrage of police gunfire silenced his would-be executioner.

13

The Honeycomb King

In families, there are no crimes beyond forgiveness.

PAT CONROY,
The Prince of Tides

Andrew Michael Christopher Chelchowski came to MCS in March 1969, in the middle of seventh grade. A shiny white jeep wagon, with "UN" painted in huge black letters on its sides, glided to a stop in front of the hostel, making the graveled driveway crackle softly as it pulled up. A skinny kid with curly hair and a funny nose got out and just stood there. After awhile, his older sister, Ania, came down and helped him find his room. She was in eleventh grade and had come to boarding the previous fall.

Two years later, "Dudley" Chelchowski was quietly on his way to becoming one of the most popular kids in the school. Those who came late, who didn't come up through the grades like most of us whose parents were career missionaries, always had a harder time. It mattered little whether our families were from the United States, Europe, Great Britain, or New Zealand; the real foreigners were those who came from non-missionary, non-evangelical Protestant homes. Newcomers were always confronted by this seemingly impenetrable wall of shared experience. Some became bitter or withdrawn; certainly few "outsiders" stayed at MCS as long as Dudley did.

Perhaps it was no longer having his sister around to comfort him, perhaps it was just growing up, but somehow Dudley had adapted to MCS with a vengeance. His lean body bulged with muscles that were the envy of much older boys. While he was not from the dominant culture in the school, he did become part of the "establishment" at MCS, active in many aspects of school life, and a leader among his cohorts. Yet he appeared indifferent to the spiritual preoccupations that most defined our community. Because of his father's secular job, many of us assumed Dudley was an atheist, not realizing that his previous education in Catholic schools had given him a religious foundation at least as thorough as our own.

Dudley seemed to know how to connect—to get into the thick of things—and still keep a low profile. He was good at sports, which certainly helped, and often hung out with boys two years older than himself—a singular exception to the usually strict social barrier between junior and senior high. Agile on both the basketball court and the soccer field, Dudley was just as good at avoiding blame. He shared most students' desire to push the rules or just to shake up the routine a little and was undoubtedly at the center of many notorious schemes and spontaneous pranks; but when the commotion erupted he was always somewhere else, smiling his angelic smile.

It was Dudley who first observed huge clusters of hemp weed growing behind the tea shop across the road from the school, prompting David Addleton and Tom Ketcham to connect this fact with the large empty brass urn which sat on the stage at the front of the high school auditorium. Such a container just begged to be put to some special use—like potting a large bouquet of marijuana bushes.

By tenth grade his friends had conferred on him that sure sign of belonging, a nickname: "the Moz"—short for Mazalovski, a famous Polish soccer player and goalkeeper. Dudley, whose parents were Polish, played that position on the MCS team, in both junior and senior high.

Dudley had dark, curly brown hair a lot like the Scottish folk-rock singer, Donovan: mod, but not too rebellious. In the 1970s all the girls wanted their hair long and straight, but they loved Dudley's curls. Other guys who had previously loathed their naturally wavy hair as girlish now let it grow out.

It was Dudley Chelchowski who, along with Steve Rasmussen and Nate Irwin, invented the terminology of "sailors and boats," a tradition that quickly became well-entrenched at MCS. A sailor and his boat meant a guy and his girlfriend who were going steady—or "sailing." Of course, Steve and Dudley and Nate were all "submarines." Their mission was to "sink the boats" (that is, expose by flashlight or other means the amorous couples on the weekly nighttime walks) and "dump the sailors into the sea." For all his popularity, Moz never had a girlfriend at MCS.

The boys in Dudley's class also popularized the habit of "teddy boy" poses for every photo opportunity—the practice of mimicking the self-important "candid" poses of college sports teams in the early 1900s, as well as the Pakistanis' compulsive seriousness when being photographed.

The MCS soccer team was called the Jesters, but it wasn't until the class of '74 that they started taking their name seriously. No matter how the games went, the team managed to make amusing drama out of every match—much to Mr. Murray's consternation. Every time they scored, the entire team would lie down on their backs and guffaw. Once they got going, this self-congratulatory ritual frequently dissolved into real laughter which wouldn't die out for several minutes. Dudley, though rarely very animated otherwise, seemed particular enthusiastic about this practice. Penalty and corner kicks provided more opportunities for indulging in grand foolishness. The whole team would huddle and then shout totally random code words as they dispersed for the play. The phrases never actually meant anything, but always left the opposing team bewildered—a mere side-effect to the Jesters' own merry parodies.

Dudley's antics just confirmed the impression that he was particularly cool, and the younger boys went around repeating his soccer field code words at choice moments to add to their own camaraderie. The Little Boys especially worshipped Chelchowski, and when, as seniors, he and Steve Rasmussen began taking care of them on Auntie Inger's day off they were beside themselves with delight. Though he never said much more than "yeah" and "shuddup," Dudley was by far their favorite substitute. His strength and tolerance made him the ideal "victim" for rough-housing: it took a lot more boys a lot longer to pull *him* down than Auntie Inger! But when he quietly gave the word, they all quickly headed for bed.

Dudley's father commanded the UN peacekeeping forces in divided Kashmir and on school breaks Dudley would be taken home in a UN plane. He would persuade the pilot to fly over MCS and make everyone jealous. He also had access to the UN commissary with its large stock of American breakfast cereals, instant coffee, and imported chocolates, which he shared generously with his companions.

I watched the camaraderie of Moz and his friends with the ache of unattainable pleasure: the exaggerated posturing, the inside jokes, the trendy slogans (which always drew withering sarcasm if I repeated them). It was always the same group shooting baskets at school, dominating the pool table in the student lounge, and playing ping-pong at Sandes. I watched them saunter up to the hostel for after-school tea, laughing at their own cleverness, so obviously reveling in the warmth and safety of assured friendships and social standing.

By the time I was in seventh grade, boarding for the high school boys had moved back to Sandes Home. Unlike many upperclassmen who singled me out for extra harassment, Dudley treated me like he treated everyone else, and that made me feel special. Although he sometimes snickered at my misfortunes—usually at the hands of his buddies—he never ridiculed me himself. I don't think he had the heart for it.

He did, however, participate in a minor extortion scheme at my expense. When I first came to Sandes I was still in my "007" phase, and everyone knew about my homemade secret agent attache case with its clever false bottom. Not long into the term, I received a cryptic note inviting me to join a highly-select spy club. If I was interested in joining, I should put five rupees—for dues—in a certain spot behind one of the houses on the hill above Sandes, after which I would be given tasks to carry out. The club's confidential couriers, the note added, were Nate Irwin and Dudley Chelchowski.

I could hardly believe that such a club existed—and one even more sophisticated than my singular efforts in sixth grade! I hastened to comply with the instructions and, much to my excitement, a couple of days later I received another communication. My first assignment, for the next several days, was to monitor who came up the shortcut between Sandes and the road to school between four and five-thirty. So each afternoon for a week I positioned myself in the bushes above "King's Cliff," carefully made note of all the boys coming home from school, and discreetly passed the list on to Dudley and Nate.

After another week or so I got a note requesting a further financial deposit "to cover preparation for special assignments," and I began to get suspicious. I launched a daring renegade operation of my own, hiding in Nate and Dudley's room one evening right after group devotions to see if I could overhear any revealing conversation. Mostly, I heard my own loud heartbeat as I waited under the bed for them to come up from study hall or perhaps a trip to a Jhika tea shop. I had lots of time to think about what might happen if I got caught.

Of course, neither Nate nor Dudley said a word about me or spy clubs as they prepared for bed. I began to realize, however, that I was stuck in that cold and cramped position for another hour or more until I could be sure they were both asleep and make my escape. Meanwhile, it would be lights-out time in the junior high section and my absence would be unavoidably noticed. Fortunately, both of them left to brush their teeth at the same time and I dashed out.

Still, I was impatient to resolve my doubts. The next night I confronted them directly and asked for some concrete evidence that this spy club really existed. They acted incredulous at my impudence and, with overly-dramatic indignation, proceeded to beat me up. That was the end of secret spy clubs.

The dining room at Sandes had a number of square tables that seated only four, like in a restaurant, besides the usual long, cafeteria-style ones. This was another thing that distinguished life at Sandes, along with food superior to what they got at the main hostel. While seating was officially first-come/first-serve, the older boys usually got dibs on the small tables. Not only was there a higher status implied in their limited availability but the serving portions tended to be more generous.

One morning I happened to be sitting at one of the small tables next to where Dudley was eating breakfast with his main buddies: Nate Irwin, Steve Rasmussen, and Tim Feldmann. They were enjoying instant coffee from the States and—a sight even more rare—Honeycomb cereal, which I really, really loved, and hadn't tasted for years. I gazed longingly at the four piles of big yellow hexagons floating in little white lakes. Tim Feldmann told me to bug off. Just then, somebody's elbow knocked the cereal box off the table, spilling much of its contents onto the concrete floor.

"Screamin' *Seaman!*" Feldmann said, as he picked up the box and went on eating. I waited a moment with my heart in my throat then climbed down onto my hands and knees and scooped the Honeycombs into my own bowl.

"Look, Moz, he's bowing down to you," Steve said.

"The Honeycomb King," Nate declared. Tim and Dudley snickered, but I was busy pouring milk onto my unexpected feast.

When I was in ninth grade, my last semester at MCS before returning to the States, I received an even greater gift—the King himself. As part of an experimental "big brother" mentoring program, the boarding staff decided to put an older boy in each of the junior high boys' rooms. The older boys were all volunteers, but must have come to the arrangement with some wariness. I, for one, was thrilled. For one glorious term—the spring of 1973—I had Dudley all to myself. Well, Dale Stock was in the room, too, but he hardly counted. He was even more of a loner than I, finding his solace tinkering with insects and diesel engines—certainly not in nighttime chats; that was against the rules. Of course, Dudley never came in till long after lights-out, and mostly the only words I heard from him during our sojourn together were "shuddup" and "yeah." Even when I said goodnight, Dudley invariably would reply, "yeah," as if acknowledging a fact rather than responding to me. But still, the idea of my officially sanctioned proximity to him made me feel important.

The mentoring program didn't always have the desired results. That same term Tom Ketcham introduced my classmate Tim Old to drugs, showed him how easy it was to buy hashish in the Jhika tea shops, and how amphetamines could be purchased *over-the-counter* at the commercial drugstore in Murree.

One night I asked Dudley about the spy club business three years earlier. He snickered and admitted that he and Nate were just looking for ways to pick up a little extra pocket money that term, and taking advantage of my imagination seemed like an interesting project.

With only a few weeks left in the school year, I felt more strongly the desire to connect somehow with Dudley. By the time my family returned from furlough, Dudley would have graduated. I never expected to see him again after the end of this term. But there was nothing I could do. Unlike many students and staff, Dudley wasn't impressed by my recent religious conversion, and my tentative efforts to seek his friendship were met with scorn. "It must be tough with your mom so far away," I offered, after hearing that his mother was ill. But my sympathy elicited an unusually vehement "*Shuddup*, Seaman!" I did not know then that the intensity of his reaction had nothing to do with me.

Another night, I was telling Dale woeful tales about my dad when Dudley came in and undressed in silence. Dale had wonderful parents and assumed, as such people commonly do, that my problems were all because I had a bad attitude.

The lights had been out for several minutes. Dudley lay in his single bed across the room from the bunk Dale and I shared.

"You're not the only one who has problems with your dad," Dudley said. That was all.

I was stunned—not only by the intimacy of his acknowledging some commonality between us, but by the sudden glimpse that maybe he knew a lot more about me than he ever let on. I didn't dare say anything; the lump in my throat would have stopped me anyway.

I couldn't find a telephone listing for Dudley—or any— Chelchowski in Alexandria, Virginia. I called the Alexandria Police Department; the woman on the switchboard had never heard of him. I left a message anyway. I didn't know then that his real name was Andrew and that Dudley (from "Dudush," in Polish) was a childhood nickname he had long since left behind. I only knew that my efforts to re-connect had once again reached a dead end.

I had become resigned to some kind of karma that deprived me of those random encounters and organized gatherings that allow people to touch their past in the flesh, and in these familiar rituals to both affirm and reflect upon the changes in their lives. I understood my longing; I didn't understand my isolation. I envied those able to gather regularly with friends from childhood or college (including those from MCS whom I occasionally heard about). Just watching beer commercials on TV, which play heavily on the joys of such camaraderie, I often found myself on the edge of tears.

My best friend from MCS days lived in Richmond, Virginia, only ninety miles away. Tim Old and I had roomed together in Auntie Inger's Little Boys department, suffered under Uncle Jim Hunter in sixth grade, and struggled into our teen years together. Yet, in ten years we had not managed to visit each other once, even though business trips occasionally brought him to Washington. The person who finally put a face on my past came from twelve thousand miles away, and could not have known how deep was the unexpected gift he brought me.

On August 4, 1993, Steve Rasmussen called me up out of the blue, saying he was in Washington for a few days and wondered if I'd like to get together with him and his wife for dinner. I was thrilled, of course, and we agreed to meet somewhere uptown the following evening.

Looking across the crowded dining room, I felt a rush of panic, fearing that after twenty years I might not recognize him. I approached the likely couple hesitantly, dragging a trunkful of emotional memories with me. Then Steve's eyes met mine and reassured me with expectation. The awkward moment was bridged by ritual comments about how much each other had changed, as the familiar details came flowing back. Steve's formerly shoulder-length hair was now professionally cropped and noticeably thinning on top. His memorable handsomeness had matured while retaining a boyish quality. Steve seemed more settled now, thoughtful; yet he still laughed easily and gently. Looking at him made me more conscious of my own adult self and the long journey that had brought me to this moment.

His Pakistani wife, Zeba, was stunningly beautiful, with an attentive, animated manner unusual in women from that part of the world. She managed to navigate the stream of earnest reminiscing between Steve and me without either getting backwatered or intruding on our separate apparitions.

Zeba had been raised in the United States. They met in Boston while attending the same college. Steve was now a health-care administrator in the mountainous frontier agency of Gilgit, a rugged tribal region in northern Pakistan. Both he and Zeba were employed by the same private Pakistani institution, not a mission board. However, the pioneering work of the Aga Khan University Hospital's health extension program did seem infused with something like a missionary spirit. And though we never talked about religion that night, Steve's obvious inner peace and compassionate insights would be the envy of many Christians.

He spoke with regret about the cruelties he had sometimes inflicted on underclassmen, acknowledging his avid participation in a system of labeling and ostracizing certain individuals that had been very hurtful to those targeted—like myself.

"So how's the book coming?" Steve asked me after a while. "Who have you heard from?" I mentioned a few names, including David Addleton. "What about Dudley Chelchowski? He lives in this area. Have you been in touch with him?"

"I've tried to contact him several times, but his number's not listed."

"I've got his number," Steve said. "In fact, I've been having trouble reaching him myself. Every time I've called, his line's been busy or no one's answered. And we're headed back to Pakistan tomorrow."

He wrote Dudley's telephone number on the back of a business card and handed it to me. "If you do get a hold of him, tell Moz I said hello and that I did try to reach him."

"Sure, I'll do that," I said, feeling an old familiar tug and the quick swell of importance, playing envoy between two of the Big Boys.

We were eating at a Thai restaurant. I watched an Indian or maybe Pakistani family at a table across from us enthusiastically dividing up various vegetable and noodle dishes. Our waiter was from El Salvador, the cab driver who brought me here, from Sierra Leone; and later an Ethiopian woman would take Steve's parking fee when he drove me home. In Washington, you could drift across global cultures without going anywhere.

"Scott Kennedy and I visited Moz in the summer of 1991, a couple of years after he was wounded," Steve continued. "We called him up and suggested we go somewhere and shoot baskets. He said, 'You know, I don't have my wheels any more,' and I thought he meant his car, but he meant he couldn't get around as well as he used to because of his legs."

"It was painful to watch him waddling around the court trying to convince himself he was fit for active duty," Steve said. "Dudley told me he still had fifty or sixty steel pellets in his thighs that would occasionally work their way to the surface and pop out."

Dudley had just gotten married to a fellow Alexandria police officer, Steve said, and was getting used to being a step-father to Sherry's three children. He was back to work by then, but itched to return full time to the K-9 patrol. The dogs were used for drug-sniffing in special operations. Just like back at MCS, whatever life threw at him, Chelchowski was not just going to handle, he'd prevail over it.

Steve told a funny story about how Dudley came to be at MCS. His father, Michael Chelchowski, was used to giving orders. But he had a personal problem. Because of his position as a UN official, the family had moved almost every year for the past ten years to various points around the world. The girls—it turns out Dudley had four older sisters—had been attending Presentation Convent, an English Catholic boarding school in Kashmir; but there was no equivalent for boys. Recently Michael Chelchowski had become concerned about the constant uprooting experienced by Dudley and Ania, his only son and his youngest daughter.

Then he heard about Murree Christian School and applied immediately. The problem was that in 1968 MCS was already over-crowded with a record number of students enrolled, and missionary families of course had priority. Mr. Chelchowski insisted on an interview with the principal, anyway, "just in case." To smooth the way for his meeting with Chuck Roub he loaded his UN jeep with goodies from the PX in Islamabad—a couple of baked hams, Swiss chocolate, a bottle of Scotch—and headed up the hill to Murree.

"I cannot take no for an answer," he pleaded with Mr. Roub, "I have no other option." Then he modestly presented his little tokens of appreciation for the hard work missionaries were doing in Pakistan. The Scotch, however, was a personal gift to the principal: a man in his position should keep a bottle handy for important visitors.

Mr. Roub was taken aback. Pakistani officials expected bribes as a matter of course, but he had never been on the receiving end of one. And the Scotch: "Don't you know we don't drink, that this is offensive to us?" he said tersely.

But Michael Chelchowski had had no experience with the morals of evangelical Protestants. "I'm sorry," he stammered. "I'm a Catholic."

Mr. Roub told him again that there just wasn't room; there was no point in trying to persuade him. Maybe they could take his daughter in the fall, but not his son.

Mr. Chelchowski was further humbled when he had to return to the Roubs' house and explain that his car wouldn't start. When a push didn't work, he asked to use their phone to have another UN car sent up from Rawalpindi. So he and the Roubs were forced to sit and chat while they waited for the new car. Much to his relief, Mr. Chelchowski found Eloise Roub very friendly and hospitable and things soon warmed up.

"Oh, I'm sure we can do something for you," she said—to Chuck's consternation. "Don't lose hope."

Of course, things did eventually work out—without the Scotch or the ham; and Mr. Chelchowski would henceforth refer to Eloise Roub as a guardian angel.

"Mr. Roub told me that story when Dudley and I were boarding parents," Steve said.

"What do you mean, When you were *boarding parents?*" I asked.

"Oh, right. You left in the summer of '73," Steve replied. "That was the beginning of our final year in school. It happened because no one else was available, so Mr. Roub asked us. It was only summer boarding with five or six senior high boys, other than ourselves, but it was a distinction that has yet to be repeated, as far as I know—with students being designated as boarding parents. We were given a staff room in the hostel with its own attached bath and shower and a few other privileges that normally went only to staff. We thought we had it made like Joe's pizza parlor," he added with a trace of the old high school exuberance.

"The one thing we weren't willing to do," Steve said, "because neither of us considered ourselves Christians at that time, was to lead evening devotions with the boys. It seemed hypocritical. Mr. Roub said that was fine, and he came over every evening to do the prayers and stuff."

"I think we were both kind of posturing—you know, rebelling against the narrow religion at MCS," he continued. "But after his mother died, Dudley was really bitter. He began to withdraw a lot his last semester at MCS; maybe I'm the only one who noticed."

"I didn't know his mother died; I knew she had been sick, but—"

"Yeah. She had colon cancer and died during the winter break in 1974. Dudley's father kept the severity of her illness from him, so her death hit him particularly hard. And he hated his dad not just for keeping it a secret—apparently, she had been ill for some time— but for keeping Dudley from being with his mother when he knew she didn't have long to live."

We paused to get our coffee refilled and remained quiet for a few minutes. I hadn't lost my mother, but I knew what it was like to hate your dad.

We talked about other things that night. We talked about their basic health work in Gilgit; I told them about the video dating service I belonged to. I had just been dumped by another girlfriend so was feeling pretty discouraged on that front.

"Oh, Paul," Zeba said, "You'll find someone who's just right for you. I know you will." Bless her heart.

The next day—Friday, August 6—I attended an evening service commemorating the victims of Hiroshima and didn't get home until late. I sat down at the kitchen table in my small basement apartment and dialed the number Steve had given me.

It turned out that Dudley's number wasn't unlisted: he lived in a small town an hour south of Alexandria. I listened to the phone ringing at the other end and tried to recapture the jovial warmth of the previous evening. I had no idea what I would say first. *Hello, Mr. Monkey Skull!* went through my head. Whenever something crazy happened, Dudley and his buddies would say that with an exaggerated Pakistani accent—imitating that looney magician who had performed at MCS a couple of times. I tried it out under my breath, but when a woman answered the phone I was flustered.

"Hi. Is Dudley, uh, Andrew Chelchowski there?"

"Who is this, please?" she said.

"Paul Seaman—a friend of his from Murree Christian School in Pakistan. Is this Sherry?"

"Yes."

She paused. "I don't know how to tell you this, but Andrew committed suicide last week."

Everything went still. The telephone, the table, the traffic beyond the window all dropped away as I grappled with the words. It felt as though someone had wrapped their arms tightly around my chest. I could hardly breath. The monkey skull tumbled slowly into the pit of my stomach, landing with a heavy thud. My body sagged.

I understood at least that my history, my feelings, my book project didn't matter at all in that moment. This was Dudley's wife. "I'm sorry," I said. "Is there anything I can do?"

Sherry immediately impressed me as a remarkably strong woman. She dealt with her pain by being forthright about the facts involved. What good was there in hiding them? And as we talked, I soon became comfortable enough to ask the obvious-but-forbidden questions.

On Wednesday, Sherry and her ten-year-old son had flown to Miami for vacation. Andrew was supposed to meet them there the next day. When Sherry spoke to him on the phone that evening he had sounded depressed. She could tell he had been drinking. She urged him to come on down, assured him that things would be better once they were together; they could talk or just relax, enjoy the time away. When Andrew didn't show up at the airport the next morning, Sherry called the house in Virginia. There was no answer. She called the airline. Their records indicated that Andrew had never boarded his intended flight. She called a neighbor and asked him to check the house. Then she called the police.

An hour later the neighbor found him leaning against a tree in a small park across the road from his house. A sixteen-year veteran of the Alexandria Police Department with forty-five letters of commendation, Moz had shot himself in the head.

"So tell me about this book you're writing," Sherry said, "about Murree Christian School." Andrew would never talk about MCS, she said. When Steve Rasmussen and Scott Kennedy came to visit, he didn't tell her until the last minute; then as soon as they arrived he went out with them, effectively shutting her out of that part of his life. "There's just some things I have to keep private from you," is all he would say.

I was surprised when Sherry told me "Andy" had been miserable at Murree. That didn't fit at all with the person I remembered. His bitter memories from his high school years had less to do with MCS, she said, than with the fact that he'd been sent away from his mother. Yes, he'd made some good friends, had some good times, but he never forgot that his dad had put him there. And twenty years later Dudley's feelings about MCS had become inseparable from the sense of helplessness and rage he associated with that period.

So he talked about neither. Not even with his wife. After the shooting at Hopkins Court, he still insisted on thinking about other people's needs, not his own. He took it as a personal failure that he had been unable to prevent his partner from getting killed, and felt he was letting the Department down by having become incapacitated.

Andrew was on crutches for six months. And he refused to leave the house all that time, unable to bear being seen as an invalid. Later he had a cane, which he used around the house but would never take outside. "Andy was so good at taking care of other people," Sherry said—and I could hear the heartbreak and frustration in her voice—"but didn't know how to let someone else take care of him. I felt completely shut out from the wounded man inside of Andy."

In less than a year, Chelchowski was back on restricted duty, doing light duties, desk jobs, coordinating drug busts. As soon as he could, he transferred back to the Vice and Narcotics unit of the K-9 squad. He was given a position in which he didn't have to enter the crime scene until the area had been contained, so he would not be directly involved with any confrontations, wouldn't have to run after a suspect. But Andrew felt useless, felt that the Department had created the position for him.

I understood the demons that can haunt even a good life, the despair that comes from feeling locked out of your own dreams, and the fear of being confined to the mundane, taunted by a false sense of failure and by the inability to control your own destiny. Tom Ketcham lived a very different life from Andrew Chelchowski, but he would have understood these things. Like Tom, Andrew had become addicted to the prescription medicine he took for the excruciating pain in his legs and was frustrated by this dependence.

Yet, many people spoke of Chelchowski as the most courageous man they knew. After the shooting, it was questionable whether he would ever be able to walk again. He easily could have signed out with a permanent disability pension, but eight months later he was working again. He cursed his physical therapists, but he kept going back. And by the fall of 1992 he had returned to a full-time position with his regular unit and his beloved dogs.

What went through Dudley's mind over the next nine months, and on that sweltering summer night as he sat under a tree in the park? Did he hear the lonesome locomotive whistle—mocking him from a distance? Or was it the constant, heart-in-the-throat clatter of a runaway freight train whipping down a mountain track? Did he watch the train approach, see the tons of screaming, tearing metal tumble off the bridge and plummet toward him in endless, unrelenting slow-motion, while he remained trapped underneath?

I was ashamed that I could have come so close to a similar ending when my pain seemed so puny compared to his. Even so, Dudley's death tapped into all the unexpressed grief, all the unfinished business log-jammed inside of me. As the first person from MCS to learn of his death, I felt a guilty responsibility, as if I were the one who'd found the body. And now, though my connection to him had been severed twenty years before, it was Dudley who thrust me into the role of messenger, comforter, coordinator.

How strange it felt, after years on the fringes, out of the loop, to be the one making the phone calls, writing letters, putting together a little announcement for the alumni newsletter. And something happened to me in the process. I discovered that things had changed. Indeed, I had become something else.

As I re-read the news clippings I had gathered from the days and weeks after Dudley died, I was struck by how conveniently the incident in March 1989 was used to explain Chelchowski's death. *". . . a sensitive man who may never have gotten over the shooting death of his partner." "Friends remembered his physical struggle to overcome the near-crippling injury and his mental anguish over his partner's death . . . the loss of his partner came to be too great a burden to bear." "However intense his physical pain, it was dwarfed by Andy's emotional anguish. He felt tremendous guilt at having survived. Perhaps he felt shame, too, at having to give up his gun facing a shotgun barrel."*

In fact, suicide among police officers is common—more than in any other profession except doctors. A *Newsweek* article (September 26, 1994) reported that "twice as many cops—about 300 annually—die by their own hands as are killed in the line of duty."

For some people the notion of suicide may be unfathomable, but I was shaken by Dudley's loss for the opposite reason. And the familiarity made me see the hollowness, the hurried quality, of people's simple explanations.

Just a week before Dudley took his own life, Vincent Foster, friend and legal counsel to President and Mrs. Clinton, shot himself. There, too—and at much greater length, of course—the media insisted that Foster must have been devastated by some professional failure; that he must have been trapped in some dark scandal for which he felt overwhelming remorse. So it was with great interest, and a very personal connection, that I read William Styron's essay in *Newsweek* which rebuked the shallowness of these interpretations.

Drawing on his own experience with depression—"an interior pain that is all but indescribable"—and knowledge of Foster's emotional and psychic struggles, Styron offered more somber and more enlightening reflections.

The uncomfortable truth is that such tragedies are unnecessary and yet they do happen, and we will never fully understand why.

I had felt awkward pressing Sherry, however gently, for the whole story. I now see that such a compulsion is not tacky curiosity, but a coping mechanism. We want the details, not out of some morbid voyeurism, but because suicide provokes a glimpse into that fearful chasm of the unknown. We need something concrete to hang onto; and maybe also, we hope that somehow in the details we will find an answer, an explanation for the incomprehensible. But such a pursuit is only a shadow play of the real story. Many of us—out of a failure of courage or imagination—are content to stop there, at the flickering screen, at the texture of the shroud.

I cover my own pain, I suppose, by attempting to sound profound. It took me three years before I was able to begin to put this account together. I still don't know what to do with that big, unspoken part that's left hanging after I'm all finished trying to honestly express what I feel. I do know that Dudley himself would have had little patience for being fussed over like this.

No one from MCS attended Dudley's funeral, except, of course, his sister, Ania. Later that summer, however, I received the following letters from two of his former classmates:

from David Addleton:

Dudley represented the larger world to me. I knew that our background at MCS was limiting; I wanted to know more. Moz represented for us a chance to break out of the MCS mold. He was a channel to the outside world, as later the inter-school conventions would be, and he was our link there to the strange world of American international schools. He had a lot of cassette tapes of popular music and, because his family made much more frequent trips to the States than ours, he had a lot of new music, which we craved for its coolness.

Missionaries were not supposed to play cards because it was associated with gambling; we played "clean" variations like Rook, but we wanted to learn how to play Bridge. When Dudley discovered that the Rook deck was essentially parallel to regular playing cards in how it was organized he taught us to play Bridge. After that, it was a short step to playing with real playing cards. Soon all the kids in boarding, in high school at least, were playing with real playing cards, which was deliciously scandalous—even, we supposed, a little revolutionary—in that straight-laced environment.

Dudley's family came from Communist Poland. His father had a respected and trusted position with the government there, which enabled him to take the family out and move them to the States where they were brought up American. But knowing Dudley was Polish, the routine Polish jokes were repressed after he came—until we discovered that most of them were coming from Dudley! How could he do this, I wondered, and how did he know so many? "Of course I know a lot of Polish jokes," the Moz replied, "I grew up in New York City." Although Dudley was not one to stand out or talk much, he was always cracking us up with the funniest jokes.

Even his appearance was a novelty at the school. His "Roman" nose and other Eastern European features distinguished him in our very homogeneous Anglo-Saxon and Scandinavian community. I was jealous of his physique. His lean, hard body bulged with muscles, often accentuated by his preference for sleeveless "muscle shirts."

In his junior year Dudley was assistant editor of the Kahani and I was annoyed because he was seeing a lot of Leslie (the editor). I was friends with both of them, but Leslie was my girlfriend at the time.

I wish I had seen more of the Moz in the years since we returned to the States. The last time I saw him was in 1975, when I visited him in New York and toured the Long Island night spots with Dudley as guide. I guess now that we're scattered to and by the four winds, many of us will regret intervening circumstances—time, geography, economics, family, work—which kept us from more frequent contact. I wish that Dudley had known more of the strength and pleasure that I get from talking with our MCS family.

from Leslie (Christy) Valencourt:

The year that I spent working closely with Dudley on the MCS yearbook (1973), was one of the happiest years of my life. And he helped to make it so. Dudley was a fun person to be with, warm and spontaneous. Yet he was just as solid as they come—loyal, dependable and trustworthy.

He held a lot inside even then. That was his strength in a way, and yet it was probably his downfall, too. He was easy to be with, had no enemies; you couldn't help but like the guy. He was unfailingly funny and entertaining, and could defuse a volatile situation just by who he was. That was the Dudley I knew and loved.

We had the opportunity to meet up again three times after graduation, at his home in New York. I sensed that he was lonely, and yet it wasn't a void that I could fill for him, much as I would have liked to. After I read the Reader's Digest *article about the shoot-out in 1989 I talked to Dudley on the phone a couple times. In retrospect, I think he said more by what he didn't say than by what he did. I wish I had been sensitive enough to do or say something that would have made a difference for him.*

Dudley's death was heartbreaking for me, as I'm sure it was for many. Just yesterday I ordered some chapstick from Avon—the same flavor Dudley used when we were kids and he'd let me borrow. We all hurt, and it's only God's grace that keeps any one of us from feeling the kind of despair Dudley must have experienced. He's gone and we'll miss him. Let's keep our eyes and ears open for others like him, for whom it is not yet too late.

Sherry Chelchowski told me recently that, in fact, she had gone to Dudley's father's house in Florida that week before Andrew's death. She had gone ahead with her son, because Dudley couldn't stand to be around his father. But lately Mr. Chelchowski had been talking about how much he wanted to be reconciled with his son and Sherry thought the time had seemed right, and that something might happen when Andrew came down for the weekend. Reconciliation requires a certain nakedness of the soul. And in the end, it was perhaps not his demons that proved too much for Dudley Chelchowski, but the fear of letting them go.

Thanks to Steve Rasmussen, Sherry Chelchowski, Jonathan Mitchell, Ania Chelchowski, Wendy Olsen-Bates, Michael Chelchowski, and Ian Murray, who contributed additional information for this chapter.

14

The Antigravity
Swimming Pool

A crazy, holy grace I have called it. Crazy
because whoever could have predicted it?
Who can ever foresee the crazy how and when
and where of a grace that wells up out of the
lostness and pain of the world and of our own
inner worlds? And holy because these moments
of grace come ultimately from farther away than
Oz and deeper down than doom, holy because
they heal and hallow.

FREDERICK BUECHNER,
Listening to Your Life

In August 1986, Carol and I and our two children from
her first marriage drove up to Ithaca, New York, where my
eldest sister Ruth still lived. I went to this family reunion
with the usual naiveté about the consequences—perhaps more so,
given the special occasion that instigated it. Mom and Dad were
finally going back onto the mission field after thirteen years in the
States. They had been re-assigned to Nigeria and would be gone for
at least three years before we saw them again. In normal families,
such occasions call for celebration, and conflicts are muted out of
respect for the impending farewell. Our family wasn't normal, and
not much had changed in thirty years. Yet, I went to Ithaca eager for
Dad to notice the positive changes in my own life.
   I had just started a new job—the best job I'd ever had, working
at the national headquarters of the Public Broadcasting Service
(PBS). I trimmed my beard for this trip and carefully selected my
best new clothes, to emphasize my new professional stature and
revitalized self-esteem. Carol and I had just come through a

tumultuous period in our marriage, in which personal issues were compounded by the stresses inherent to being a step-parent to half-grown children. I was proud of our success.

"Has Paul told you about all his previous girlfriends?" Dad asked my wife in front of a whole living room full of people. "He's had quite a few, you know. You're not the first older woman he's been involved with."

Like Dad, Carol was a United Methodist pastor and he related to her affectionately as a colleague as well as a daughter-in-law. She understood that such comments were not *intended* to be put-downs of her, but of me. What Dad failed to see, of course, was how humiliating this was for Carol, to have him constantly making derogatory comments about her husband. Even his "professional" friendship with her, I came to see much later, had the effect of putting her on a level with him, rather than me.

On the way home from Ithaca that summer I finally confronted the evidence that my dad didn't like me. (He didn't seem to like anyone much, but that was a bigger issue.) Every time our family got together at Christmas or for a weekend visit I would come away feeling tense, depressed, and with my own very large supply of insecurities much closer to the surface. The consequences of this invariably played themselves out in my relationships with Carol and the children. For awhile I would revert to immature, petty, and authoritarian behavior, until I recognized the pattern and could get myself on an even keel again.

In retrospect, the reasons for this were obvious. Whenever we visited my parents, Dad would tell me by almost every act, word, and posture that I was immature, irresponsible, and of dubious moral standing; in short—childish. His "sharing" memories from the past consisted of negative anecdotes and innuendos apparently designed to remind me—and Carol—that all those "bad" things were still a part of me and somehow made me suspect and unworthy.

Even when not directed at me, Dad's manipulative social techniques and obsessively self-centered behavior required a lot of patience, especially when he bullied my sister, Martha. Her already fragile sense of personhood had few resources to cope with his systematic insinuations. But, in general, the whole family learned to work around him, successfully navigating circumstantial necessities without ever really acknowledging the internal damage that occurred to all of us.

For years I had repetitious dreams about my dad, reliving the fights we used to have when I was in high school. The situations were typically fragmented and discontinuous, but the fear, guilt, indignation, rage, and helplessness were always vivid and I would wake up tense, sometimes for days. This time, I did not come back from Ithaca depressed or thrown off balance by the encounters with Dad. My self-esteem was finally stronger than him (thanks in part to a very loving wife). I came home deeply troubled, but I did not squabble with Carol. I knew who I was angry at. The dreams came back, but with a different ending. Now, I confronted Dad with his behavior and I did not feel confusion or fear, only self-confident anger. In one dream, I was so angry I beat him up; we were physically tussling on the floor. I woke up in a sweat and knew it was time to write my father a letter from the heart. What I composed over the next several days confronted Dad with how I experienced him, as I have described it here, and included these three paragraphs:

"As to the event that triggered this letter, I was frankly astounded by your rudeness during our visit this past weekend. It was all the more blatant because there were no circumstantial factors to help explain it, such as Christmas rush or Martha's presence. Other people have observed that your attitude changes when I come into the room, as I have seen happen with Martha. That was troubling to hear, but consistent with my growing sense that you don't like me—resent me, in fact. Why else would you do the things mentioned above; or hole up in your attic "office" the whole evening and all day, and then criticize me for not riding in the same car with you—as if I were the one who didn't want to be sociable?! As I said at the time, it's hard to comprehend how updating your address list could be more important than visiting with your only son, the last chance to do so for at least three years.

"My biggest immaturity in the past few years has been wanting your approval. That has been a debilitating dependency. I looked forward to this last visit more than to any other family gathering I can remember in recent years. I felt that at last I could hold my head high, as an adult, as a son you could be proud of. But not once did you affirm any of my accomplishments. . . .

"All that I have said points to something that our society has been giving a lot of attention to lately and there is a word for it: child abuse. Child abusers are often well-meaning and mild-mannered in other areas, but that does not excuse or justify their sick behavior. I want you to stop abusing me. I want you to stop abusing all of us. You can't help the past; you can't help the scars from your own childhood that caused you to treat us the way you did—in spite of God's grace and healing, and your best efforts (which you deserve a lot of credit for). But you need to be aware of the damage you continue to inflict, and learn to stop. It seems like a good step would be to realize and accept that other people are not out to *get you, that they are doing the best they can, and that a lot of people actually love you—and would show it a lot more if you didn't spend all your time either hiding or cutting them down. "*

I mailed the letter off to my parents' address in Nigeria, with copies to my three sisters, and waited for a reply.

Dad never received the letter. When I realized this a few months later, after making subtle inquiries, I decided not to send another copy. I felt like the moment had passed, that it would no longer be a constructive encounter. The letter had served its purpose for me. I had crossed the line. And by becoming free of an emotional dependence on my father I discovered I was becoming free to love him.

In May 1990, Ruth called to let me know that Mom and Dad were coming home—for good. I was stunned. They had just completed a three-month furlough in the States. But when my parents returned to Nigeria, the local church authorities had apparently already decided to ask Dad to leave. They waited, however, until *after* Mom and Dad had spent their home leave going around the country raising financial support for the well-drilling project Dad had designed from scratch and was in the process of implementing—"2,000 wells by the year 2000."

I suspect Dad has cried for me many times, though I never saw it. Once, after a confrontation when I was in ninth grade, I told him to go to hell. Surprisingly, he didn't hit me, or even react with angry threats of discipline. Instead, I saw a look of overwhelming sadness in his eyes. Given his beliefs, my defiant words caused him to truly fear for my soul; and I glimpsed in him then, however twisted and deeply buried, something beyond wrath and judgment. Now the gash had split wide open and I couldn't help but see through all the layers of crap and concertina wire to the fragile beating heart of the man. And it made me cry.

I had cried for my father just once before in my life. In the summer of 1974—the year we were supposed to have gone back to Pakistan—our family attended a spiritual retreat called "Camp Farthest Out." It was the first and, it turned out, the only time all six of us were together for such an event. The participants included several other families, single people, and older folk. Children, youth, and adults were divided into small groups that met together at various times throughout the week. By the time everyone gathered for the closing ritual of sharing, a deep sense of community—rare and exhilarating—had permeated the group. We sat on folding chairs set up on the front lawn of the main building. The camp center was all modern red-brick and low roofs, angling steeply at the far end where the chapel spire knifed upward. Behind it, a wide expanse of grass sloped away and flattened again between two wooded hills. Three narrow bridges on the camp road indicated where the creek snaked back and forth out of sight.

Then my dad, a man with little social life and few close friends (most of them long-distance and formed much earlier in his life), got up to speak.

"I have mixed feelings about death, like I suppose most people do," he began, "and I'm not saying I want to cut short what time the Lord has allotted to me on this earth; but I look forward to getting to heaven, so that the small group I've been privileged to be part of this week can get back together." Before he finished the sentence, his voice cracked and tears began streaming down his cheeks.

That did it. I had never seen Dad so vulnerable. It was like someone flipped a lever inside of me; a rush of emotions filled me to overflowing and I wept. For a long, glorious and painful moment I felt closer to my father than all the world.

Sixteen years later it was not the courage of his openness that moved me but the long tragedy of his life. When I heard that Mom and Dad were coming home from Nigeria unexpectedly my first thought was, "It isn't fair." No one deserved to be shattered like this, certainly not someone as earnestly and selflessly dedicated in his call to serve as was my father. I knew about shattered dreams, about doing the best you can and having other people turn on you anyway, about never being given the chance to prove what you're capable of because it interferes with someone else's agenda. And my heart broke for Dad. This time the tears were not for a cleansing of my own tormented soul, but in solidarity with another's. For weeks after I got the news I was angry and uncomprehending, sharing in the sense of utter defeat that my father must have felt.

The mission board's decision not to let our family go back to Pakistan in 1974 had far-reaching consequences, especially for Dad, who lost what he was sure was his life's calling—and the only thing at which he felt really successful. Yet, he never lost his vision and never abandoned his hope of returning. Every day he practiced Urdu, writing his notes and daily reminders in Persian script. When the time came to return to overseas service the mission board asked him to go to Nigeria, even though this meant learning a new language and adjusting again to an unfamiliar culture. He had, in fact, felt called to Africa thirty years earlier, but post-colonial turmoil, continuing to escalate in the early sixties, had prevented an assignment there.

Soon after arriving in Nigeria as an agricultural consultant, he was asked to shift his emphasis to the urgent water-supply needs of church villages in the bush country of Gongola State. Dad had no experience in this area, but studying and organizing were two of the things he did best. He ordered the latest literature on the subject (with some help from me in Washington), arranged ecumenical funding, and found the technical support he needed. By the end of his first three-year term he had laid the groundwork for a sustainable self-help Village Wells Project. When the first wells were put down they provided not only clean drinking water but a model of grassroots development: local, cooperative, and free of corruption.

And then, after an unsuspecting furlough, this sudden, humiliating turn of events. After his career had been derailed the first time, Dad suffered through a series of demeaning make-do jobs. This was to be his zenith, his sunset glow of belonging and usefulness, his calling finally fulfilled one last time before he retired. And then it abruptly ended. A part of me died, too, as I readily connected with my father's crushing disappointment; years of bitterness and estrangement were washed clean by a flood of empathy.

I know there are at least two sides to every story and I never assumed Dad was entirely innocent. I knew him too well. But, as in an uncannily similar on-the-job crisis I myself had experienced just a few years before, it seemed that a lot of people had made mistakes and Dad was the only one paying the price.

Dad was always impatient with the social niceties commonly used to develop trust and loyalty, the "small" rituals that are even more important in non-Western cultures. I remember the farewell dinner in Raiwind the last week before our family left Pakistan in 1973. My father's Pakistani assistant had invited us to his home and we all sat on rope beds in the open courtyard, as was the custom, waiting for the food to be cooked. We chatted awkwardly with the men and boys of his extended family; they didn't speak much English and Dad was the only one of us really conversant in Urdu. The women cloistered themselves in the kitchen, leaving my mother and sisters even more isolated.

"When is it going to be ready?" Dad asked, looking at his watch.

"Just coming, just coming," his assistant assured him, unfazed by my father's mannerisms after working with him for several years.

"Does that mean ten minutes from now or two hours from now," Dad persisted, "because I've still got a lot of packing to do. If it's going to be a while, I can go get some work done and come back."

Even at fifteen, I understood that Dad was missing the point of the occasion, and his lack of graciousness embarrassed me. After they returned from Nigeria, Mom told me that he had been the same there. He didn't have time for "superficial" socializing when there was important work that needed to be done. He never learned the importance of *being,* not just doing. So when the currents of corrupt church politics swung against him, there was no one willing to stand up for him. He hadn't invested enough in the people, only "the work," as if you could separate the two. And it was the same in subsequent years when he returned to pastoral work, until he reluctantly agreed to retire in 1996.

The emotional solidarity I felt with my father quickly eroded. Just a few months after their return I visited my parents again at Ruth's house. One night I picked up a video copy of "On Golden Pond" for us to watch. Jane Fonda plays the grown daughter to Henry Fonda's grumpy old man who never lets her feel that she's good enough. Dad actually watched the whole movie—a rare concession—but I don't know how much sunk in. The next morning I was wearing one of my favorite T-shirts: a replica of the plaque bolted to the side of *Pioneer 10,* an interstellar space probe. Prominently featured on the plaque, along with other scientific information about our solar system, is a sketch of a naked man and woman—so that any extraterrestrials who might intercept the probe would know what earthlings look like.

"How do you reconcile your Christian faith with the moral implications of wearing a picture of a nude woman on your shirt?" Dad asked me.

Later, when Dad's negative attitude and "practical" concerns were making it impossible for the family—the group of families—to make a simple decision about which restaurant to go to, I suddenly stomped my foot and screamed—quite to my own surprise. Immediately, I felt exceedingly sheepish. At some level, though, I understood that my reaction was at least more honest than the way we usually catered to Dad, dealing so delicately with his whims for fear of making matters worse. I also knew, with great frustration, that my reaction reflected only on me, not on him.

At the end of that visit I told Dad, without animosity and with only a little tension in my throat, how fed up I was and that if he couldn't start being more respectful I didn't want to see him anymore. It just wasn't worth it.

Predictably, in a phone conversation sometime later he tried to use my "ultimatum" against me, trying to make me feel guilty for "censoring" our relationship, for wanting it to be "artificial." Whatever. At some level he must have got the point, but I didn't go back to Ithaca for three years.

When I began writing this book, I started with Auntie Inger and the Little Boys department. And then, knowing I could not go on until I faced it, I wrote about the most traumatic event of my childhood—getting suspended from school in ninth grade and my parents' complicity in the way that incident was handled. Even now, I cannot write those words without a sudden tightening in my chest as the weight of it comes back for a moment. But I did write about it. I did not "censor" anything; I did not try to be kind; and when I finished, I was finally free of it—not that all the pain was gone (as I am reminded again just now)—but it no longer controls my emotional identity.

If I had not first written that chapter ("The Legendary Screamin' Seaman"), I could not have written this one. I certainly did not anticipate the chain of events I was setting in motion that would unfold over the next four years. I thought I was writing a book about the past, about Murree Christian School, about cross-culture identity and the enigma of "home." But the most dramatic story turned out to be the journey—in process—of father and son to find each other.

Father's Day is an occasion I have typically ignored, but in the spring of 1993, I was deeply immersed in childhood memories. I had recently exorcised my most painful memories on paper and I thought it would be an interesting challenge to see how many positive memories I could recollect, specifically about Dad—as a kind of narrative Father's Day card. I figured that with a little effort I could manage a couple of pages. A few days later I had filled *ten* type-written pages of anecdotes, and more kept coming to me.

One of my earliest and most prominent memories was of Dad sitting in his office, at that big desk with all the pigeon holes in it— one for each day of the week, for each month, even A.M. and P.M. *"I remember your old Underwood portable,"* I began, *"a permanent fixture beside your desk. I was proud that you could type so fast: clackety-clackety-clackety, whizzz-CHUNK; clackety-clack-clack-clackety, whizzz-CHUNK! It was amazing. Sometimes, when I was sure you were gone for the afternoon I would sneak into your office, roll in a piece of paper, and poke the keys randomly as fast as I could. It didn't matter that I wasn't writing anything; I just wanted to get the rhythm—the sound of it—so I could imagine that I was typing, just like you."*

I remembered the little knights he drew for me on three-by-five cards that I could cut out and use in my backyard sand castles; the bullet train and revolving restaurant in Japan; our trip across the United States in 1968; and watching the first moon landing on our neighbor's little black-and-white TV. I remembered the long voyage around Africa by ship and our family's safari in Kenya; Dad's generosity with money matters, his patience with my Pentecostal phase, and of course, that memorable week at Camp Farthest Out at Watson Homestead, near the town of Painted Post (the next town over from the thriving metropolis of Horseheads, New York).

I closed this "Reministle from Son Paul" by expressing my shared grief about Mom and Dad's premature return from Nigeria, acknowledging how much that must have affected him, and encouraging him to write down some of *his* happy memories.

Dad's response—fitting, perhaps, if somewhat short of my hopes—came in the form of a brief note of appreciation and a "rain check" that promised a longer reply when he had time. Meanwhile, two events—a funeral and a parcel of letters—prepared the way for the fulfillment of that promise a year-and-a-half later.

My grandma died in the fall of 1993. Etta Kunz Quinlan, my mother's mom and the only grandparent I had known at all, had been ninety-three. Like my mother's sister, she had spent her whole life in Louisville, Kentucky. At the viewing, people greeted one another in quiet but curiously animated voices, expressing both the grief of the occasion and gladness for those who came. Dampened by the heavy carpeting, pockets of hushed chatter spilled into the large adjoining sitting rooms along with the lavish and plentiful floral arrangements. The faint smell of hospitals and motel rooms lurked just below the lilies.

Dad and I sat at the back of the room; I thought about the last funeral he and I had attended together. His younger brother, Joe— my favorite uncle—had committed suicide twelve years before. Uncle Joe pastored a small United Methodist church in central Pennsylvania, just up the river from Three Mile Island. His teenage son found him hanging from a pipe in the basement.

The viewing for Grandma was like a cocktail party compared to Uncle Joe's wake. That event was a much more intimate affair— family members only—and austere, reflecting both the occasion and the Appalachian context. But we were a big family (Dad had nine living brothers and sisters) and, with no one skilled in grief counseling or assertive enough to try, the whole big group of us sat in oppressive silence. Finally, one of my aunts suggested we pull our chairs around in a circle and talk about what we were feeling. So everyone got up and rearranged the folding chairs with a great clatter, more, I suspect, from relief at having something to do than from enthusiasm for the suggestion.

Then we sat in uncomfortable silence again, this time having to work harder at avoiding each other's eyes.

Uncle Joe, who graduated from the same seminary in Washington, DC, where I now work, had a history of depression. In spite of recent progress through therapy, in the end, he surrendered to his demons. Mental illness and family violence snaked through my genes, back through the generations on both sides of the family. My father's mother had gone after one of her young children with a butcher knife and was temporarily jailed for attempted murder. My mother's grandfather clubbed a Black man to death one Fourth of July in an unprovoked fit of rage; he was sent to a mental hospital to avoid a criminal trial and never came out. Until I began research for this book, I did not know that my sister Martha had made at least one suicide gesture in boarding school, or how frightened the other junior high girls were of her furious temper. I only knew that one day she was gone and would be finishing the rest of the semester at home. No one ever told me why.

I did not know any of this at Uncle Joe's wake.

"I'll say something," I blurted out, my chest pounding. I stood up, blinking back tears. "I'm really angry at Uncle Joe. I think what he did was a fucking selfish thing to do. He abandoned his family and hurt a lot of people who loved him."

Well, that didn't exactly prime the pump. I think Aunt Sandy and my cousins understood, or did later, the pain behind my outburst, but Dad never forgave me. Recently, in better times, I asked him what he thought was the worst thing I ever did. Without hesitation he mentioned this incident. I always thought it was the obscenity that bothered him, but in fact he still thought I had just been trying to get attention.

Dad and I sat in the well-appointed funeral parlor in Louisville, Kentucky, watching the mostly overweight relatives filing past Grandma's casket. It seemed to me as good a time as any for a little man-to-man chat. "You had a vasectomy done while you were in Pakistan, right?" I asked him. "How come?" I had been "fixed" three years earlier and for some time now had wanted to ask Dad about the circumstances surrounding his decision. He replied matter-of-factly, as though it were a rehearsed question for a radio talk show.

"The Pakistan government, through the UN's population control program, was encouraging married men to have the operation," he said. "We already had four kids and I wanted to set an example. Most of the local men were uneducated, as you know, and I wanted to show them that the procedure was harmless, that it wouldn't affect their sexual functioning."

Of course, in order to accomplish this, he had to be very public about his intended operation (which was performed by an American doctor at the Christian mission hospital in Lahore). This caused quite a bit of embarrassment for Mom.

After Grandma's funeral, we all went back to her church where some of her friends had prepared lunch for all the relatives. As it turned out, this was the same church where my parents had been married forty-two years before.

While the others were eating in the basement fellowship hall, I asked Mom to come up to the sanctuary with me. It was a small church, warmly furnished, and the wooden pews fanned out from the communion railing in a large semi-circle.

"This must bring back a lot of memories," I prodded Mom as we sat close together in the back row.

Immediately, she started crying and told me how hard all the years since then had been. "So many times I've wondered how different life might have been if I'd made a different choice forty years ago," she said.

Never before had she let so much pain show through the "good missionary wife" image she had constructed for herself. Mom's faith in God had always been unwavering, but the accumulated grief of so many dashed hopes, so many pretty-girl dreams lost along the way, was finally beginning to leak through.

Later, I did the same thing with Dad, sitting with him alone at the back of the church. His version of their courtship, especially about the other woman he was engaged to at the time, was quite different from Mom's. It didn't matter. For the first time in my life I had gotten a glimpse of my parents as young people.

One day, a few months after Grandma's funeral, I received a package from Mom—some old correspondence she was "getting rid of" that she thought I might be interested in. Sorting through the papers, I quickly realized that here was fifty years of family history that almost had been thrown away! Especially interesting to me was a packet of the newsletters my parents had written to their supporters and relatives while they were in Pakistan, including several from the years following the unexpected decision that kept us in the States after 1974. Their struggles to change course professionally in midlife and to make sense of what had happened were all recorded here. It would serve no good purpose to be too tactful with their prayer partners, but neither was it easy, I suspect, to be blunt without also expressing bitterness.

This never seemed to be a problem for my mother, who always transcended whatever life gave her to bear. Except for the grief. Until we grew apart in my late teens, Mom had always been there for me, for all of us kids, giving us hugs and kisses, never holding back an I-love-you or a good-night back rub. She taught us pride, applauding our accomplishments, even at play; she modeled hospitality at its finest, and lived by the strength of grace. Even as she broke, which often happened in front of us, she picked herself up with an elegance of spirit that kept her going, kept her beautiful. Only many years later did I begin to comprehend just how cruelly her heart had been torn apart because of Dad—caught between her Christian duty to her husband and her motherly instincts to protect her children from him. As an adult, I knew how difficult Dad could be for one weekend a year, but she still lived with him.

After reading my parents' general newsletters, and their "prayer letters" to closer friends, from 1974 to 1976—years of harsh adjustments, emotionally, financially, spiritually—I had a new sense of the challenges *they* had had to overcome while I was busy "finding myself" and doing my own thing. After running a demonstration farm and heading the agriculture department of Raiwind Christian Institute for ten years, the only employment my father could find was as a fertilizer salesman. Mom got a job as an industrial nurse at a "sheltered workshop" for handicapped people. She loved the work, but it meant being gone from home all day. With Dad unemployed or underemployed for much of this period, Mom became the primary breadwinner.

On short notice, they had to find a new place to live, find furniture, buy a car, buy clothes and otherwise provide for three growing children and a daughter who had just started college. Since they were no longer employed by the United Methodist Church, they now had to pay back the mission board for Dad's graduate school expenses at Cornell. Then there was the psychological embarrassment of not fulfilling their pre-publicized plans to return to Pakistan, and the ongoing revelation of Martha's real mental illness.

When I asked Mom if these had been the hardest years of her adult life, she replied, "They were hard, but the trials get more severe the farther we go." I knew she meant living with Dad. Yet, she stayed. She would not dye her prematurely white hair to accentuate her otherwise youthful beauty because Dad didn't believe in make-up. And she would not leave him. For the last several years, before and after their brief assignment to Nigeria, Dad had worked as an itinerant pastor. Because of the United Methodist Church's "connectional system," and Dad's limitations, this meant moving every couple of years, preventing Mom from effectively pursuing her own career or putting down social roots in a community.

But she did not stand still. Some of her passion and creativity got channeled into mission education presentations in churches throughout central Ohio and other charitable work. Several articles she wrote were published in United Methodist mission and women's magazines. Yet the grief remained, like a fist clenched around her heart.

Toward the end of 1994, Dad sent me a page clipped from a religious publisher's catalogue. He had circled a book called *Listening to Your Life: Daily Meditations with Frederick Buechner* and suggested it as something I could get him for Christmas. I had never heard of Frederick Buechner, but I was happy for the convenience—one gift to check off my list of holiday dilemmas. When the book arrived, I learned that Buechner was in fact a well-known theologian, a minister, and the author of over twenty novels and nonfiction works. Unlike the glib affirmations and admonitions that fill most daily "inspirational" books I've seen, each entry in this one was a substantial excerpt from one of Buechner's books—sermons, novels, and personal memoirs.

I ordered a copy for myself, too, and at Christmas time, when Dad opened his present, I suggested a "gift that would keep on giving" for the whole year. I proposed that we both read the daily meditations in Buechner's book, write down our thoughts, and mail them to the other person. He agreed, and for all of 1995 we listened to each other's lives.

Two weeks after we began this exercise, Dad preached a sermon that opened with an anecdote about an incident we both remembered clearly: the time when I was five years old that our family visited New York City, and I had gotten on the wrong subway train by myself. The sermon then went on:

> Subway tracks are dangerous, not just because of the
> chance of being run over by a speeding train, but because

of what they call the third rail that provides the electric power.

This past week, against the background of Human Relations Day and Martin Luther King's birthday, I studied the suggested scriptures for today. And it came to me that, in the two special observances, and in all four scriptures, there are three common threads or themes; or, if you will, three rails running through all of them. The first one is highlighted in the sermon title: in each special-day and scripture segment there is *something for everyone.* The second rail is the recurring theme of unity-in-diversity. And, in the third rail, the power source; along each segment, or at each station, we find an epiphany, or manifestation—God being revealed in a special way. So don't be left standing on the platform. Let's get on this train together, and see how this three-rail track will take us to our destination . . .

Dad had not then seen any of the manuscript for this book, which by then I had been working on for over two years, and knew nothing of its recurring train motif. But those last few sentences quoted above proved apt for the journey Dad and I had just begun.

What started out as a shared spiritual discipline developed almost immediately into a lush and intimate correspondence. I believe in Providence, but much of the credit for being the instrument of God's grace must go to Buechner himself. A man of deep personal faith whose theology was down to earth—I mean, tugging-at-the-roots, bruising-your-fingers-in-the-gravel down to earth—Frederick Buechner was also a writer of breathtaking eloquence. For all our differences, both Dad and I felt comfortable—and challenged—in both of these areas. As both a preacher and a novelist, Frederick Buechner turned out to be the perfect meeting ground for my father and me.

"I wonder how many other relationships have had new avenues and vistas and bridges opened up by this catalytic writer!" Dad wrote soon after we had started this project. One early passage from *Listening to Your Life* sums up the divine serendipity of Buechner's prose, which resonated so precisely with our own life experiences and theological struggles:

> . . . and again we are tempted to see God's meaning as clarity itself. But what is God saying through a good man's suicide? . . . . What about sin itself as a means of grace? What about grace, when misappropriated and misunderstood, becoming an occasion for sin? To try to express in

even the most insightful and theologically sophisticated terms the meaning of what God speaks through the events of our lives is as precarious a business as to try to express the meaning of the sound of rain on the roof or the spectacle of the setting sun. But I choose to believe that he speaks nonetheless . . . (p. 3)

We didn't learn until page 318, in an entry for December, that Buechner's own father had committed suicide.

Repeatedly, Buechner's personal vignettes connected uncannily with my current writing project, while for Dad, they inspired reflection on the whole of his life and provided a structure for him to share meaningfully about his childhood for the first time:

I guess the only President I've seen in person was F. D. Roosevelt, on the back platform of a train that came through Connellsville during his whistle-stop campaign for a second term in 1936. I sat on my father's shoulder with a big crowd of hopeful poor people in between.

My early life was spent on a hill overlooking this dirty, hilly town (pop. 15,000). Besides a passenger depot (where I saw FDR), there was a large freight yard—with many steam engines—of the Baltimore and Ohio Railroad, mostly for the numerous coal mines and coke ovens in the region. A century ago, my hometown was the coke (roasted coal) center of the world, feeding the steel mills downriver at Pittsburgh. (The Loughiogheny River was non-bargeable.) My first train ride as a boy was from Connellsville to California—Pennsylvania; I didn't see Pittsburgh until I was thirteen when my father and I bicycled and hitchhiked up to his birthplace in Auburn, New York, passing through Ithaca on the way.

My personal coal-mining experience was upriver near Confluence in a dangerous, non-commercial slope mine owned by my foster parents and their relatives. I associate many educational memories with this period, but mostly unpleasant ones.

Your grandfather trudged the hills of Connellsville as a mail carrier for about forty years, covering nearly all the city routes at various times. Failing health and a lifetime of overwork forced his retirement at age sixty-nine. I was a high school senior when he died in February 1947, less than two months after he retired. My only keepsake from him was the last Connellsville Post Office badge (number 3) he wore on his cap, which I was regrettably over-eager to give to my only son, long before he was old enough to appreciate its value, and care for it accordingly.

I don't know what ever happened to the only souvenir from my own grandfather that I think we used to have—his moustache cup.

❁

I immediately recognized the archival value of such material, and asked Dad if he could please start typing his replies so they would be easier to save. In his next letter, after explaining why typing would inhibit his spontaneity, he wrote: *"I confess that I was not initially thinking so much of their usefulness to you. Buechner was just the catalyst who helped me get out some too-long-bottled-up heart to heart stuff for the beginning of a new relationship with my son.* [The exercise] *has had inestimable usefulness in opening my heart and life for me, to you, and to Mom perhaps, when she gets around to reading my comments."*

Consistent with the flow of the daily meditations, Dad's responses moved from nostalgic to philosophical to confessional: *"— A poignant final paragraph, at the beginning of what may be the final year in the latest chapter of a long series of failures in my life that seem to far outnumber the occasional gratifying successes . . ."* he wrote at one point. Often he commented on a passage's relevance to the book I was writing about my life and about Murree Christian School. Neither Dad nor I managed to get to the Buechner readings every day, but we always caught up. We did not comment on every entry, and it was striking how repeatedly we chose the same passage to highlight and respond to.

Six months after we completed this pilgrimage-through-correspondence, my first book was published. (Though its release preceded this one, *Far Above the Plain,* an oral history of Murree Christian School, was actually a spin-off of the present work.) A few weeks later I received a lengthy letter from Dad, which I have come to think of as "The Albert Essay."

"I have been trying to move away from the negatives associated with my retirement being mostly involuntary, and enjoy the positives," it began. Now that he had time, he wanted to say more about his father, Albert Seaman, and other influential people in his life who had come to mind during our reading of Buechner's book together. *"Along the way, there were other stimuli to also write about some other Alberts in my life that affected me personally or indirectly—and, therefore, have also affected you and others whose lives I have touched these sixty-six-and-a-half years."*

"Part of what got me to finally sit down and set this down on paper was reading one of the epigraphs at the beginning of your long-awaited Far Above the Plain: *'Growing up is like a blow to the head: It makes partial amnesiacs of us all' [Tom DeHaven, Entertainment Weekly]. Much of my early life (and later life!) was so painful that, at times, the*

only way to deal with it was to block it out. And our continuing need for marriage counseling suggests that the healing of harmful memories is still incomplete for both Mom and me.

"Another stimulus is remembering that my father died at age sixty-nine, only months after retiring, with still a lot to share in his head and heart. Only too late did I come to at least a partial realization that the Great Depression and World War II and the Cold War, one after another, must have made a large contribution to what seemed like personal paternal cruelty from my childhood perspective." Albert Seaman's father had been a Methodist Protestant pastor whose wife was a poet.

Then he went on to describe the preferred aroma of "Prince Albert" pipe tobacco among those used by his father's friends when he was a boy. ("*Albert of Saxe-Coburg-Gotha, 1819-1861, prince consort of Queen Victoria,*" for anyone who wanted to know.) Albert Schweitzer, the pioneering missionary, physician, theologian, philosopher, and musician. Albert Einstein, "*the physicist who affected every creature in the universe more than we can imagine, contributed (albeit with serious reservations) to the beginning of nuclear warfare at Hiroshima on August 6, 1945.*" Albert Fulmer—still living—an early spiritual mentor and Sunday School teacher at Apple Street Methodist Protestant Church in Connellsville, where his grandfather had been pastor years earlier.

And, finally, Albert Leighty, "*retired owner-operator of Point Valley Dairy Farm, which had supplied milk to our family from my infancy. He still lives in the house that I helped him build as his hired hand/foster son while I was there for my last two years of high school. My previous foster fathers had been abusive, so Albert Leighty seemed like a gift from heaven for me. Losing his wife to cancer several years earlier had probably mellowed him, besides having a different personality. We shared the same room in the old homeplace, rising at 4:00 a.m. to go get the cows in and milk them before I went off to school, sometimes hiking the two miles over the hills in trackless deep snow, wishing for snow shoes like the ones I had seen in pictures.*

"In recent years, with links to my past dwindling, I have renewed contact with Albert Leighty, widowed again ten years ago. I've been writing to him at Christmas and for his birthday in July. He was so pleased to get my card last month that he called me right away—even on day-rate. It's hard and scary to imagine what might have happened had he not done so much during those crisis years to restore my faith in human nature and in a meaningful future for my life.*"

I had hoped that *Far Above the Plain* would encourage other missionary kids to write about their past, to recover a sense of connectedness in their lives, to see the sometimes hidden threads of continuity and grace. I never expected that my own father would be the first to do so.

Soon after I received "The Albert Essay" Dad and I were talking on the phone. "You've been writing for a long time," he said. "You've come a long way since that science-fiction novel you were working on in high school."

I reminded him how disapproving he had been of my obsession with that effort, but also how proud he had been when my bound copy of *Stolen from the Stars* sat side by side with his thesis on the living room coffee table.

He laughed, acknowledging the mixed messages he had sometimes given. "You were always involved in some creative project back then," Dad said. "Wasn't it around that time that you were trying to invent an antigravity swimming pool?"

Apparently, Dad had noticed a lot more of what I was doing than I ever realized. I was simultaneously startled that he knew anything about that and embarrassed that I had, indeed, been working on something so ridiculous. But in many ways that idea was no more ridiculous than my asking Dad to review a copy of this manuscript before it went to press.

Which is exactly what I did.

Of course, reconciliation did not mean that Dad underwent a personality transformation. Ever since high school, I had stopped sharing my writing with Dad because his only response was to correct the spelling and punctuation. This time I made him promise that his "helpful" proof-reading would be balanced by some more personal feedback. Still, his comments required a lot of patience, not for anything overly-critical he said, but for his long-windedness in expounding upon minutiae. (I involuntarily learned a lot about the geography and geology of Pennsylvania by accidentally placing the coal fields of his childhood in the central rather than western part of that state.)

Then he read chapter eight, "The Legendary Screamin' Seaman." Tucked among the numbered page and paragraph references to minor grammatical points was the following sentence: *"I don't recall some of the incidents involving me in this chapter. Is some of it fictionalized/poetic license?"* Of course, it wasn't; but, after a few more spelling corrections, he went on to say, *"If this is completely accurate —Sorry! Regrets. Apologies."* And with reference to my comment about being the only victim, when a lot of people shared responsibility for the circumstances leading up to my being suspended from school, he said, *"The pain was shared, though evidently not obviously or helpfully enough. Sorry again."*

A few page references further he again wrote, *"I'm sorry!"*

Two simple words that I had waited twenty-four years to hear. And this time I didn't mind the repetition. Dad's apology was sweeter because I had, in fact, already forgiven him. Writing that chapter was a sort of ritual act of cleansing for me, naming the residual pain that often lingers even after genuine forgiveness has occurred. And now, whenever we talk on the phone and he says "I love you" just before hanging up, it is so much more full of meaning because we have acknowledged the depth of each other's pain, not just "set aside our differences" to be civil to each other.

"A crazy, holy grace," Frederick Buechner called it. *Crazy because whoever could have predicted it? Who can ever foresee the crazy how and when and where of a grace that wells up out of the lostness and pain of the world and of our own inner worlds? And holy because these moments of grace come ultimately from farther away than Oz and deeper down than doom, holy because they heal and hallow."*

15

Obscure Paradise

Life is a mystery, everyone must stand alone.
I hear you call my name, and it feels like home.

MADONNA,
"Like a Prayer"

When, as a teenager, I first began trying to discern what
was God's will for my life, and wondering what my "calling" might be, my father would sometimes quote Samuel
Shoemaker's words to me, remembered from his Asbury Seminary
days: "The will of God is like the path of a ship, not the track of a
railroad: you do not see the way laid out plainly before you as far as
eye can reach, but you see the wake when you look behind you, and
you know that the evidence of the leading of God is unmistakable."
   Judging by my wake, it seems likely that a lot of confusion,
restlessness, meandering, and emotional whirlpools will continue to
characterize my journey. Yet, in my better moments, I can discern a
pattern or triangulation that charts, however incrementally, a dis-
tinctly forward motion, a kind of spiritual mean. I do seem to have
emerged from typhoon country intact and with some useful stories
to tell.
   It is hard for me to recapture now the emotional agony and
spiritual chaos that characterized my life just three-and-a-half years
ago. But I can retrace the key elements that have contributed to
whatever measure of healing, wholeness, and contentment I feel
today. Growth is a slippery process with overlapping currents of
influence and circumstance that make it hard to clearly delineate
each stage. I can trace the roots of this book, at least, to July 1989,
when I returned to college to finish a long-postponed bachelor's

degree. The APEL Program at American University in Washington, DC, deserves a lot of the credit.

APEL is an acronym for "Assessment of Prior Experiential Learning"—no connection to the well-known computer company. The APEL Program offers academic credit for professional and other life experiences, to give returning adult students a boost toward completing degree requirements. Through this program, students can achieve up to thirty credits—the equivalent of a year's worth of full-time classes. One of the first exercises in the two-semester seminar involved compiling a chronology of every significant event in our lives, year by year, since graduation from high school: moves, marriages, career changes, and any other milestones of circumstance or personal growth. We were all amazed how full and rich our lives had been for people who "never got a college degree" and despite, for many of us, no discernible career path. Through the simple act of writing it all down systematically—not as personal as a diary nor as pious as a resume—some unexpected patterns emerged from the jumble of dates and seemingly random events, and, often, a reassuring sense of progress.

I did not realize then, however, that as a tool for personal reflection my list had been profoundly incomplete. By starting with the year I graduated from high school, my chronology left out one of the most shaping facts of my life—growing up in Pakistan. I have subsequently come to think of this as The Great Divide and refer to events in my life as either "B.C."—*Before Coming* back to the States, or "A.D."—*After Departing* Pakistan.

As part of my APEL "Portfolio," I wrote a paper on cross-cultural adaptation. When the university awarded me six credits in that subject area (the equivalent of a year's class work) it was the first official acknowledgement I had ever received for the value of that seemingly obscure experience. A few months later, I discovered a whole movement dedicated to recognizing the unique benefits and challenges of a childhood abroad and to naming the community of those who share this experience.

In September 1989, American University sponsored a seminar on "Third Culture Kids," led by David Pollock, Director of Inter-action, Inc. The immediate impact of this workshop came simply from who the participants were: all sixty-five of us had been raised outside the United States. As the seminar progressed, it quickly became apparent that despite widely varying backgrounds we had a surprising number of other things in common, too. We learned that studies have consistently shown some predictable patterns in the emotional experience and social adjustments of children raised overseas because of a parent's occupation.

David Pollock described himself as a "TCK wanna-be." He said that third culture kids were "the prototype citizens of the twenty-first century," exhibiting the skills and character traits that will be critical for leadership in an ever more interdependent world with increasingly multicultural societies. Pollock looked like a stereotypical anthropology professor—or career missionary—with kind eyes, graying hair, and a white beard. He did, in fact, serve as a missionary for several years and, consequently, became the father of three "TCKs." He was currently Director of Intercultural Programs at a Christian college outside New York City. This shared faith perspective increased the rapport I felt, which his earnest manner and relaxed, interactive speaking style quickly elicited anyway.

According to Pollock, third culture kids *are those who have spent a significant part of their developmental years in a culture other than their parents' culture, developing a sense of relationship to all those cultures while not having full ownership in any. Elements of each culture are incorporated into their lives, but their sense of belonging is in relationship to others of similar experience.*

That sense of belonging quickly became apparent from the participants' very engaged responses as David sketched out this model, illustrating his points with poignant anecdotes that pulled on chords deep in my soul, stirring places that had been buried under years of scar tissue and presumed irrelevance. In small groups we shared the most vulnerable and precious secrets of our "unique" background the way others might talk about last night's TV program or basketball scores. For the first time in my life I didn't have to explain myself—and when I did, people actually *wanted* to know. I finally began to understand that there was nothing wrong with me for being who I was, and that I wasn't alone. People kept prefacing their remarks with: "I don't mean to repeat what everybody else has said, but . . ." For the first time, I had the odd experience of feeling *ordinary*. It was exhilarating—but also left me a little unsure of myself.

We talked about the positive aspects of the TCK experience: cross-cultural skills, ease in learning new languages (not true in my case!), a wider world view, adaptability, and maturity. Third culture kids are often two to three years more mature—in some ways—than their monocultural peers "back home." My inclination in high school to hang out with college students now made sense, given my experience; I wasn't just being pretentious or rebellious.

Then we talked about the down side of growing up global, the hidden costs of this "wonderful privilege" that adults seemed so impressed with and our peers had met with boredom—or resentment, thinking we were stuck up. Words such as "boarding school," "servants," "missionary," "London," "India" and "Africa" have very different connotations in the States, we quickly learned, than they did for us abroad—connotations based on fantasies, ignorance, and moral judgments. I wasn't the only one who felt out of sync and misunderstood. Loneliness and confusion were a common experience for those returning from a childhood abroad, whether the time away had been twelve years or only two.

When I came back to the States in tenth grade and saw signs for "body shops," I thought they were massage parlors. I knew that America was a decadent place, but I was surprised to find so many of them in the small towns of upstate New York. Nobody snickered when I shared that story.

Increasing the pain of isolation was the sense of rootlessness that our backgrounds had bred: TCKs will move an average of eight times in their first eighteen years. A majority of us will attend at least five different colleges before getting a bachelor's degree. Check, again: American University was my fifth.

Two of the hardest questions for a third culture kid to answer are, "Where are you from?" and "Where is home?" Because our families moved so much, there is often no place where TCKs feel geographically rooted. For the same reason, they may be unable to adequately maintain lasting relationships. This experience, as many of us could testify, frequently carries into adulthood: as difficulty with commitment or intimacy or as a constant, underlying anxiety about losing the friendships or romantic attachments that we do develop.

Not all of these traits are unique to third culture kids, but taken together they are more likely to be found in us *as a group* than in other social groupings.

Unresolved grief was the single issue that resonated most deeply with everyone—all the friendships and familiar places, people, pets, and things that were left behind so many times. Everyone experiences losses growing up, but those from an internationally mobile childhood experience losses that are multiple, simultaneous, intense, and often unresolved when families move from posting to posting or base to base—sometimes on very short notice. For many of us the result is a lifelong legacy of powerlessness, distrust, and confusion about loyalty placement. But the hardest transition came when we moved "home" to America for high school or college and lost both the family connections and the comfort of peers, even the mere acquaintances with whom shared an understanding of the expatriate lifestyle and values.

David then described what commonly happens during this "transition phase," when TCKs move or return to whatever country their parents call home. I felt like I was listening to a fortune teller. Hearing others describe their feelings and share familiar stories opened up emotional memories of my own. Finally, I was being given permission to feel the pain, to let go of the repressed grief that I had tried to ignore—or hadn't even recognized—for so many years. I heard sobbing coming from several places around the room, and I wept with relief. As the tears streamed down my cheeks, I felt the pain of the confused little boy and the self-loathing man, and I felt the spiritual rush from revealed brokenness and the paradoxical pain of accepting comfort.

The fourth floor lounge in the Butler Pavilion at American University, where the TCK seminar was held that Sunday afternoon, has become one of the sacred places in my life's journey. Subsequently, trying to hold onto something of the sense of community that I experienced then, I tried to help start a Third Culture Association at A.U. But I was ten to twelve years older than the other members of the group and the compelling issues for me were different from theirs. It was another year before I discovered that an organization already existed to serve adult TCKs.

When Norma McCaig founded Global Nomads International in 1986, she had never heard the term "third culture kid." She only knew what her experience had been. She defined global nomads as *"persons of any age or nationality who have spent childhood years living in one or more countries outside their passport country because of a parent's occupation."* Whether our parents served with government, voluntary, or missionary agencies, as diplomats, international businesspeople, or military personnel, global nomads share a common cultural heritage.

The term *global nomads* refers to both the transient nature of such a childhood (when a parent's occupation may cause the family to live in several different countries) and also the resulting sense of cultural rootlessness that often remains well into adulthood. Some people (mostly academics) quibble that the term "third culture kid" is patronizing or too obscure, but it does point to the particular social identity of growing up in an expatriate community that is neither the culture of the host society nor that of the home country, and something other than just a blending of the two—a *third culture,* the impact of which is most significant when experienced during one's formative years; thus, third culture *kid.*

Norma McCaig conducts workshops similar to David Pollock's TCK Profile, and the weekend retreat I attended with both of them and fourteen other global nomads was another watershed experience. Her approach is to list the relevant categories—mobility, leavetaking, relationships, personal development, cross-cultural issues, global perspective—and ask the participants to explore the upsides and downsides of each. This emphasizes the possibility of choice in our perceptions and actions, and reduces the tendency to take on a "victim mentality" about our experience.

Even so, the emotional core of these workshops often deals with the painful aspects of the global nomad legacy. This does not mean they focus on the negative. On the contrary, we are well aware of the benefits of our unusual upbringing. But to finally be able to identify and talk about the more difficult sides is an effective way to let go of the pain. The TCK profile offers helpful insights for gaining better control of our lives, not excuses for our weak points. Learning how much our experience was shared by others helps put things in perspective, but certainly not every aspect of our personalities or personal situations can be handily explained by our unusual background.

Norma McCaig's defining axiom for the goals of Global Nomads International is *Exploration, Affirmation, and Action,* emphasizing that, ultimately, the point of untangling the web of confusion and pain is to allow the skills and wisdom we have gained —including through the grief—to be utilized in service to others.

In fact, people are sometimes confused about what exactly a "global nomad" is, partly because we like to emphasize the positive. We do feel special; and we are grateful for the privilege of such rich and varied cultural exposure. The early experience of learning to relate to people not like ourselves and having repeatedly to adapt to new circumstances often has given global nomads a social edge. In an unfamiliar group, we tend to be less uncomfortable than others, and we have a heightened sensitivity to intercultural issues. We tend to be less judgmental and more cautious about accepting simplistic explanations or easy generalizations. It is easy to trace how our background has influenced our political perspectives and material values, but what about its emotional and spiritual consequences and its impact on relationships?

Many of the positive aspects of a childhood abroad are similar to those we share with our international fellow-travelers. But internally, global nomads sometimes struggle with issues that are distinct to our particular heritage—issues that are hard to define because they often go unrecognized or are not easy to talk about. When high school or college students decide to participate in a foreign exchange program or join the Peace Corps, they may come back with a radically altered sense of their identity or place in society, but they do have someplace to come home to. And they have the inner foundation of having _chosen_ their foreign experience and the knowledge that it is _temporary_. Global nomads have neither. They did not choose their circumstances and they had no assurance of when the cycles of separation and loss would end. The landscape changed repeatedly, socially as well as geographically, as the family moved from base to base, or the children moved back and forth to boarding school; and if my family didn't go on furlough or get transferred, my best friend's did. Later in life, global nomads often have no place to come home to when things get rough, no sanctuary of acceptance where the rules are comfortably familiar.

Culture shock or "re-entry" (reverse culture shock) may be common to a number of groups; there are certainly both benefits and challenges for anyone discovering and adapting to a different culture. But global nomads experience these transitions _repeatedly_, during their _formative years_, with _no choice_ in the matter, and must cope with _shifting social identities_ often before even forming a primary one. The self-reliance that global nomads are forced to develop in order to survive, for example, is not at all the same as the self-confidence and curiosity that allows exchange students to leave their families and venture abroad. Both refugees and immigrants tend to maintain a sense of family and cultural identity, often heightened by their circumstances, and when they long for home they know exactly where and what they are longing for.

Global nomads must not only deal with the accumulated grief of successive losses, but must do so without the comfort of a clear sense of home. Our longing is for something more obscure, something always intangible.

We all need to tell our stories, for we long to be assured that we are not alone. There are few places in our modern society for this to happen—which, I suspect, may be a primary reason for the popularity of psychotherapy, the many twelve step programs, and other support groups. I am repeatedly struck by the similarity of results when people feel seen and heard—when their troubled hearts are witnessed by others—whether the context is an adult Sunday school forum, a personal growth retreat, a workshop for parents and children of divorce, or any gathering of global nomads. People bond quickly with those who've shared this experience, and feel a sense of release and empowerment from recognizing their common humanity.

Trauma experts emphasize that talking is a critical step in healing. Whether the people involved are survivors of an airplane crash or victims of a hurricane, simply describing *what happened* in detail, while difficult, significantly hastens their recovery from shock and helplessness. Like Vietnam veterans, global nomads have until recently been deprived of social validation of their experience. Friends, relatives, school officials, even our parents' sponsoring agencies, usually couldn't appreciate the "big deal" about what had happened to us, because the trauma of uprooting and cultural dislocation was beyond their own experience.

Global nomads themselves often overlook or deny the accumulated grief that is also part of our heritage—partly, perhaps, because we have had no empathetic place in which to express that grief. (Psychologists call this "disenfranchised grief," a term that strikes me as particularly appropriate.) Many are unwilling to acknowledge their grief because they think that to do so would mean there was something wrong with them, not understanding that grief is a normal and inevitable part of life. It is ludicrous to say, in effect, "I had a happy childhood, therefore I have no grief from that period of my life." Not all grief is the result of bad things that happened to us. Often grief is a kind of paying respect—honoring the value of what is gone.

Psychologists generally agree that most depression is repressed anger; and most anger is related to unresolved grief. In the revised edition of her landmark work, *The Drama of the Gifted Child*, psychotherapist Alice Miller states that, in her view, *all* violence comes from unresolved grief.

In *A Guide for the Perplexed*, E. F. Schumacher (author of *Small Is Beautiful*) emphasizes that knowing oneself is a *prerequisite* to understanding others. It is not frivolous or even optional. Forget guilt. In our fear that we are being self-indulgent or feeling sorry for ourselves, we grimly go about "getting on with life," "being responsible," and being "mindful of those more needy" while we ourselves are half-lame and half-blind. This is false maturity and dishonest altruism.

Many of us feel guilty that our grief is trivial in comparison with the "real" suffering in the world—in Bosnia, Rwanda, or America's inner cities. But a child doesn't make these comparisons, and long after we have intellectually gained some perspective on the particular traumas we experienced while growing up, it is the child's emotional scars that remain.

Ruth Van Reken's book, *Letters Never Sent,* a remarkably vulnerable exploration of one woman's lifelong struggle with this legacy of grief, has been criticized for focusing on the negative side of being an MK, a missionary kid. In some circles she has been dismissed as an aberration, someone with personal problems. (Notably few of her detractors, however, have been fellow MKs.) Ruth's response is simply to remind people of the parable of the lost sheep and the Good Shepherd's concern, not for the ninety-nine safe and healthy sheep, but for the one who was left out in the cold, frightened and alone.

During this project, I encountered similar concerns from some alumni of Murree Christian School who felt I ought to focus on the "typically wholesome, victorious life" of missionary kids—meaning as *they* experienced it or chose to remember it, or thought it should be portrayed. Jesus' words seem relevant here, when he said, "It is not the healthy who need a doctor, but the sick. But go and learn what this means: 'I desire mercy, not sacrifice.' For I have not come to call the righteous, but sinners" (Matthew 9:12-13).

I don't think we need to defend God's reputation. And I think the "Christian witness" is better served by an honest portrayal of human frailty than one glossed over by spiritual-sounding language that, in fact, offers a very superficial form of redemption. It is also interesting to note that Ruth Van Reken's supposedly exceptional perspective struck enough familiar chords to sell 25,000 copies— almost exclusively by word of mouth. *Letters Never Sent* has become something of an underground classic in the missions community and has been well-received in the larger community of global nomads, in spite of its overtly Christian perspective.

There is something powerful, of course, in hearing your own private story articulated by someone else. It is a healing revelation, one that moves us from isolation to a bond with the rest of humanity. That is why certain songs have such strong appeal. Someone else has expressed my own experience with music. In an interview about his book, *Shot in the Heart,* Mikal Gilmore, a long-time *Rolling Stone* music critic, said, "Music has been my best friend. It has counseled me. It spoke for me when I didn't know how to speak for myself. I took from it vicarious strength. It gave me at times a moral center, moral guidance. Music really spoke to my imagination—passionately. I heard lyrics that seemed to speak for me—for pain I couldn't articulate better, or beauty or transcendence" (*The Washington Post,* July 8, 1994).

Mikal Gilmore's childhood was hardly typical. His older brother, Gary Gilmore, the Utah murderer executed by firing squad in 1977, was the subject of Norman Mailer's Pulitzer Prize-winning book, *The Executioner's Song*. *Shot in the Heart* is a memoir about Mikal's family, and he wrote the book to put his own ghosts to rest. It is the same reason many writers write. It is a purification process, an exorcism, a pilgrimage. The appeal of story-telling, the appeal of reading good books, is not just to experience another's life vicariously, but to find out if at the essential levels their story is the same as ours. Good songwriters do this in bite-size pieces, giving us a little nugget of the universal human condition that we can suck on. Over the last few years I have encountered many songs that illustrate TCK themes.

Here is a list of my personal nominees for "The Top Ten Songs on TCK Themes," drawn from popular music of the last few decades:

Just a Song Before I Go	Crosby, Stills and Nash
Leaving on a Jet Plane	John Denver
Changes	David Bowie
Like a Rolling Stone	Bob Dylan
Somebody's Always Saying Goodbye	Anne Murray
The Stranger Song	Leonard Cohen
Homeward Bound	Simon & Garfunkel
Dweller on the Threshold	Van Morrison
On the Road Again	Willie Nelson
Can't Find My Way Home	Blind Faith/Eric Clapton

Several more equally relevant songs come to mind without any effort: Pink Floyd's "Wish You Were Here," Roseanne Cash's "On the Surface (Everything's Okay)," Simon & Garfunkel's "I Am a Rock," former Eagle Don Henley's "The Heart of the Matter (is Forgiveness)," the Beach Boys' "Winds of Change," the Beatles' "In My Life," and John Denver's "Goodbye Again." (Denver ought to know: he is himself a global nomad, having been raised in a military family.) Then there are Nancy Griffith's emblematic lyrics from the title song of her album, *Leaving the Harbor:*

> When you are leaving the harbor
> Do you cry out to the shore?
> Do you bless the wave of the ocean
> Do you call your vessel home?

Hearing other people articulate the emotional essence of my experience has comforted me greatly over the years. But ultimately,

192 PAPER AIRPLANES IN THE HIMALAYAS

knowing that a lot of other people were lonely, confused, grieving, or spiritually hungry didn't really nurture my soul. All the sympathetic miserable company in the world wasn't going to bring me into the Promised Land. Even the healing revelations about my TCK identity and the new sense of my special place in the world that it gave me weren't enough. Something was still missing.

In 1991, I became president of Global Nomads Washington Area and joined the Board of Directors of Global Nomads International. A year later I received the first GNI Leadership Award. But I continued to be disoriented by the number of social misunderstandings in both my professional and personal life, and bewildered by my inability to find lasting companionship. It was the weariness from these contradictions that brought me down to the Potomac River in March 1993, to that pivotal encounter with myself underneath an abandoned railway trestle.

My evangelical friends tell me, of course, that the problem was that I hadn't given my life fully to Jesus—in whom the only true peace and comfort can be found. God knows I've tried that solution. And those who've known me for years, and know my childhood background, and can still glibly say, "I'm so glad we can recommend Jesus to you," only illustrate the just-doesn't-get-it mentality that is precisely one of the reasons I can no longer subscribe to the kind of Christianity they think is the answer. Such platitudes as "Maybe you've never *really* given your heart to Jesus" totally dismiss the authenticity of my spiritual journey so far, and the earnestness with which I repeatedly pursued a relationship with Christ.

Because I *have* taken that journey seriously, and approached it honestly, the result has been theological ambiguity, not a denial of faith. Matters of the soul, it turns out, are no more subject to doctrine than matters of the heart are to logic. The road to spiritual clarity and contentment is not so clearly mapped out as I was led to believe at Murree Christian School. Sometimes there is no road at all, or the numbers on the sign posts don't match those on the map. Contrary to what I was taught, there is no reliable equation between the practice of faith and the experience of God's presence.

In the fall of 1984, I lost an important political-action job with a progressive nonprofit organization in Washington. Two months later—while I was still unemployed—my wife asked me to leave, saying that a temporary separation might save our marriage. The way in which these two incidents were handled, more than the end results, shattered my idealism about both institutions; and I soon lost my faith in a third. After finding a small inner city apartment, I joined a weekly Bible study group associated with the church my wife and I attended. One evening that winter I shared, with great awkwardness, that I was contemplating suicide and would appreciate their prayers. Yet, during the following week no one from the group called to see how I was doing or to offer support.

I got through the "deadly February" blues, but I never went back to the group. Or to that church.

My efforts to find a home in the Body of Christ have repeatedly been inhibited by the insensitivity, whether by righteousness or neglect, of those who would most recommend their Savior to me.

"You can't blame God for human weaknesses," they say; but I cannot separate my need for reliable community from my hunger for spiritual truth. I believe in the Incarnation, that God is somehow—and passionately—involved in human affairs. Yet the seemingly random quality of divine intervention prevents me from embracing one particular creed with certitude. I know God's grace when I experience it, whether in daily hope and sustenance, or in the power of transformative moments. I am grateful for the Compassionate Mystery—beyond a recognizable combination of factors—that led me away from self-destruction in the spring of 1993. And though writing this book began as a very personal pilgrimage, I quickly found myself moving in the stream of "divine serendipity," part of some larger purpose, and felt closer to God than I had for a long time.

Yet, a restlessness remained.

In June 1994, I attended a weekend retreat called "Legacy of the Heart: The Spiritual Advantages of a Painful Childhood" by Wayne Muller, which is also the title of a book he wrote on the same topic. Though Muller is an ordained Christian minister, he works as a therapist and community activist, and has assimilated wisdom from many religious traditions. For example, he incorporates into his life and his workshops "centering meditations," a practice that conservative Christians too often dismiss as "New Age" heresy or therapeutic mumbo jumbo. As it turned out, half the workshop participants were therapists who had come for professional development, but soon discovered they were really there for personal reasons. In fact, given the weekend's topic, and the reverent tone of the presentations, I kept forgetting that this was not a religious retreat.

Wayne's presence was its own testimony, the most compelling evidence for the credibility of his ideas. The gentle confidence he

quickly created a remarkable atmosphere of safety and
ility. (Participants began referring to the retreat as "Wayne's
ld," an affectionately ludicrous reference to the goofy adolescent
omedy that had recently been a hit movie.) Wayne showed us the
liberating power of honoring everything that life has to offer, from
pain to potatoes to opposing viewpoints. For the first time, I understood this discipline—for that is certainly what it is—not as passive
acceptance, but as a tool for insight and a way of staying connected
rather than self-absorbed. Christians are fond of quoting (often out
of context) St. Paul's reassuring maxim, "All things work together for
good to them that love God" (Romans 8:28), but it usually sounds
more like grim—or insensitively perky—consolation rather than
respectful alertness to what life has to teach us.

I came away from Wayne's world with two other important
truths. First, each of us has within ourselves a "core of goodness"
that has never been spoiled, violated, or perverted. For decades, psychotherapy has operated under the mistaken assumption that people
have been damaged and need to be repaired. Wayne Muller believes
that people's true selves, both innocent and powerful, have become
trapped behind emotional barbed wire, smothered under layers of
brokenness, neglect, and cruel self-images. Yes, we need healing, but
not the kind of therapy that reinforces our sense of being sick people.
What we need is help in stripping away these layers of mud and
dried blood so we can draw strength from what is pure and
undamaged within ourselves.

Second, people need to develop an awareness of our common
humanity, not what sets us apart. Some people have lived with their
pain, their brokenness, or sense of loss, for so long it has become an
essential part of their identity. And even when they want to be
healed, it is hard for them to let go of the thing that has defined their
being for so long. Their "exceptional" circumstances, their "unique"
suffering, is what makes them special. This pattern had certainly
been true for me.

During my senior year at Ithaca High School I dropped my obsolete nickname from Murree, "Screamin' Seaman," to embrace one
a current girlfriend conferred on me: "Crazy Diamond"—inspired by
the Pink Floyd song, which perfectly matched my self-image as a
misunderstood pilgrim with unique qualifications for some sacred
mission, some great contribution to society. In fact, "Shine on You
Crazy Diamond" became something of a personal credo: *Come on
you stranger, you legend, you martyr, and shine!*

Such self-absorbed earnestness is not uncommon in adolescents,
but like many TCKs, much of my emotional life remained in adol-

escence for a very long time. Therapists call this condition in adults "terminal uniqueness," when a person feels that their problems are so unusual that no one could ever understand, let alone be able to help, or assumes that their lives are uniquely gifted; or, as in my case, feels both are true. Either way, this position greatly inhibits our emotional and spiritual growth, both of which depend on our recognizing our connections to others and realizing how common are most of our struggles.

Learning about the common characteristics of third culture kids was the single greatest step in helping me overcome the paralysis of my own "uniqueness." One of the primary functions of Global Nomads (the organization) is to facilitate the coming together of people who share the same distinct heritage, and here I found a place where I no longer felt like an outsider, where at last I could feel at home. One way to define home, perhaps, is the place where you're always someone special without trying to be, and where you don't ever have to explain yourself because people already know who you are. When a healthy understanding of what makes me distinct is balanced by the profound comfort of *not* being different, then a true sense of belonging becomes possible.

I was amazed by the diversity of experience included in the family of global nomads or TCKs. How could people from such different backgrounds have so much in common? When I first got involved with Global Nomads International, I was convinced that, as a missionary kid, I had little in common with military brats or foreign service dependents who had lived in "little Americas," completely out of touch with the country around them. In fact, the bond of commonality is greater than our differences. When global nomads get together there is a catharsis of recognition that transcends our stereotypes about each other.

My heritage turned out to be quite different from the rootless, maladjusted stereotype I had accepted. As I looked more deeply into my experience, I was confronted with how many of my emotional and cultural struggles were key elements of the American character. The "TCK" songs listed earlier—none of which was written to describe the global nomad experience—provide a dramatic illustration of this connection.

The culture of the United States, perhaps more than that of any other country, resonates with many aspects of the TCK profile. Ambiguously rooted in various cultures, constantly in search of its own identity, America is powerful yet naive, well-meaning yet often misunderstood.

A *Washington Post* article called "Black Unlike Me" had this startling subtitle: "Larry Graham Lives in Two Worlds and Feels Truly at Home in Neither" (Tuesday, July 11, 1995). Startling, because there in front of me in large black type across the page of a major national newspaper was one of the classic descriptions of a third culture kid. In fact, the article was about Graham's recently published book of essays, *Member of the Club*, which describes his struggles with the social contradictions of growing up upper-middle-class and black in a racially charged society.

The more I examined the distinctive combination of grief, alienation, and nostalgia that I associated with the TCK legacy, the more I noticed that these "unique" characteristics were also shared by immigrants, refugees, ethnic minorities, and various types of exiles. Similar issues of rootlessness and cultural confusion are articulated passionately, perceptively, and poignantly in the many well-known works by international writers such as Derek Walcott, V.S. Naipaul, Salman Rushdie, Pico Iyer, and Michael Ondaatje—all but Walcott with family roots in South Asia.

Ondaatje, author of *The English Patient*, was born in Sri Lanka, moved to London as a young boy, and has lived in Toronto, Canada, for the past thirty-five years. Iyer, who spent part of his childhood in America, is a true global nomad—as the term is used here. So is Masako Owada, the Crown Princess of Japan, who grew up in the Soviet Union and the United States because of her father's position in the Japanese Foreign Ministry. Likewise, celebrated American authors Pearl Buck, Thornton Wilder, Katherine Paterson (*Bridge to Terabithia*), and John Hersey were all raised in China because of missionary parents.

The greater portion of American blues, folk, and rock and roll lyrics are motivated by a nagging sense of loss, a need to belong, and a desire for wholeness that is often phrased as a longing for home. The Christian sacrament of communion—by its very name a celebration of community—expresses these same yearnings. Once you get past the theological jargon, the mumble-dee-magic of "transubstantiation," the Eucharistic message is: *"Do this in remembrance of me." Share . . . and be made whole. Be assured that you will find your way home.*

My own pilgrimage to remember and be reconciled with a fragmented past has been no less of a redemptive experience—and one equally dependent on the power of community. Discovering the multiple layers of commonality—the bond of ordinariness—I share with the rest of humanity has been humbling; it has increased my compassion for others and given me a greater sense of my place as part of the whole. Yet, the journey toward wholeness has also required honoring the particulars of my own history. And realizing, at this very personal level, the extent to which I share a common emotional experience with others from Murree Christian School has affected me even more deeply. When people responded to my invitation with their own reflections on growing up at MCS, I was surprised again and again by the number of people who also had felt like outsiders there, some whose popularity had obscured incredibly deep insecurity and pain. (Such a paradox: that, unknowingly, the biggest thing we had in common was our sense of being alone.) One woman—the valedictorian of her class—wrote: *"I have spent the rest of my life trying to please people, in response to my fear of rejection, and wondering what I did that was so bad that my parents sent me away."*

I had supposed that my difficulties as an adult were also a solitary suffering, unique to me. When I solicited each member of the class of '73 to write about their twenty-year reunion (for the Supplement to this book), I envied their classically successful profile: all ten of them seemed happily married with children; among them were doctors and lawyers. All of them still professed a strong Christian faith. Yet they, too, wrote of childhood pain—loneliness, insecurity, and a sense of abandonment—that seems to affect them even now.

And in my own class (1976), I can hardly claim any unique status as an outsider, unduly troubled by social alienation. Of the eight or nine of us who grew up together, two are gay, one is a single woman who has never married, two struggle like me with depression; another experienced sexual abuse as a child—at the hands of a well-respected missionary who was a family friend. Three of my classmates have been career missionaries. One of these recently got divorced, however, after spending his entire life within the insular community of an evangelical mission organization—essentially, a continuation of the sheltered environment of boarding school. At thirty-eight, he is unprepared for the real world. Not only is he coping with a spiritual identity crisis, with no support structure to lean on or guide him, but for the first time in his life, he has to find a real job—with less experience at job hunting than the average sixteen-year-old. Clearly, to paraphrase one of the counselors in *I Never Promised You a Rose Garden,* I never had a corner on suffering or alienation.

By the time I attended Wayne Muller's workshop I had been working on this book for a year and a half. More than 120 former students of Murree Christian School had responded to the survey I sent out, and many of them were eager to share their stories. Wayne said that when we were growing up no one talked about their feelings so everyone thought they were the only one who was sad or lonely or afraid. But we were all in pain. I thought about MCS as he continued: "Since our feelings were kept secret, we felt our wounds set us apart from those we loved, not comprehending that everyone hurts, feels confused. Our particular pain, rather than making us unique, actually invites us into a deeper communion with all living beings.

"When we stop taking ourselves so seriously," Wayne said, "we are set free to more playfully engage the world in which we live. We are free to explore our boundaries and to experiment with what is possible."

I met Rosalie Anderson at Wayne's workshop, and our relationship has been significantly shaped by the insights and the challenges of that weekend. Three months later, Rosalie convinced me to participate in a four-day intensive personal growth workshop that took my interior journey to yet another stage. I had never heard of Temenos, the organization conducting the workshop—"It's like Lifespring with soul," Rosalie explained. It sounded like a lot of New Age mind games to me. Lifespring was a cult, wasn't it? The coercive techniques of their instructors had been widely publicized. But her offer to pay the considerable registration fee helped temper some of my initial skepticism.

Although Rosalie had already been separated from her husband for several months when I met her, he blamed me for the breakup of their marriage. Rosalie, being Rosalie, also invited—and paid for—her husband to attend the same workshop, because she thought it would be good for him. This added an unusual dimension to the proceedings. So did getting stuck alone in the hotel elevator for two and a half hours the first night.

The Temenos workshops are distinct from a lot of self-improvement programs because they combine inner healing with relationship skills, self-expression with social accountability, and empowerment with an acknowledgement of our connection to the Great Mystery. Although a Jungian perspective has clearly been a major influence, Temenos draws on the wisdom of many different psychological and spiritual traditions. Its programs are "consciousness work" and they are *work*. They are about pressing beyond our comfortable habits and familiar ways of seeing—or protecting—ourselves, and require honest engagement. The Temenos Basic

Workshop reaffirmed many of the things I had been learning. It gave me tools for a more disciplined self-awareness and a better understanding of both the patterns that hinder me and the resources available for a conscious life.

In addition to the primary instructor, a number of trained volunteers staffed the workshop. We were divided into eight small groups, containing no more than six or seven people, and each of these had two "facilitators." Then there were logistics people who ran the sound, set up the room, and provided a conscious spiritual presence that contributed immensely to the power of the experience. With such a carefully planned structure and such an incredible amount of hands-on support, instead of running amok, internally at least, like a bunch of lab rats in a maze, fifty-two total strangers were able to come together, be vulnerable, and confront volatile issues in often serendipitous ways. Small-group exercises repeatedly tested our determination to apply the "inner work" we were doing to situations in the real world. Combining this with the sanctuary-like support of the secondary staff, Temenos provided a model of ideal community.

The instructor, Jodi Pliskin, was not at all like Dave Pollock or Wayne Muller, however. She came from New York City, from an upper-middle-class Jewish family, and her abrasive manner did nothing to dispel my stereotypes in either of those categories. She talked down to us and her approach seemed unnecessarily negative. Several times during the first two days I considered quitting and going home. But by the third day, I had become so in awe of Jodi's wisdom and discernment I was practically worshipping her as a saint. I also came to sense something of the tremendous personal cost she had paid to gain the wisdom that she shared with us.

Among the lasting gifts that Temenos gave me were two visions I had during guided meditations. The instructor led us into these exercises, sometimes accompanied by music, with gentle words that set the stage and merely suggested the topic that might be explored. We all closed our eyes and Jodi asked us to become conscious of our breathing, to be aware of each breath, to consciously relax our bodies, becoming more and more focused on the person within; then, very intentionally, to visualize ourselves going to a place where we felt safe, content.

I am floating through a narrow gorge, moving upriver, around a bend to a little beach. I climb a steep path up the canyon wall to the rim. A little farther through the underbrush I come to an overlook. Here I build my "sacred circle" by symbolically placing a few stones around where I sit, legs dangling over the edge of a great drop. I watch myself meditating, like an Indian seeking his guide.

Then, I am paddling a canoe across a large lake at night. I am almost naked and feel my strength, my manhood, and it seems as though I could paddle forever. I feel the rhythm of each stroke, the smoothness of the water, as the canoe glides forward, moonlight glistening off the ripples. And then it happens—like an apparition, like King Arthur's Lady of the Lake—she comes up out of the water, soft and beautiful: my feminine self. She is smiling, confident, good-humored, and relaxed. She has my face, but without the beard, of course. For the rest of the meditation I focus on her, become her, and she is with me wherever I am guided to.

It was a transcendent experience—like the circumstances surrounding my religious conversion at age fifteen, and just as liberating. This revelation had a lasting impact on my self-image and on my understanding of the divine within me. Best of all, it is an image that I can now recall at will—always accepting, full of grace and wisdom—whenever I seek discernment or tranquility. Indeed, many people's spiritual journeys have been radically transformed after similarly discovering, in a personal way, the female image or manifestation of God.

The following afternoon we did another visualization exercise that took us back to our childhood home, as a small child. But first we were to select a guide to take with us, to keep us safe and advise us. I knew immediately that it would be Her. I remembered the big brick duplex at Ospring in Murree, where we lived during the summers after my family first arrived in Pakistan. I was six or seven years old. That house had thick walls; we lived in the lower unit and it was always cold and damp. In the evenings, my mother would spend hours huddled in front of the fireplace, kneeling down and fiddling with the wood or blowing to encourage the timid flames.

In separate sequences, the instructor asked us to find our parents, one at a time, and call out to them—aloud. I will never forget the sound of that little boy calling out through my voice, "Mom! Mom. Mom?" and later, "Dad . . . Dad . . . Hey, Dad." I found Mom in the back bedroom. Dad was at his big desk in the living room, just to the left of the front door. In both cases, they were happy encounters, and when we were asked to say anything to them that might come to mind I was content just to crawl into their laps and sit quietly.

Then Jodi asked us to bring both of them into the room together, and I realized how compartmentalized our family life had been. Though we always ate meals together when my sisters and I weren't in boarding school, and had occasional family outings, most of the time we seem to have gone our separate ways. I never saw Mom and Dad together—except those times when Dad, usually in passing, would plant a loud kiss on Mom's lips, which always ended with a dramatic sigh by both of them. In my guided meditation I wanted to ask them to do things with me together, so we could be a family.

As I was watching this scene, it came to me that I could do this in my own soul by bringing together my feminine aspect, my aware adult self, and the little boy I still carried within me. *We* were a family, in the sacred circle of my own heart. I felt the deep waters of a great truth stir inside me as a rush of goose-bumps rippled across my skin. I had never felt so complete. And though an unbelievable sense of relief flooded over me, I did not cry. I felt solid, expectant.

After all the longing and loneliness, it seemed like such a simple discovery. I had found within me the companionship I had ached for, and no matter where I went or who passed through—or stayed—in my life, I would never be alone again. I had come home.

Understanding our roots in the past is only a tool for finding our place in the present. Indeed, we are social animals, and my search for identity, purpose, and contentment was incomplete without a tangible experience of *community*—a concept inseparable from the definition of home.

Mary Edward Wertsch's landmark work, *Military Brats: Legacies of Childhood Inside the Fortress* (Aletheia Publications, 1996), is, in spite of the specificity of its intended audience, the most thorough, thought-provoking, and deeply moving examination of global nomad issues yet to be published anywhere. Toward the end of the book, Mary lists four key tasks that military brats must undertake to bring "balance and interiority to their lives." "These tasks are: dismantling one's myths, healing the wounds, making peace with one's parents, and addressing the question of belonging" (p. 390). Obviously, this list is equally relevant for all global nomads, and I found it interesting to note that through the process of writing this book, I seem to have largely completed the first three tasks.

The question of belonging remains unresolved. It may be that the lingering grief I feel is not so much for what I've lost, but for what I haven't yet attained.

❂

At one point when I was a senior in high school, I was trying to make up my mind whether to become a monk or join the Marines. Understood in the context of my background, this apparent polarity makes perfect sense: both would satisfy my need to belong and to know what the rules were, the need for a clear sense of identity and for community—two things I had at MCS.

I recently identified *nine* different communities to which I feel a partial sense of belonging—and, significantly, *none of them overlap*. These are not just social activities, but groups with clearly understood, self-perceived identities—and well-defined if unspoken rules. They include the neighborhood where I live, church, Global Nomads, contra dancing, various writers' groups, MCS, Wesley Seminary, Temenos, and my extended biological family. Even Global Nomads, where I clearly feel most at home, provides only an illusive sense of community. Like rock and roll, it is mostly not a reciprocal relationship. Its gatherings are cathartic, but the participants tend not to be joiners, shy away from commitment, or simply aren't around long enough to make the investment.

I myself have moved thirteen times in the last fifteen years, for various reasons that all seemed rationally compelling, but this pattern has certainly disrupted my efforts to build community and a relational network where I can feel at home. (As I write this, I realize that all these moves were motivated by or the result of relationships.) But after more than nine years at the United Methodist seminary where I work, I still feel like an outsider even there. I have recently begun to apply the principles I learned from revisiting my perceptions of my childhood to current situations. As at MCS, I discovered that many other people feel like outsiders at the seminary, and I've learned that one's place in a community may depend more on one's self-perception than on any particular position determined by others.

I also acknowledge that the social displacement I bemoan is well-suited to the writer's life, which needs both a level of detachment and large blocks of solitary time.

One of the major themes in Christianity is this sense of in-betweenness, from the Exodus motif of God's people in exile and wandering in the desert, to the Apostle Paul's description of Christians as "strangers and exiles on the earth" (Hebrews 11:13, I Peter 2:11); just as Christ prayed for his disciples who, like himself, were "not of the world" yet had to live in it (John 17:14-6). Paul understood the reign of God to be breaking-in-but-not-yet, seen "through a glass darkly" (I Corinthians 13:12). And he knew what it was to be caught between worlds. After all, he was a Jew raised in Persia. Could his fanatical persecution of the Christians have been at least partly an effort to prove something to himself, to assert his Hebrew identity? Jesus himself spent a significant portion of his early childhood in a foreign country—as a refugee in Egypt. Yet, I have never heard a sermon about how this cross-cultural experience might have shaped him.

Victor Perera, author of *The Cross and the Pear Tree: A Sephardic Journey,* says of his own multicultural experiences: "To be a wandering Jew teaches you tolerance of other cultures, so that you go from exile to universalism" (*The Washington Post,* Wednesday, May 31, 1995).

Religion, I am convinced, is a powerful draw for many people for reasons quite separate from doctrine and belief. It answers two of humanity's most basic needs, for spirituality and community. It took me a long time to make the connection, to realize that all these years my search for the right religious community, my passionate dedication to political causes, my intense romantic attachments, all reflected my effort to recapture a sense of belonging.

Yet, part of my global nomad legacy—the tendency to see at least two sides to every issue—has hampered this desire. In high school and college, every church I tried seemed either too liberal or too conservative. The United Methodist Church had a good awareness of global issues and religious diversity but little sense of community. Independent "faith" churches were more clear about their identity and commitments, but generally held cultural assumptions about America's divinely-ordained superiority that I found offensive.

It is here that the legacy of Murree Christian School continues to affect me most. I am no longer comfortable with the narrow doctrine that Christianity is the only true spiritual path. Yet, the evangelical faith taught at MCS is so ingrained in me that I can not freely embrace any other religious expression. So I sing with Van Morrison,

> I'm a dweller on the threshold
> And I'm waiting at the door
> And I'm standing in the darkness
> I don't want to wait no more.

Bono, the lead singer and songwriter of the popular Irish rock band, U2, once said, "People are always interested in bridges. I'm more interested in what's underneath them." That is what I have tried to do with this book—see what's underneath the cross-cultural bridge that is my heritage as an MK. I've learned a lot; I've experienced a lot of healing; but as Bono sings in the title line of one well-known song, *I still haven't found what I'm looking for.*

Like many global nomads, I have a tendency to feel more comfortable on the bridge, in between, but this can sometimes be an excuse—an arrogance, even—for not making commitments, not making decisions or deciding loyalties. Ambiguity is a fundamental part of the human experience; recognizing this can justify an irresponsible aloofness, or can bring deeper wisdom to a humble engagement with life's sticky but compelling issues, empowered by the insights and skills that our distinct experience has given us.

> I'm a dweller on the threshold
> As I cross the burning ground
> Let me go down to the water
> Watch the great illusion drown.

On Saturday, March 16, 1996, as I was completing this chapter, Auntie Inger Gardner died following heart surgery. She was eighty-three. For the past few years she had lived at the missionary retirement center near St. Petersburg, Florida. Just seven months ago, Rosalie and I had flown down to see her. I knew that she was then recovering from her second heart attack and realized that there might not be that many more chances to make this pilgrimage.

Much to my relief, Auntie Inger's illness had not left her incapacitated or frail beyond recognition. She still drove her own car, at least locally, and she had the same twinkle in her eyes. Her apartment was half of a little ranch house with a driveway and carport at each end—like the cookie-cutter suburbs of the 1950s. But it was a spooky place, a whole community full of nothing but elderly evangelicals happily waiting to "go be with the Lord," like an episode of the "Twilight Zone." And my dear boarding mother, so generous and sincere, had become a Rush Limbaugh fan! We had to cut short our first dinner together in twenty-five years so she could get home in time to watch his ten o'clock TV show.

When I got the telephone call the morning she died, my first thought was, "I'm so glad that I made the decision to go down to visit her last summer." My second thought was, "I wonder what she found on the other side?" She was so certain of her Savior, the Lord

Jesus Christ. Whatever form of glory she found, I'm sure she wasn't disappointed.

And no one I knew in my daily life could possibly comprehend what had happened. I felt that an era had ended.

A few weeks later a newspaper article reported that the town I live in has decided to discontinue the use of sirens by the local volunteer fire departments. Neighbors have complained of noise pollution; and in an era of beepers and cellular phones, the siren as a means of summoning emergency teams has become obsolete. It seemed fitting.

I still have dreams about MCS. They usually involve some sort of reunion and a peculiar blend of past and present that seems perfectly natural. Previously, I always woke from these dreams in a state of anxiety or drained from their emotional intensity.

Lately, the recurring dream is that I am on the bus going up to Murree. I am happy, even as the tears stream down my cheeks. My stomach is all in knots, not knowing what to expect; I am tired but eager to be there. Then the bus always breaks down at the halfway bridge. I get my bicycle off the roof thinking I can ride the rest of the way, but the tires are flat. I try to find an air pump to borrow, but then it doesn't work or the effort gets lost in a jumble of the dreamworld trivia that always seems so earnest in the midst of it: the bike is really muddy and I keep trying to clean it, or people keep asking me to do things, distracting me, and I never get started up the hill. I am an adult in these scenes, but sometimes see myself through the eyes of a little boy—coming back up the steep, rocky trail from the river with Auntie Inger, after spending the day swimming.

Last night I had the same dream. This time the bus doesn't break down at the bridge. As we cross over and begin the real ascent, I see the mountains for the first time. On one side, the road snakes upward and into the distance, disappearing where dark monsoon clouds roll down from the ridge like a forest fire. Across the valley, terraced slopes float endlessly up into great shafts of sunlight. Here, close to the road, a splash of wild strawberries runs laughing down an unexpected meadow. And beyond, the rich green hues of forested hills fold back, layer upon layer, into broken silver shadows against the sky.

SUPPLEMENT

The Alumni Letters

The self-absorption that seems to be the impetus and embarrassment of autobiography turns into (or perhaps always was) a hunger for the world. Actually, it begins as hunger for a world, one gone or lost, effaced by time or a more sudden brutality. But in the act of remembering, the personal environment expands, resonates beyond itself, beyond its "subject". . . . We do "live again" in memory, but differently: in history as well as in biography.

PATRICIA HAMPL
A Romantic Education

Nestled 'neath the great Himalayas
Far above the plain,
Stands the school we love and cherish
More than earthly gain.

> *Built upon a firm foundation,*
> *In God's hands a tool,*
> *Shaping lives of dedication—*
> *Murree Christian School.*

There within her halls of learning
Wisdom's torch burns bright;
Where indeed her students grasp
The Good and True and Right.

MCS SCHOOL HYMN
(words by Ralph E. Brown)

Sandes Home

❀

Author's Note

The following selections by former students of Murree
Christian School were collected between 1993 and
1995. (The titles are mine.) Reconstructing this larger
community perspective—both familiar and sometimes
different from my experience—was a vital part of my
own re-examination of memories. These letters are
part of my story.

Too Old for Teddy Bears

Roy Montgomery '73

I remember eagerly anticipating boarding school. With three siblings there before me, I felt certain that I must be missing out. During the ten-day vacation at the conclusion of the summer term of first grade, at the height of the monsoon season in Murree, preparations were well under way for the momentous event. The family *dhersi* (tailor), Karim, sat cross-legged on the verandah of our summer cottage for a week, making over barter sale clothing with his hand-cranked sewing machine. We children were indulged by having permission to sew our little name tags onto our every possession. What a lot of them there seemed to be! I was issued an old footlocker which I painted bright green. What joy, what thrills, what pompous delights to step back and read my very own name cunningly crafted thereupon in black paint which ran like a schoolboy's nose! Prized possessions which entered that trunk included a dinky lorry, from Esajee's general store on the Mall, a new coloring book of racing autos with cheap wax crayons from the corner store, and the teddy bear that had tenderly comforted three siblings before me—the same bear that had never regrown the fur I had barbered when Bruce was still its owner.

I don't recall ever seeing a teddy return for a second semester of boarding with the same six-year-old. Generally, after one semester the little rogues had become hardened veterans without tender affections, choosing the afflictions of missing one's bear rather than enduring the teasing of upperclassmen for a season. Anyway, these delights, the necessaries, and a few unnecessaries like a toothbrush, were fondly packed away in readiness. (My mother taped a mysterious and intricate message to the inside lid of my footlocker, which I now suspect was a detailed list of its contents, as per boarding regulation.) When the fateful day arrived, the bedding was rolled up into the *bister-bunds* of their rightful owners, mine with a favorite wool blanket of faded royal Stewart tartan.

Skipping merrily off to the fall term as a sheep to the slaughter, followed by four well-laden Kashmiri coolies, including my childhood strongman-hero, Habib, I was so intoxicated by the novelty I scarcely remember the inevitable goodbye—I didn't know the weight of the word. I was that green.

By the first night the novelty had burnt off, leaving a wretched residue of dull, lonesome ache. Mommy and Daddy were a lifetime away. Oh, to just back up a day, but how to advance three months? The pain gradually, but only partially, subsided as those first days and nights slowly ground by. Somehow, I managed to distance myself from all who were close and at the same time find solace in the camaraderie at hand. Thank God for those mischief-making comrades! I most likely wouldn't have survived without them. My big sisters snuck in goodnight kisses for the first while until I pushed them away to silence the sneers of jealous boys, thus foolishly deepening my loneliness. A boy who wanted to cry did so quietly after dark under his pillow, but it was somehow reassuring to hear muffled sobs issuing from the darkness amidst the sounds of squeaking bunk beds. If you couldn't talk about it, at least you knew you weren't alone.

I hungrily awaited letters from home. They were read by the matron to each illiterate beginner in turn during the Saturday afternoon rest hour, while we provided correct pronunciation for the mixed-language vocabulary of home. The dread of my week, however, was the moment of torment when the teacher would say, "And now, children, take out your stationery pads and envelopes to write your letters home." Like a prisoner sharpening the sword with which he will be beheaded, I remember painfully lifting the hinged top of that little wooden desk, slowly sifting the debris for paper and pencil and finally emerging with the crumpled bundle of despised envelopes—tokens of my own death warrant, to be sealed with those blood-red one anna stamps. That first term I'm quite sure I never got past the customary "How are you? I am fin." without losing it. It was a disgrace among schoolboys to cry, but that was the moment of truth and the concealed pain could no longer remain hidden. I'm so grateful for the marvelous grade one teacher we had, Miss Joan Larsen. I don't remember if any of the others were such babies, but I will never forget her compassion for me, taking me tenderly upon her lap until at length I was able to regain a semblance of composure.

My feelings? Shock and shame with myself for losing control, and bewilderment for why I had. My brain would not explain to me why my heart hurt. That weekly scene has fixed itself in my mind as the embodiment of the painting of Jesus carrying one lamb whilst the others walk. Somehow the little stuffed kid goat that Miss Larsen had perched upon the top shelf works its way into the picture as well. It doesn't quite fit in with all those nice white sheep, but nor did I. Those later MCSers who hadn't the privilege of having Miss Larsen for grade one can blame their misfortunes upon Keith Mitchell, who wooed her and wed her and took her away from us.

Watching the Descent of the Nomads in the Cold Sunshine

John Mitchell '81

A young boy walks alone through the noisy chinar leaves behind the big school on a Sunday afternoon with twelve-and-a-half days to go before leaving for winter break. No leaving school bounds without permission—can't wait till he's a big guy. Time stands still. Autumn sunshine crystal clear and cold. Silence. He's leaning against the ancient fence of iron railings and granite, staring at the empty upper field, deserted army houses; no one at the tea shop across the road. Nothing moving except a trickle of urine draining down the wall.

What a mess on the road—goat marbs everywhere—must have been a big group of gypsies, the nomads, I bet. Oh, I hope some more come soon. The sun is weirdly bright but barely warm. I like it this way. It'll be different down in Sind. Everyone will be taking their mid-day rest and I can ride my bike all over, all around the empty streets. I wonder how my birds are, has the gardener been giving them fresh water and seed? Twelve-and-a-half days isn't so long, but it's not moving. When I get up tomorrow it will be barely eleven days. Then it will be another whole day till I see Mom and Dad, and sometimes the train is hours and hours late. I wish Mom were accompanying the train party this year. Mrs. K— is so strict she probably won't even let us off at any of the stations; but the train is long and the platforms are crowded. We'll see. Mmmm— some really good *aloo pakordas* in Lahore, and some *halva* in Multan . . .

It's so quiet even the birds are not making any noise. No wonder time isn't moving. Maybe it's the Second Coming . . . wow. Some nomads coming round the corner up from the lower field.

The dog is huge, walking slowly; all the goats follow him. Does he already know I'm watching him? I wonder where they're coming from, where they're going to? Billy said some camp near his house in Guj. Do they walk all the way? The guy looks tired but he walks with long strides. His *chappals* have thick soles made from truck tires and his beard is long and black (all of the men look like that). There's another one. The ladies walk, too; their heads are not covered and they have huge earrings, the kind Mom would probably use as Christmas decorations. Does that boy have to go to school? I bet he doesn't. What will he have to do if he can't read and write. As long as he can count, I guess: how many goats and how many rupees. That baby can hardly be comfortable tied onto the mule like that. No crying though. In fact, none of them are talking. Now they are close: all I can hear are the feet of the goats—kind of like hail falling on hard dirt. The ladies' skirts are nice. None of them looks at me; everyone else in Pakistan stares like crazy. They probably don't stare because everyone stares at them also. They're different and they don't belong anywhere.

Maybe one day I could walk with them. Where will they camp tonight? I walked over twenty-five miles with Dad one day. If I left now, maybe I could walk to Pindi and meet the train party at the station. That would be cool. I wonder if they'd let me come with them. Boy, those goats smell. I could help them and maybe they'd pay me and I could buy really nice Christmas presents for everyone. But I've got a spelling test on Tuesday and we've got to win the soccer game against those guys this weekend. Would our team win without me? There's singspiration tonight: oh no, yuk—I have to go. If I fake sick they'll make me go in a bathrobe, that's all. If I jump over the fence now and follow them, I'd be sitting by a fire under the trees somewhere, smelling the smoke and the goats, eating a nice hot curry instead of singing Surely Goodness and Mercy. These nomads are probably too tired to sing. Look at them walking away, their shoulders down. In the spring they'll be back. They might come past in the morning when I'm at school and I'll miss them. I'll never see them or the baby on the mule again. I wonder if they'll look for me, or remember there was a white boy at the fence looking at them. No fences or school bells for them. The bearer always hits the gong so hard; maybe he imagines it's some sassy kid or bossy missahib's face.

They think of the strangest things to give us for high tea at the hostel: "elephant eggs" and *jalabies,* or fakey potato stew and watermelon. (Mmm . . . it'll be guava season when we get home.) The gypsies are gone for the winter. It's getting cold and dark;

they'll have to stop soon. The line will be finishing now—I'll run to get there just before they start seconds. Probably KZ pizza or something. Only one more high tea after this one. After the next high tea there will be barely four days left. I wish I had some American candies to swap for L-J's *paratas* at feastings tonight. Ready, steady, GO.

Breathing deeply lungfuls of fresh mountain air, moving freely, barely touching the ground; flying past the water shortage nightmare toilets behind the school, then up the slope through the dizzyingly tall pine trees, up the shortcut, each stone familiar; past the monkey bars and tennis court—colossal battle grounds, sites of unimaginable heroism, gallantry, and bitter rivalry left behind in a dozen steps—to crash through the forbidden cook's door just as they're about to start serving seconds.

NOTE: John Mitchell '81 is the son of Joan (Larsen) and Keith Mitchell of New Zealand, and unrelated to Jonathan Mitchell '79, an American, whose reminiscences appear later in this section.

The Near Touch of Romance

Deborah (Nygren) Willow '75

One Friday night when I was in ninth grade there was a skating party in the gym. John Huffaker, whom, through the secret and mysterious machinations of junior high girls, I found myself "going with," asked me to go up to the library with him. I could tell from his solemn demeanor that something serious was afoot and it was with anxious excitement that I followed him up those steep steps to the deserted library. (Girls avoided going first up those stairs for reasons of modesty.) We sat down across from each other at one of the tables, and after some silence during which I became even more anxious, he came out with it:

"How do you feel about holding hands?"

It was a big question, full of implications, I suppose. Ninth grade was the magic line after which such contact was allowed. I was astonished, confused, embarrassed, but managed to blurt out that I thought it was okay. He nodded once, seriously, and we left the library in silence, without touching once. Nothing more was said on the subject, but two weeks later, during the after-singspiration walk, he tentatively took my hand and we suffered sweaty palms in utter silence for a mile or two.

Tricky business, being a staff kid at MCS; at least for me. I suspect my siblings were better at it. On the one hand, I knew I should feel grateful for the privilege of being able to live with my parents all the time when none of the other kids had that. On the other hand, my privilege set me apart. I never felt I knew exactly what was going on. I sometimes believed myself to be the object of secret jokes and laughter. I never had a really close friend the way the other kids seemed to. I still have trouble developing close friendships. Perhaps this is just the way I am. Perhaps it is a consequence of not really being a part of my peer group for so long. I don't know and I don't lay any blame. Even then, it was not a straightforward enough situation for self-pity. After all, I was so lucky to live at home.

A Heart-Shaped Fish Bowl

Judi (Fidge) Cox '84

I was eight years old when I first came to MCS, my brother Richard was ten, and we were excited by the independence that boarding represented. But a dark, musty-smelling hostel with endless corridors and lots of regimented bedrooms, bathrooms and playrooms quickly dampened my enthusiasm. I had to be traumatically, physically restrained, in fact, while my anxious parents drove back to their home in Islamabad.

Being an English kid, I was teased for my accent straight away in the dining room. I was put in a cold, tiny room with four other girls. And after the lights were out, I clutched my hot water bottle and buried my head in my pillow, too embarrassed to let the others hear me cry. I must have nearly suffocated that first night.

It wasn't long, though, before I made friends with Sharon Simpson on the monkey bars below the principal's house. My time was soon filled listening to stories by Elaine Roub about the "little people" who lived in the grass behind the hostel, or playing in the old broken-up canoe down there. I once found a snake by the big bush at the bottom of that hill. Having best friends and a very special older friend certainly made boarding happier.

After-school games included Three Feet in the Mud Puddle, Four-square, and Prisoner's Base, down on the outdoor basketball court. Prisoner's Base was a good running-around game: two teams occupy bases behind the opposite back lines of the court and try to capture members of the other team in the neutral area between these lines. When captured, you have to line up waiting to be tagged, forming a line starting behind the opposite base line. When there are lots of prisoners, the line is longer so it's easier to be freed by your team members tagging the first person in the line. Behind the other team's base line is a desirable place to be as you can catch opponents as they run out into neutral territory. We played this game so often, all the strategies became second nature.

Indoor games, played in the girls' lounge, often involved sagas that went on over a few days, in which families were formed, personalities developed, and conflicts and tragedies were acted out. They fell apart when bickering or boredom took over. Rearranging our rooms and seeing how many different ways bunkbeds could be stacked always provided a change of routine. Barbies were a cult for awhile.

I can still remember the cold, lumpy breakfast porridge that made me dry retch and reduced me to tears my first year in boarding. And the huge "no thank you helpings" at other meals, forced on us by self-important table monitors. But then I can't help smiling as I remember Mr. Roub striding through the dining room on his way somewhere and yelling, "Hi, kids!"

Until high school, when the boys moved to Sandes, the girls' and boys' departments were in the same hostel, at opposite ends of the hall on the same floor. We ate together, and played Tin Can Sally or Run Sheep Run together after supper; or Flashlight Beacon on Friday nights, when we were allowed to stay out later. It was like one big family, especially on weekends when we could sit with our older brothers or sisters for Saturday night films, Sunday dinner, and "Singspiration" on Sunday evenings.

Such proximity also made late night mischief that much more tempting. Only rarely did we become giddy and reckless enough to actually raid the boys' rooms. It was so strictly against the rules that even monitors wouldn't let us do it on the houseparent's day off. But I fondly remember a few brave pillow fights, messing up beds, repressing squeals, and tangling with unidentified bodies in the dark. On one occasion I was dragged down the boys' hall and stuffed into a closet as a captive. Then the houseparents arrived back, and with great embarrassment I walked down the hall back to the Middle Girls section in the stony silence that signified we were in BIG TROUBLE.

When the boys raided us, it was mass destruction on a grand scale, plus horrors such as panty theft and kidnapped teddy bears.

In junior high, we sometimes met up with the boys in the woods at night without the houseparents knowing. One time we were just pulling out all the food we'd brought with us for a feast— we were right down near the fence at the back of the hostel, sitting among the tree trunks—and before we realized it we were surrounded by monkeys. We all got spooked and left very quickly.

❀

Auntie Eunice stands out among my early memories. I remember her singing down the hall and just the way she always seemed to be there when you needed her. Memories from her Little Girls department include: being tucked up into bed each night with her favorite saying, "snug as a bug in a rug"; pretending (most of the time) to be homesick after lights out in order to have a comforting bit of "goop" or a hot drink (I'm afraid to say, this soon got recognized as fake!); memorizing verse by verse the first chapter of John's Gospel; and having my hair cut because Stephen Gordon kept pulling it in the breakfast line and Auntie Eunice just couldn't brush through my tangles!

I remember Miss Kitti Clarke reading stories to us while she sat on her rocking chair; we all sat on the matching stools and got distracted playing with the wrinkles on our dirty knees.

Without a doubt, Miss Cheryl Chapman was my favorite early teacher. She made learning fun and had a great sense of humor. I remember her challenging us to learn the scriptures by setting up a competition against a Pakistani school on the plains to learn the five chapters of the Epistle of John. I would work on a few verses then work at getting up the courage to go to Miss Chapman's room and recite them to her. She was always so encouraging and friendly. I managed to learn only the first two chapters but remember vividly the great feeling of challenge and how hard I worked to learn those verses.

I can't mention Miss Chapman without also recalling how in her classroom she used to make us stick our heads in the garbage can for three minutes for saying "shut up." I also remember her saying once how she has always wanted a heart-shaped bath tub and hoped she would get one in heaven. I'm sure she'll get much more!

I remember a lot of romances right from third and fourth grade up—some with guys I "sailed" with in high school. I will never forget the excitement of holding hands for the first time—and even breaking up with someone because they wanted to hold my hand on the school bus as I thought that was "going too far"! I remember sneaking my first kiss with a new guy on the Sunday night walk back from Jhika—right before the *last* bend before school, simply because it had taken the whole walk home for him to get the guts up to do it!

And, I remember feeling as if the whole world had ended when someone broke up with you—only to find that both of you were going back out with someone else (or even with each other) within a few weeks.

I went through some very difficult and heartbreaking times at MCS. Some of it was just part of growing up, but other things were made harder by our unique circumstances: being away from home, and around the same people all the time; getting boxed into a type (such as "always happy"); not being able to find time or space alone, especially for girls; loneliness and unhappy times when I was excluded from a group, made worse by the fact that we lived together, not just saw each other at school; and conflicts with the staff—too many parents! There were so many regulations about what we could wear or what music we could listen to. Our tapes always got censored and the guys' music didn't—that made us mad!

Camp-outs provided a major break in the routine a couple of times each term. Who could forget those mountain rest houses (government bungalows), with their spectacular views? Or the long, rugged hikes; singing around a crackling fire with someone playing a guitar; flashlights and sleeping bags out under the stars; cold mornings with the grass soaked with dew; and hot pancakes for breakfast.

MCS became home to me, and one that I will always cherish. There was a great feeling of adventure and a unique sense of community; the closeness of friends and teachers at MCS has been unmatched in my experience since. And I have never forgotten how to tuck in sheet corners the proper way, how to polish shoes correctly, how to keep my drawers and living area tidy enough to be ready for a "white-glove" inspection at the drop of the hat.

Nor will I forget the cool, clean freshness of mountain air, or the awesome displays of lightning that crackled across the whole length of a night sky; the tiny pink-and-white flowers that bloomed only at Easter; the wind whining through the pine needles—distinct from just wind in trees. These things will remain with me always.

Kicking Fire in
the Monkey House

Jonathan Mitchell '79

The rambling elegance of Sandes Home was a wonderful contrast to the modern, functional efficiency of the main hostel. Sandes had little recognizable organization or sense of purpose about it. Filled with sudden passageways, trap doors, isolated attics and hidden crawl spaces, it unapologetically offered both spacious verandas big enough to land an airplane on and closet-size bedrooms. Reputedly, there were underground tunnels and even dungeons beneath Sandes. We discovered many other wonderful secrets about the place, and though we searched in vain for these Gothic artifacts, the thought that they might exist gave our residence an added aura. The more tangible quirks of the place, however, were not so enchanting.

The showers at Sandes were a source of endless aggravation. The hot water heaters were small and worth only five or six showers before you had to wait an hour for the water to reheat. Consequently, the best time for a shower was at six-fifteen a.m. when the gong—that famous Sandes gong which everyone tried to steal on April Fools—announced the beginning of the day. Most of us avoided the mad rush for the showers and rolled out of bed with only seconds to spare for seven o'clock breakfast. Showers could also be had about four o'clock in the afternoon, if the tank hadn't run dry. Of course, the water could run out at any time, and many an uninitiated chap has had to spend half an hour under a tiny trickle of water in order to rinse off the soap he so ecstatically and imprudently worked into a rich lather. We soon became proficient at alternately soaping and rinsing small portions at a time.

The showers were downstairs and separated from the stairwell by a dressing room of sorts in which, for reasons unknown to any of us, there was always a *hammom* (a water barrel with legs and a faucet). The light switch for the showers was also in this room. You left your clothes and towel here since everything in the shower room got soaked. The shower room was about ten feet by ten feet and only two of the five showers worked properly. The floor was always cold. There were a number of rough wooden platforms you could stand on, but these had a way of absorbing old soap and toe jam, and some of the more fastidious types would wear rubber thongs.

It was not unusual for the electricity to fail several times a day, and in such cases one had to grope his way to the stairwell in a most vulnerable position. There were a number of trouble-making types, Dennis Sherbeck coming most immediately to mind, who would fill a bucket with cold water, turn off the light, and wait for the unsuspecting bather to venture out. This poor soul rarely made this mistake twice, as he not only bore the brunt of the freezing water but had to face his irate co-bathers who were also sprayed. In such situations the shower on the left, just inside the door, received the least spray and was thus the station of choice.

But there was one occasion when this was definitely not the case. Ketcham and I had returned from an exhausting and challenging afternoon sitting in tea shops, taking pictures of wizened old men, and I had beaten him to the favored shower. The water was very hot and we were whooping it up and carrying on as usual when a rat shot out of the drain and up the hot water pipe. About half way up it wisely abandoned this route and leapt onto my shoulder. Ketcham and I both scrambled out of the room in a mad rush with visions of sharp teeth and claws—not to mention rabies shots—flashing before us; I still get goose bumps thinking about it. I don't know what happened to the rat, but I watched the drain very carefully after that.

In the showers you had to guard your shampoo very closely. Quite a number of us did not have shampoo or did not consider it important enough to buy, but this was not usually a problem since someone invariably left their bottle behind. It was a rather unfortunate event, however, if you left yours, for it would be empty by the time you remembered it. I only made this mistake once, and it left me determined to teach these shampoo-thieving vermin a lesson. That bottle of Colibri Egg Shampoo had cost me thirteen rupees at Esajee's in Murree (never mind that I had benefitted more than once from forgotten shampoo bottles). Marty "Fartha" Ketcham and I set the trap, gleefully mixing motor oil with some of his Jovan "Sex Appeal" cologne (I always wondered how he got away with that sort of cologne at Murree). As luck would have it, Ketcham happened to be showering the next morning when little Mark "Moppy" Heaton arrived, minus his shampoo. This gave Ketcham the chance to set the hook a bit deeper. We had assumed that the unfortunate chap would immediately realize the trick and waste an entire bottle of shampoo trying to remove the oil. Ketcham saw to it that things didn't end there.

"Funny stuff, this. It doesn't seem to lather," said Moppy.

"Oh, it must be that new stuff, Mountain Dew. It's designed not to lather," Ketcham explained.

"Not bad," said Moppy, unsuspecting. After all, anything new from the States was special and bound to be great. And so Moppy headed for school not realizing that his hair would never dry.

By this time quite a few people knew a prank was going down. We let it be known that Brian Calderwood, one of those mighty seniors, had left his hair removing lotion in the shower room. This was expensive stuff and he was bound to be upset if any was missing. Besides, his henchman Dan Cutler was always eager to avenge a wrong, real or imagined. Meanwhile, Moppy's hair kept dripping and he was becoming rather anxious concerning what Brian and his cronies might do to him when they saw his hair falling out. Fortunately, Moppy's older brother David came to the rescue and put an end to the festivities. We were feeling rather chuffed with our success, and even Moppy put a decent face on it. At the same time, we firstborns couldn't help wishing that we had an older brother to look out for us.

I am surprised that Sandes Home never burned down. The wiring could have come out of a Rube Goldberg arrangement and was something to behold. More than once, I saw an electric wire burn all the way up a wall. We would stack as many as seven plugs on a single outlet to power our stereos, immersion heaters, hot plates, lamps, hair dryers, electric blankets, torture devices, and who knows what else. Then there were match fights, in which we would flick flaming matches at one another along the big wooden veranda. The best brand was "Vulcan," much like the "Ohio Blue Tips" we used for stink bombs back in the States. The "Vulcan" matches would flare for quite a while and could give you a good burn if they went down your neck. The best trick of all was to shove a roll of toilet paper ("Po Pap") into a Bournvita or Ovaltine can and douse it with ethanol (unwittingly courtesy of the chemistry lab). Once lit, this device smoldered marvelously and when kicked, flared like a flamethrower. We would kick these around for ages and I attribute my modest soccer skills, with the exception of the "butt trap," to this high stakes game.

One Saturday night Sandes almost did burn down. Everyone had gone to the movies at the main hostel. The tamer fare of science and cultural films provided by the United States Information Service was sometimes supplemented by Buster Keaton on a railroad inspection buggy, or in a sauna with cute Finnish girls, which staff member Derek Tovey would unsuccessfully try to edit by putting his hand in front of the projector lens. Us guys would try to disguise our keen interest in these scenes, while the girls would try to hide their embarrassment with equal lack of success. When these movies lost their appeal we played them backwards.

On this particular evening, Ketcham and I were enjoying the rare quiet of an empty dorm and decided to indulge in a little private repast in our room. We set out the ingredients for cooking a twenty-pepper omelet which we planned to eat with prodigious quantities of mustard and unripe mangoes marinated in vinegar. While boiling water in a bucket on my primus stove, we wondered what would happen if we added kerosene to it. The results were most uninspiring. The next obvious question concerned whether the kerosene-water mixture would light or not. To our delight it did. After a minute of admiring our handiwork, the smoke was getting rather thick and we began to consider putting the contraption out. We added more water to no avail—this merely brought the fire higher in the bucket. We turned off the primus. Sand from the ever-present fire buckets didn't help either. We were obviously in a pickle. I saw that the bucket bottom was beginning to leak from the heat, and I knew that the hot dripping kerosene was going to ignite at any moment. I don't know who thought of it, but we finally put the fire out by placing a wet towel over the top of the bucket. At that moment the solder gave way and spilled the contents all over the floor. But no matter, the strange smells were easily explained. We liberally applied a mixture of bed bug killer and Ketcham's trusty "Sex Appeal" to the affected area and maintained that our shelf had fallen over.

Then there was the Haunted House, which we "hosted" for the elementary kids one Halloween. The setting was Sandes Home, naturally, and the inspiration the haunted houses of our own grade school days, when Auntie Inger appeared as a cackling witch who passed out gooseberry "eyeballs." Our little guests were guided through a complicated obstacle course, mainly on the top floor of Sandes, with former student Roy Montgomery (bald and bearded at the time) as a chained fiend, scenes of barbaric rituals, and a horrible ghost who chased the group down the stairs at the end. We had rigged up the lighting with an improvised switchboard, which melted during rehearsal from the electrical overload. We probably left a number of kids deeply traumatized, and nearly burned down Sandes again that night, but it was good fun.

Returning to Murree in March, after the long winter break, was always a bittersweet experience. It signalled the end of the great holiday and the beginning of another semester of classes. It meant that you would miss the coming of spring on the plains—the sweet peas and jasmine, the mynas and brain fever birds, the warm weather. It also meant you would be separated from your family again. But at the same time, all the chaps would be there and there would be plenty of time to horse around and plan mischief.

March was cold and gloomy in Murree. It was stormy and your hands and feet were always wet. We used to keep our hard boiled eggs from breakfast as these would retain their heat for the longest time. When they got cold, you could place them on a classroom heater and they would be ready to serve as a handwarmer for another half hour or so. Indoors, it always smelled heavily of the fumes from those kerosene heaters.

In the early spring, we often found large piles of old snow where it had slid off the roof and accumulated over the winter. These were perfect for building tunnels and forts, for storing your homemade yogurt, or for riding your bikes onto the roof. This was a dense, heavy snow—good for packing into snowballs or making snowmen. Not that we made many snowmen, it somehow seemed too pedestrian and lacked the excitement to which we were accustomed. You couldn't brag about your snowman. On the other hand, large clumps of snow could still be used for brave and wonderful things. Like roadblocks, for example. The snow ploughs would leave enormous ready-rolled piles of snow on the side of the road, and it was a simple matter for five or six of us to sneak down to the road after dark and shift a series of these into the middle of the road.

We then positioned ourselves in the woods to observe the frustrations of the hapless driver who happened that way.

Our first victim was a three star general who, with the aid of his chauffeur, had to push his way through six of these obstacles. We had not anticipated this event. If only it had been Irv Nygren or Ian Murray in their little Morris Minors, even an old Opel taxi full of woodsmen heading for the tea shops would do. A three star general, on the other hand, could cause trouble—maybe he could get the school closed down. We would be forever remembered as the ones who put an end to this fabulous institution. We spent the next several days sweating it out and wondering why we had ever gotten involved in such foolishness. And for all our suffering we received no reward; it just wouldn't do to brag about harassing the military.

Roadblocks of snow, however, was a fundamentally sound idea. We had merely carelessly chosen our test site. Sandes Hill was really the perfect spot. This road from Jhika Gali up to the boys' dorm was phenomenally steep. We could judge the power of cars by how well they performed on this particular incline. The best part of all was the sharp corner just where the gradient was greatest. Many an inexperienced driver stalled here and had to reverse down for another attempt. Only legitimate victims would venture here, and the corner would hide the roadblock from view until the critical moment. Nor could the quarry emerge from the vehicle to seek out the perpetrators: parking brakes are fickle things and it would be imprudent to park a car on such a steep spot.

We set the trap at four-thirty one afternoon, and the results were beyond anything we could have anticipated. We heard a vehicle rev up and make a run for it from the other end of Jhika. There was only one vehicle which needed that much help—our favorite green 1951 Chevy pickup which used to belong to Dick Thompson ("Tom Hussain," as he was otherwise known). Up the hill it chugged, losing speed steadily. As it rounded the corner we strained to see who was driving. What a stroke of luck. It was our new houseparent—I shall call him "Damian"—whose fiery and unpredictable temper we had come to loath. What a fitting fate! Had Mr. Nygren or Mr. Murray strayed into our trap we would have felt a twinge of remorse, but we could revel in this with abandon. The truck groaned to a halt and immediately began to roll slowly backwards as Uncle Damian madly wiped off the fog from the rear window—Tom Hussain had often complained about the brakes. We waited to see what would happen. A few minutes later we heard the heavy footsteps and labored breathing of Damian as he fought his way up the icy road. Aware that he was probably being observed, he tried to casually push the snowball aside. But like I said, this snow was extraordinarily heavy, and it took him several mighty heaves to roll it to the side. He then turned and staggered down the hill for another attempt.

At that moment the same idea occurred to all three of us: *We could move it back again!* This was historic—what a story we would have to tell. We heard the truck make its run through Jhika; our hearts raced as it approached the corner. This time Damian gave full vent to his frustrations, and I was sure someone from staff housing would hear him. We slunk further into the protective cover of the woods. After the third episode he was in a right rage and we declared our operation successful. We nonchalantly sauntered in to supper that evening as though nothing had happened, but to our great surprise and disappointment, so did Uncle Damian.

The snow usually was gone by the middle of April, which put an end to late-night snowball ambushes from King's Cliff on unsuspecting—actually, quite suspecting—couples, trying to enjoy the rare privacy of a Sunday night group walk. Certainly by the middle of May, though, the lack of snow precluded such ambushes, and the romantic pairs would drop their guard. But the snow melt was not strictly over—there was a well in Murree which was filled with snow every winter for the purpose of supplying summer ice for cold drinks. This snow was also suitable for snow balls. One Saturday afternoon two of us headed into Murree and borrowed a tin tub from my parent's summer apartment at Bexley Cottage. We purchased as much snow as we could carry and hitched a ride with thirteen woodsmen and two goats on an old Opel taxi to the base of King's Cliff. Needless to say, the element of surprise that evening was total. In fact, the threats of retaliation from those who had been humiliated in front of their girlfriends were so fierce that we prudently chose not to take credit for the event. We even claimed to have narrowly escaped ourselves and loudly wished that the fleas of ten thousand camels would infest the armpits of the perpetrators forever. Sometimes, if it had been a heavy winter, large accumulations of snow still remained on the sloped roofs. As the weather grew warmer these accumulations would lose their adhesion to the roof and slide down to the ground thirty feet below with great effect. There was always plenty of warning while the snow gathered speed and no one was ever buried. On Sunday evenings, however, it was customary to eat supper ("high tea" we called it) out on the edge of the downstairs veranda. When snow was on the roof, the unsuspecting chaps downstairs were tempting targets. Usually a healthy whack at the roof with a long handled broom was enough to set a huge hunk of snow into motion. This always resulted in a mad rush for safety by those downstairs, and frequently they would leave their food behind in their haste. The snow would land with a mighty crash, burying for several weeks anything which happened to be in the way.

Occasionally, these strategies could backfire. It was a dark and stormy night at the end of the fall semester, and David Hennessey was due to leave for the airport at four a.m. to return to his home in Dubai. He told us in no uncertain terms that he was on no account to be disturbed. As luck would have it, the girls took this opportunity to conduct their version of a raid on the guys' dorm. This consisted of a loud cacophony of tuneless Christmas carols interspersed with giggles and other typical female carryings-on. David Hennessey eventually woke up in a rather foul temper, and, failing to see any humor in the situation, soon began throwing shoes and other handy objects at the girls; but Ruth Longjohn calmly gathered whatever came sailing over the veranda and tossed it down the hill. This was not the intended effect and called for sterner measures. The fire buckets were naturally empty, so David Hennessey was reduced to lifting a *hammom* from one of the bathrooms and staggering with it towards the veranda. He only got halfway before he fell, spilling forty gallons of water on the floor, which rapidly seeped through to the dining room. This was not the intended result either. Heroic stories were made of more than this, and he had to think of something quickly.

It didn't take him long. About six inches of snow had accumulated on the roof from an early winter storm the previous week, and the girls were foolishly standing right in the target area. Unfortunately, the broom on the ceiling trick didn't dislodge it. This snow needed a little more encouragement. So David Hennessey, still in his underwear, quietly crept out the bathroom window onto the steeply-sloped roof and made his way to the side where the offending women were gleefully caterwauling. We watched with much anticipation; this promised to be memorable. At that moment, there was a yell followed by a crash, followed by the sound of David Hennessey sliding down the roof. He went sailing past us and landed in a heap at the girls feet. This was the ultimate in humiliation. No time to check for broken bones or missing pieces of flesh. David Hennessey roared up the stairs in great haste into the comforting arms of his delighted roommates. It wasn't till he reached home that he realized his toe was broken. But better that than his neck.

❀

Truth be told, most of the time it was we who got our kicks from harassing the fairer sex. A popular group activity of the guys, and an ancient Murree tradition, was pataka raids on the girls' hostel. Patakas were small, "impact-type" firecrackers readily available in the local bazaars. As Little Boys, we shared the hostel with the girls and longed for the excitement of such a raid. We dreamed of the day when we would carry out raids of our own. Unfortunately, by the time we were at Sandes the school Board had banned patakas. I guess they didn't make for good relations with the local army commander. However, our imaginations were fertile, and we were undaunted.

Marty Ketcham, Tweets Burton, Slugger Lall and I had been making a burp tape. This was a stereo collection of our choicest belches. Slug, after a meal of dahl, would get a warm coke, shake it, and drink till he was bloated. Some of his belches would last as long as five seconds and he could shape his mouth to make them resonate wonderfully. We had close to half an hour of this on tape. Now, we had heard that Maylene Dalton would throw up at the sound of a burp, and this proved to be an added incentive. As plans for a raid developed we settled on the use of stink bombs and the burp tape in place of patakas.

But these were not the only innovations on this raid. We also involved both sets of senior high houseparents. Wayne Hildebrand, having never seen a rule that said boarding staff couldn't participate in a raid, agreed to accompany us, and Debby Rupe agreed to open the hostel door. Neither needed any persuasion, and the whole operation went without a hitch. At midnight, Deb furtively let Ketcham and me into the girls' dorm and crept back to her room. The two of us tiptoed down the hall, quietly opened each girl's room, and placed a mixture of calcium carbide and water behind the door. After closing the door we propped prepared sticks under the door handles so they couldn't be opened from the inside. We then squirted some ammonia through the keyhole for good measure. We had only completed four rooms when a series of screeches and howls forced us to reconsider our strategy and beat a hasty retreat. We locked the outside door and climbed up on to the second-floor ledge outside of Maylene's room. There, Ketcham turned on the belch tape.

The two of us sat there nonchalantly swinging our legs and basking in the sounds of belches and shrieks. I crept over to Deb's window and could see her on the floor laughing uncontrollably.

This was better than a pataka raid. The rotten egg smell of carbide never smelled so good. And there was more excitement to come. The commotion had roused the night watchman and he announced his approach by menacingly banging his stick on the trash barrels. But Uncle Wayne, our faithful "back-up," blinded the chowkidar with the strobe flash from a fancy camera we had brought for just that purpose. Thus, we made good our escape, without being identified, and the chowkidar had an excuse to abandon his intervention—much to our relief. Roub Sahib, the principal, tended to believe the chowkidar's tales, and rightly so.

As we walked back to Sandes by the light of the moon, we topped off the evening by doing the needful at Pee Corner. I have a flash picture of us there, which we wanted to put in the *Kahani*, under the caption "Pee Corner or Bust." Rob Bailey, student editor of the yearbook, was most supportive, but we were later persuaded to leave this image of male bonding to our own scrap books. And we took comfort in the rumor that Maylene—unable to rid her mind of the sound of belches—felt ill for a week.

Lords of the Flies

Rob Bailey '78

I felt very alone the first night at Sandes, after being used to the constant presence of a parent. All of the others in my room were strangers to me, despite the fact that I may have remembered their names from my earlier years in Pakistan. Sandes was quite cold in early March, and there was no heat. The water in the bathroom *hammom* was ice cold, and often there was no running water from the tap. I didn't have the freedom to get out of bed in the middle of the night and wander around the house, because the house was someone else's room. If I was hungry, I couldn't get something to snack on. I had to wait until breakfast. And it was darker and more silent than I could remember it ever having been before—perhaps the effect of not feeling at home. That first night I was startled out of sleep by the eerie wailing sound of a chorus of jackals. The sound was frightening, and made me feel a little better about being inside the dorm—at least for a few moments.

My family had just returned to Pakistan after almost eight years away, so many of my memories of Pakistan and of MCS were quite cloudy. My brother and I arrived in boarding after the winter break, half way through my eighth grade year. Prior to this, my parents had heard much about recent incidents of drug use in the school, and were alarmed at the possibility that we might be exposed to such activity in their absence. They did their best to fortify our minds against every imaginable temptation or corruption that we might encounter. While they never intended to produce anti-social militants, that was in effect what we became. I was only thirteen, and didn't have the maturity of judgement to know what sorts of things I should openly oppose, and what things I should stay quiet about. I took it as my moral duty to vocally oppose everything with which I disagreed, even if I knew absolutely nothing about it.

I had the particular misfortune of having chosen an issue—rock and roll—which had unique importance in boarding. Music was much more than entertainment for junior and senior high boys. Music was a catalyst which permeated and shaped the entire boarding environment. Whenever I hear any Three Dog Night song, I am reminded of that first semester at MCS. The same is true for Carole King's *Tapestry* album, Love Song with Chuck Girard, and Paul Revere and the Raiders' *Indian Reservation*. A year later there would be other favorites.

Having their "own" music is important to most teenagers in Western societies. But we had no radio, television, or videos, only recorded music. So, the importance of music as an expression of the collective spirit and for the formation of personal identity, was even greater for us than for our Western counterparts.

During that first semester at Murree, I learned that my assumption about Christians having a unique trustworthiness because of their faith was false. Two of my roommates had exceptionally violent tempers, which I had a talent for provoking with my self-righteous attitude. One of these guys seemed very well-mannered and shy. But once his will was thwarted he could become a quick and silent raging fury. I bested him in a game of dominoes one evening, and once the game was over he quietly got up, walked over to his bed, seized a metal pipe intended as a bed support, and attacked me with it. This onslaught was so quickly executed, without any expression of rage, that I didn't begin to imagine what he was going to do until he landed his first blow on my back. I soon learned that he always kept one of these things handy for just that purpose. When he failed to gain the advantage with the pipe, he bit me instead—right through a coat, sweater, flannel shirt, undershirt, and through the skin of my shoulder—successfully drawing blood. When the other roommate heard about the incident, he rushed to the defense of my attacker and literally picked me up and hurled me across the room. I learned to lose an appropriate number of games of dominoes in future matches, unless I absolutely couldn't help winning.

The roommate who had tossed me across the room like I were so much baggage had managed to embroil himself in financial controversy by embezzling funds from our class peanut butter concession the semester before. Early in the spring semester this fact had not yet become known, but he had been asked for a financial accounting. Somehow, he managed to persuade me to help him figure out the ledger, which he claimed he could not make heads or tails of. I was puzzled at the fact that I seemed to be much more concerned about straightening out the mess than was he. In the end I concluded that a vast amount of money was unaccounted-for due to several missing pages from the books he had kept. When I told him that I felt this was what we should report to the class, he objected strenuously, and suggested that we make up some other reason instead. Shortly after I had reported the unaccounted for funds despite his objections, he showed me a large knife which he had bought in the bazaar, and told me that some night while I was asleep he was going to kill me with it. I immediately offered to buy the knife for almost all of the money I had, and kept it locked in my foot locker where I felt sure he wouldn't be able to get it.

The third roommate was probably the only sensible person of the four of us. He would listen to my arguments with others about the evils of rock music, and say little. Whenever I would speak as an authority—even quoting song lyrics—he would ask me if I had ever listened to that particular song. Not wanting to appear stupid, I would lie. Then he would ask me to hum a few bars of the melody. I didn't like him very much for that sort of thing. He also had a way of being very critical, even caustic at times, whenever I paraded my righteousness in front of others. It was all too easy for him to point out my own weaknesses in the same areas where I judged others. After all, he had the dubious pleasure of having to live with me.

I did not find a parade of drugs in boarding, as I had been led to expect. There were many tales of the previous semesters, when things had reached a saturation point, resulting in the simultaneous suspension of virtually 25% of the high school. But that was all hearsay. I had no firsthand knowledge of any such activity. On one occasion, someone tauntingly dangled a small bar of brown, bark-like material in front of my nose, and asked me if I knew what it was. I didn't, but said "yes" anyway, just to get the offending object out of my face. I later learned it was hashish, which was quite easily available at low cost in the bazaars.

Many events took place during that first year which at the time I took to be the norm of behavior, but came to realize were in fact quite aberrant by MCS standards. The spectacle of two senior boys running naked down the road was such an incident. In the fall of '74 "streaking" had apparently become all the rage back in the States, producing some excellent stories for *Time* and *Newsweek* (decidedly the diet on which MCSers cut their political teeth). Wanting to keep pace with the times, everyone was daring everyone else to try it.

And one morning David Hover and Mark Pegors decided to put words into action from Sandes Home via the shortcut down to the staff housing half way up the hill from Jhika Gali. I couldn't imagine wanting to do such a thing, but I nonetheless took my place with virtually every other soul at Sandes as part of the raucous audience eager to view such an outrage.

The event was duly photographed (though the negatives and prints were subsequently destroyed on staff orders) and one spectator observed later that Mark had looked like a Greek athlete, while David had too much flab. David was deeply offended by this comment and responded with typical philosophical earnestness that "cosmetic values occult the spirit," confounding any rejoinder.

For this historic feat, Mark and David were made to dig a new garbage pit behind Sandes—a rather functional punishment, I thought. But the impact of this incident went far beyond what the foolhardy pair might have imagined. David was a monitor at the time and was promptly defrocked. Some members of the cast of the play he was directing for the Kabul inter-school arts festival threatened to resign. Mr. Roub angrily (and quite rightly) pointed out that the fragile relationship maintained with the Islamic community could have been seriously shaken had Mark and David been seen.

I draw a distinction between raids and mischief. Mischief is the sort of activity which can be done without much planning; it might involve some minor infraction of the rules. A raid, on the other hand, was an event intended for conspicuous notice, and was by definition both a major infraction of the rules, and a blatant affront to the peace and dignity of the establishment. A raid's success was measured entirely in terms of the magnitude of the disturbance it caused. But if the participants were caught, its degree of success invariably seemed to be diminished. For this reason raids required planning, organized tactics, and above all, secrecy. This was another reason for rule one of our boarding school raid policy—never include women, because they could seldom maintain secrecy. Many were the sorry cases of raids which became known well in advance of their occurrence as a result of telling a woman. These raids all have their place in the folklore, and are often used as reminders of the many pitfalls and dangers one may encounter by failing to heed the "rules" of raids. But the raids that do not fit the rule are seldom remembered in the folklore; instead they are deliberately erased from the collective memory of MCS students. On one occasion, the girls raided the guys using the tactic of disclosing a secret before the event.

It was during the early fall, when the nights are still fairly warm, and the weather is mostly clear and dry. Stan Brown, a recent MCS graduate, was visiting Murree that week, and he was approached by one of the high school girls as to whether he would be willing to chaperon them on a midnight raid to Sandes Home. They felt it would be a little risky wandering around in the woods late at night without someone to guide them in the darkness. As anyone who lived there knows, on moonless nights the shortcut to Sandes was negotiated more by memory and touch than by sight and it was all too easy to take a wrong turn and end up off the trail in the middle of the woods. Stan was in the mood for some adventure, and he consented to act as their guide. The leader of this raid was to be Maylene Dalton. At least it was she who told Bruce Rasmussen what was going to happen that night, and swore him to secrecy. To this day, I don't know whether that tactic was intentional or accidental. But the girls could not have hoped to have victimized the boys to better effect than the way it happened.

Bruce, of course, was a leader among the guys, the admiral of the fleet at that time, and while his affections for Maylene were well established, and his loyalty was beyond question, he was also a resident of Sandes Home and a man himself. In cases of such a moral dilemma, there was never any question as to what was the proper thing to do, and Bruce did exactly that. He returned to Sandes and announced that the girls would be leading a raid against Sandes that night. Of course, we would never dream of trying to stop the raid. We all enjoyed being raided, as well as raiding, but also felt that the raid must not be allowed to succeed without an appropriate response. In such situations, of course, the dorm parents were willing to grant broad and generous liberties. We were permitted to troop down to Jhika Gali and purchase whatever ordnance we felt we needed to defend ourselves, and anyone who so chose could stay up past their bedtime to participate. Maylene had even disclosed the time set for the raid, so we were able to plan our response in an orderly fashion and with confidence.

Stan (the graduate, the traitor) knew nothing of our intentions, so when he quietly slipped out that evening we continued with our normal activities and pretended to take no notice. The moment he was gone, however, the preparations stepped up into high gear. It had been decided that since the route of retreat was going to be the shortcut, we would permit the girls to come up the shortcut and carry out their raid. They would be given a full response, however, on their way back down the shortcut. We had purchased the late tomato crop at Jhika. These tomatoes were beyond ripe, to say the least, and were better used as missiles than as food. We also had appropriated the water buckets off the Sandes balconies. These buckets were intended to be used to put out fires, but at that moment we had a much more important use for them in mind.

We all dressed in our darkest clothes, and lined the shortcut on both sides of the path. We positioned ourselves every ten feet for perhaps thirty or forty yards. Our intention was to permit them to enter the shortcut as they retreated until the entire group was inside the trap. Despite their hurry, progress down the path would be slow at best due to the engulfing darkness. Once the last girls had passed them, the guys at the end of the gauntlet nearest the top of the shortcut would close in behind the retreating women to close off their exit. The signal to begin the barrage of rotten tomatoes and buckets of water was to be a loud whoop from the men at the top of the shortcut once the exit had been closed off. What we anticipated as the inevitable outcome of our strategy would be worth the wait.

Now, imagine you are a high school girl, scared of the dark, beating a hasty retreat from the guys dorm in total darkness, on unfamiliar ground, having just pulled a raid which you are certain will tweak the ego of every red-blooded male in the place. The skin on your back is already crawling with the thought that you may be pursued in the darkness, and a good head start and speed are essential. As you are groping down the most difficult part of your escape route, passing directly below the walls of the dorm itself, you can hear the sounds of muffled cries from within the building. The hornets nest has been riled. In addition, you are passing through dense woods, from which wild animals may emerge at any time to devour you. At that moment you hear from directly behind you a loud bloodcurdling shriek, followed by a chorus of grunts, growls, and withering war cries both to your left and your right. Panic engulfs you. You understand that you are now surrounded in the darkness by the very persons you had hoped to elude. You heave yourself into a trot, tripping over the equally terrified girl in front of you on the path. All mayhem and disorder ensues. You cannot tell what has become of the leaders of your group, or your chaperon. The cries and screams of the other girls ahead and behind mingle with the sounds coming from the woods on either side. Suddenly, you are hit by something soft and wet—you imagine it to be garbage, or something fresh from the refuse piles of the local meat market. It is followed by something liquid which drenches your clothing and hair. The air is filled with missiles. What do you do? You scream, and tear off into the endless woods, away from the screams and cries for mercy of your comrades.

The prospect was delightful beyond estimation.

We calculated their time of arrival to be between 11:30 and midnight, depending on how quickly they walked and how long it took them to get out of the dorm. By 11:00 we had lined the shortcut, and had lookouts posted atop King's Cliff at the base of the shortcut to alert us when they heard the girls approaching. Then we waited.

It is difficult to sit still for thirty minutes, and of course time crawls when you are eager for something to happen. Thirty minutes dragged into forty-five, and then an hour. Suddenly, the lookouts called up that they saw a flashlight on the road. It was now after midnight, and we were becoming impatient with the unanticipated delay. But when the signal came up that they were coming, the wait was forgotten, and total silence ensued.

As the light came up the path, it became apparent that it was Stan, but he was alone. Bruce stepped out onto the path and soon learned that the girls' plan had been discovered by Debby Rupe, the Senior Girls dorm parent. Doubtless, one of the girls had told someone else in the hostel, swearing them to secrecy, and before the hour was up, everyone knew about the coming raid. Debby could tell that something was up by the strange behavior of the girls and the fact that there was so much activity after lights-out. So she maintained a vigil and locked the doors. When Stan came up the back stairwell to collect his charges, he heard Debby's voice from inside the door announce:

"The door is locked!"

Stan deduced that no one would be leaving on any raids that night. Debby had unwittingly spared the girls from a humiliating rout in the darkness, something for which, at that moment, none of the girls felt in the least grateful to her. But the group most disappointed and humiliated by the failure of the expected raid were the guys who had spent all evening planning for it. We quickly decided that the whole episode had been a setup in which the girls had "raided" the guys without even getting out of their beds.

Not long after this reverse raid didn't happen, I devised a scheme to retaliate against the girls for not raiding Sandes Home as expected. Of course, the act would have to be perpetrated at night, under cover of darkness, and would have to involve rousing noise. Patakas were out of the question—not worth the wrath of the principalities and powers that would inevitably be brought against us were we to use the forbidden firecrackers. So noise would have to be more creatively generated. It occurred to me that musical instruments could be used quite effectively for that purpose, and they could be kept at Sandes under the pretense of practice. I was, at that time, an avid student of the tuba. Of course, I chose that instrument because of its size and impressive volume. During my practice sessions behind the hostel, I would do a few of the compulsory scales before resorting to full-throated blasts into the silent woods. The echoes were quite impressive. How much more effective if done at night, in the silent darkness. We would rouse the entire hostel with bellowing blasts.

Those of us who intended to participate saw to it that we had our musical instruments at Sandes that night. Originally, there were eight or nine persons who intended to participate. But someone must have talked, and before dinner that night the Senior Boys dorm father issued a warning that any plans to pursue late night activities outside of the dorm with musical instruments would be punished. The company of those now willing to participate immediately dropped to three. Those of us who remained calculated that, since the long weekend was to begin the following noon, we could not possibly be punished. They would not dare to keep us from our families. So despite the warning and well after lights-out, once we were sure that the entire place was asleep, we grabbed our horns and ventured out into the softly sighing woods of a moonless night.

There was little traffic on the road to school, and we had no concern that we might be seen. If we heard the sound of an engine, we headed over the kud—the steep slope below the road—until the vehicle had passed. The only stretch of road where one could neither go over the kud, or up the hillside to escape detection was the long stretch of road from Apple Turnover (that's another story), past Elephant Rock, and up to the next turn in the road. We approached Apple Turnover with hearts pounding. We paused to listen closely for engine noises. Hearing nothing but the sound of the murmuring forest, we moved on, out into the abyss of road ahead. When we had almost reached Elephant Rock, to our horror, the sound of a Morris engine came up from behind, and before we could hope to run to a point of concealment, the car came around the corner. It was Irv Nygren, with a car full of missahibs from the elementary school staff quarters on their way back to school from a late night staff outing in Murree.

There may be many effective ways to conceal a trumpet. My two comrades did this quite handily, one by stuffing it inside his pants, the other, under his coat. But concealing a tuba inside one's pants is difficult, and so I had to assume a manner which would give the impression that there was nothing at all out of the ordinary about taking a stroll in the woods at 12:30 a.m. with my tuba. As the car passed us, to our amazement, it did not even slow down. Perhaps the ploy had worked! Dared we hope? Yet, we all realized that the element of surprise had been blown. A few hundred yards down the road, the Morris, now empty except for Mr. Nygren, returned on its way back to the staff housing near Sandes. This time, the car slowed and stopped as it approached us. We knew already that it was silly to hide, so we stopped to converse.

"Well, what a surprise meeting you here!" Mr. Nygren said. "How do you fellows happen to be out so late?"

"We just thought a breath of fresh air would be nice."

"I guess so! I see you brought your tuba along for better resuscitation, am I right?"

"Oh, absolutely!"

"Well, I hope you enjoy your stroll. Good night."

The fact that we had not been instructed to get in, and carted back to the dorm was a clear signal that, although our intentions had been discovered, we would also be allowed to proceed without hindrance. And so with complete confidence, we walked up to the hostel. Our fear of detection was gone and so we selected spots along the steep road that headed up toward the cantonment area adjacent to the hostel, where we were fully visible to every unfortunate soul who lived on the school compound.

We began our serenade with a roundhouse, full-volume blast. While I huffed and puffed on my tuba, emitting one blast after another, my comrades resorted to random, senseless scales. The noise was quite remarkable. We saw one or two heads pop up in the windows of the second and third floors, but there was no other response. No cheering, no screams of delight at being roused from sound slumber at midnight. The exertion had not provoked the anticipated reaction, and we were out of breath and dizzy from our hyperventilation. So we stopped to rest, and the silence closed in once again. To our astonishment, even the chowkidar, who should have been out of his quarters like a shot to protect the compound from such a violation to its peace and dignity, didn't stir. *What? Was the whole place dead?* We shook our heads in disbelief.

Our anticipation of a rueful response was sorely disappointed. The other two wanted to leave. But I insisted that the last thing on earth they would expect was for us to remain, and do it again. So we waited. While we waited, one of the graduates of MCS and his fiancee, both of whom were visiting MCS at the time, drove up to the school compound in their car and parked in the garage area under the water tower between the principal's residence and the hostel. While we watched, they remained in the vehicle. I do not know for a fact what they were doing. They could have been discussing some pertinent issue of theology over which they disagreed. However, they remained there for some thirty minutes. And during that time, even though it was a warm night, the windows of the car gradually got more and more steamed up.

Finally, she got out, and he started the car, and drove off into the night. We waited another few minutes, trying to decide when the time was right. Then we began to blast them again. This time we swore to continue until some response was provoked. Somewhere in the midst of my moose-like blasts, I had a blinding inspiration. I stopped and bellowed out, "Wake up you lumps, it's Howdy Doody time!"

Pat Nye emerged from the second floor of the elementary school building in only her nightgown and slippers, and yelled, "Robert Bailey and Tim Sherbeck, that is *enough!*"

We thought this was quite amusing, since Tim Sherbeck wasn't even there, and one of us gave her a sassy little toot on the trumpet in reply. She didn't regard that toot to convey the proper attitude for persons being admonished by an authority figure, so she continued down the steps, out into the driveway in front of the hostel, and came thundering up the road toward us. We decided that she meant business, and scrambled for the bushes and trees on either side of the road where we had been sitting. Her approach was so rapid and so unanticipated that we scarcely had time to find adequate cover. I felt certain that the lights of the dorm would reflect off my brass instrument in the darkness and disclose my hiding spot. But we had no choice other than to sit perfectly still. Pat walked up to within ten feet of me, directly in front of the bell of my tuba. It was apparent from her hesitation that she could not see us, and was unsure whether we had left or were still lurking nearby. I was nearly overcome with a gnawing temptation—all I had to do was put my mouth to my tuba, give it a mighty blast, and watch her leap out of her skin. It was tough, but I resisted.

After a minute of standing directly in front of me, closely scrutinizing every bush for signs, Pat concluded that we must have left, and she retreated to her quarters once again. After she was inside and the lights were out, we emerged slowly onto the road. This time, we felt more pleased with ourselves. It had succeeded. We had annoyed someone to the point of blowing their stack.

After a quick vote, we decided to venture one more serenade, and then flee. Once more we began to issue blasts, and scales. While we were playing at top volume, the chowkidar, in fulfillment of his night watchman duties at last, came leisurely strolling up the road toward us. I paused to greet him, and he made some gesture of supplication, as if to plead with us to cease and desist from our most unmusical activity. I told him that this would be our last song, and then returned to my playing. Finally we had our fill, and quickly left, getting back to Sandes Home around two a.m. As we snuck back up the steps to our rooms, we were greeted by the dorm parent, who was sitting and waiting for us like a spider. He had received a call from Mr. Roub while the first blast was going on; the principal had asked him if any of the boys were missing. So all he had to do was take a body count, and we were caught. We were told to see him in the morning, before breakfast, to receive our punishment.

The following morning, we were given the task of cleaning out the showers . . . with toothbrushes. "Use your own," he replied to our disbelieving inquiry.

Each dorm parent had their own style, and their own likes and dislikes among the individuals whom they had responsibility for. Uncle Damian had a talent for devising mindless and irrelevant punishments, and he had shown a particular distaste for the Bailey brothers. It did not bother us that we would be required to pay for our deliberate violation of the warning we had been issued. But to require us to use *our own* toothbrushes for a purpose which would certainly destroy them was both unnecessary and mean-spirited. But we found a way around it. We began with toothbrushes, and when he had left to supervise breakfast, we broke open the mop closet adjacent to the showers and found corn brooms, which worked much better and much faster. Imagine what astonishment he displayed when he returned an hour later and we were done; the whole shower was spotless, and there was not much he could say about it.

That day, despite many questions, I kept saying that I had no comment on whether I was involved. Mr. Roub called for me at some point during the morning to stop and see him.

"I don't know whether you heard about the serenading that we had here last night?" he began.

"Oh yes! I have been hearing about it all morning. Sounds like it was quite something!"

"Yes, it was. At first, I thought that you may have had something to do with it, since you are the only tuba player in the school."

Here he gave me a penetrating look, and paused for my reply. I remained silent, wearing my most innocent look.

"But I got a call from Colonel Butt at the Upper Topa Cantonment, and he was calling to apologize for the behavior of his men last night. Apparently the Colonel heard the noise, and he happens to know that it was some of his men who did it."

"I see."

"So, I'm relieved to hear that something like that won't be happening again."

"No, I'm sure it won't, if the Colonel says so."

I believe that Mr. Roub suspected beyond much doubt that I had been involved, but he also treated me as if I were an intelligent person, even when my actions gave him no cause to believe that I was. He also knew what kind of mischief to overlook, and what kind truly deserved punishment. I always respected him for that reason, even though I gave him many reasons to be annoyed with me.

Much of the relationship between authority and our natural inclination to defy or circumvent it was a game—played by both sides, I think—of dignity and equilibrium, a balance between respect and flexibility. The school had plenty of rules, most of them intended to keep us manageable with a minimum of effort, and also to keep us from offending the culture in which we were guests. The great unspoken rule, which I think we instinctively understood, was that we might tangle with the details, but we wouldn't violate this dual intent behind the rules. And when we did cross the line, most of us were sane enough to regret it—at least later when our character had seasoned a bit. Mr. Roub understood this balance and responded to our adolescent mischief with great forbearance. More importantly, he had a deep belief in our innate respect for the codes of fair play.

Himalayan Roller Coaster

Jonathan Mitchell '79

We had a motley collection of bikes, purchased largely from graduating seniors. I was the envy of the crowd when I replaced my old three speed with a 15-geared outfit inherited from Dale Stock. No matter that the rear derailleur spring was so weak that I had to attach a horseshoe and a rubber catheter tube to restore the chain tension. It was ugly but it worked. We spent hours sitting on the big veranda of Sandes Home preparing our bikes for weekend rides to Pindi, with grease, extra parts, and brake cable pieces spread all over the place.

Once the weather got warm, we traditionally began these trips at five a.m. Even in the late spring, it was rather chilly at that time in the morning and, lacking gloves, we would put socks over our hands to cut the cold wind. We flew down that hill at reckless speeds, trying to break the thirty-minute barrier, but I never made it to the bridge in less than that. Legend has it that Sam McMillan made it in twenty-eight minutes, but no one has been able to verify this. However, I did have a record of sorts: I rode from Sandes to the Inter-Continental Hotel in one hour forty minutes—about as good a time as a car would make in those days.

Rawalpindi was a good forty miles from Murree, but fortunately most of it was downhill. Actually, the first seventeen miles were downhill and the rest was up and down—a fact which many novices were dismayed to discover. Typically, we stopped for breakfast at Company Bagh where we savored hot tea, *parathas*, and omelets. By the time we got to the bridge, which ended the downhill portion of the ride, the temperature would be over 100 degrees; and if you stopped, the burning sensation was overpowering.

I am surprised that no one was ever killed on the Murree-Pindi road. I hardly remember a trip without one of the party having a close call. Once, a car overtaking a bus left Tim Wilder no choice but to collide with a large rock on the side of the road. Tim Johnson promptly rode over him; but apart from a front wheel which emerged in the shape of a figure eight, both walked away unhurt. We loaded Wilder and his bike on a Suzuki pickup, and by the time we reached Pindi he had everything repaired. Unfortunately, he again crunched his rim when forced onto a curb. At the same time as we found the situation amusing, we were rather sympathetic to his misfortune since rims were not easily replaced.

Traffic was not the only hazard. Bikes with pedal brakes were particularly treacherous. They had only a rear brake—rarely enough for the hairpins at Chara Pani, as many unfortunate souls will attest. Furthermore, the chains on these bikes had a way of coming off at the most inopportune moments, leaving them with no brakes at all. This happened to Danny Norkko, and I will never forget him sailing through Company Bagh waving his legs and screaming at the top of his lungs. Fortunately, someone cleaning a truck dashed out and rescued him at the last moment.

Gene Stoddard, Dale Stock, and I often rode to Pindi together. We invariably agreed to meet at Bolan Radios on Kashmir Road at four o'clock sharp for the return trip. We soon learned to remind Gene that he had to be there at exactly four p.m., as we liked to make it up the hill before dark. Gene had the best intentions, but he had a way of running into fantastic deals that fully justified a late arrival. He would show up with goats or civet cats in tow, which wouldn't normally be a problem, but we were on bikes. Neither the goat nor the civet cat was impressed with this mode of transport, and on both occasions we were forced to walk to Murree Road and wait for a truck going up the hill.

On our last trip Gene was again late, but this time he had found something more easily transported. He had a pair of partridges in a bag. These were no ordinary partridges, he assured us, these ones could fight—and they would make for great entertainment in Jhika tea shops after study hall. We headed for Murree, hoping to catch a ride along the way. Sure enough, as we neared Rawal Lake, an old Bedford stopped to pick us up. And what a stroke of luck this turned out to be. No load of buffaloes here, where you had to dodge cowpies and drool: this truck was headed for a wedding at Ghora

Gali and was carrying all the huge pots of food. By the time the truck stopped for the obligatory radiator fill-up at Company Bagh we were stuffed.

There we were, seated comfortably on greasy quilts above the driver's compartment, sipping on tea and remarking on our good luck. This was naturally a great moment to check on the health of the partridges. Gene pulled one out and began gently massaging its neck, as one does with fighting partridges. What we failed to observe was that the string tying its legs together had come off. This minor detail did not escape the notice of the partridge. Off it went, fluttering to the ground and running down the bazaar. With a great shout, Gene got the attention of half a dozen truck *wallahs* and coolies, and soon half the bazaar was out to watch and participate in the chase. What a sight—three Americans shouting and jumping up and down on a truck, with a mass of people falling over each other, chasing a partridge. They finally caught it, and we heaved a sigh of relief. It would have been a sad end to a perfect day to have lost the partridge; but to tell the truth, we never could get those birds to fight.

David Addleton '73

One of the more difficult chapters in my life at MCS occurred during eighth and ninth grades. The "big" boys had recently begun a program of hazing the younger boys when they entered boarding school in junior high. The hazing they intended to apply to each new boy was a "pink belly" and a "dry shave." Failure to cooperate—that is, to accept this torture without a fight—meant they would administer their torment with extra zeal. A single "pink belly" ordeal I went through lasted more than half an hour, included putting water on my belly to increase the pain, and left my stomach covered with blood blisters. When they came at me for the "dry shave," I fought back with what strength I could against half-a-dozen boys much larger and stronger than me. They could not hold me sufficiently still to accomplish their task, and knew they could not hide the bloody results if they tried anyway. David McCurry told them to quit. Thus, I avoided the second half of the hazing by fighting back.

About the same time, the school installed a system of monitors, based loosely on the British system of prefects. High school seniors and juniors, the same people who hazed us, were selected to monitor our behavior. The school gave them authority to punish infractions of the rules by demanding that we write lines, copy dictionary pages in the library, and work in the garden behind Sandes Home. They were not given any authority to administer corporal punishment. Some of the monitors remained upset that they had failed to put me through their hazing routine. As a result, I received enormous numbers of lines and dictionary pages to copy, and more than fifty hours in the garden. One monitor in particular ordered me to copy twenty-five pages from the dictionary "because I don't like your face."

Near the end of the fall term in ninth grade, Mr. Roub called me into his office to discuss my "misbehavior"—my failure to cooperate with the monitors. I told him I would cooperate with any and all fair authority; but that I would not cooperate with the monitor system as they had organized it. I demanded punishment for the monitors for their behavior towards the junior high boys. He agreed that their plans for the monitors had not worked out as they had hoped, but said he would have to support the monitors if the system were to work at all. He offered a compromise: I could shovel chicken manure from the coop during a Friday night skating party and then sweep the gym after the party and my slate would be wiped clean. He would also see about making changes in the system of monitors and try to prevent hazing in the next, spring term. I shoveled the chicken shit, swept the gym, and missed the skating party.

The monitors remained unchanged the next term, and I continued my refusal to cooperate with them. I promised myself never to require anyone else to undergo hazing, and would not cooperate with efforts to inflict a similar pain upon other new boys. I returned to the States during my tenth-grade year with some bitter memories of MCS.

Even so, while my family was on furlough, I determined that I would enjoy my last two years in Pakistan to the fullest. Something about my experience in the States made me realize what a unique opportunity I enjoyed by growing up in Pakistan. I recalled playing marbles during recess as a little boy, when the big guys would play with us; or the times we played "Eagle's Nest" (a variation of dodge ball) with older kids. When I returned to MCS the next year I sought out little kids to play marbles with during recess. By the time I reached eleventh grade, organized hazings were no longer in vogue. And I didn't use my own monitor status to punish anyone. Instead, during their boarding parent's day off, I put the Middle boys to bed after reading them stories—and tried to keep them in bed until their boarding parent returned.

I remember my last two years at MCS with considerable pleasure. One summer my siblings and I stayed in boarding. We had a ball. We would take early morning picnics in the woods with the girls, raiding the lab for a primus or two and the kitchen for pots and pans and food. We'd meet the girls outside behind the hostel, walk to a fine spot in the woods, and sit out under the stars, eating cookies and bread, tea and eggs, and talking about our lives at MCS and our futures until the first rays of daybreak began fading the stars. We'd be back in bed half an hour before the wake up call and sleepy the rest of the day.

Little Diplomats

Rob Bailey '78

THE CHOWKIDAR AND THE CHURDAIL

During my sophomore year at MCS, there occurred a changing of the guard at Sandes Home which had a profound effect upon all of us. Fortunately, though, we only felt the discomfort of that change for a brief time. When faced with adverse circumstances, the boys in the dorm were capable of banding together to destroy anyone who threatened to make any uncomfortable changes. While I was there, we trained several dorm parents and drove one out of the place in this manner. We also drove away one particularly troublesome night watchman—the chowkidar.

This gentleman was hired when the regular chowkidar, a man of much skill and many years' tenure, was fired for sleeping on the job. It seemed rather ridiculous to us to fire a man with whom we were all satisfied because he did what people normally do at night. Instead, the dorm administrator argued, he should have stayed up and wandered the grounds at night to ward off burglars and thieves. But in the entire time I was there, and for years prior to that as far back as anyone could remember, the place had not been robbed even once. It seemed highly unlikely, therefore, that they should begin to rob us at that particular moment in time. There was something about Sandes, it would seem, which so terrified the local burglars and thieves that they dared not venture up the hill for fear of being devoured. Why else should someone be so reluctant to rob an isolated building occupied by thirty to forty defenseless foreign boys?

So the old chowkidar had to be fired, and a new, more eminently qualified, more high tech chowkidar was hired in his place.

This man was one in a million where chowkidars were concerned—a true ace, with an impressively lengthy resume. He was hired in from the outside, with no local connections to compromise his integrity, so he could be counted on not to be bribed into complacency by friends and relatives. This man had no friends, and his relatives were all distant ones.

In a spectacular departure from precedent, this chowkidar conspicuously armed himself with a Moses-like staff. He would make regular rounds, about once every thirty minutes, beginning the moment the sun went down. The irony of this was that it made his exact whereabouts completely predictable. In addition, he would loudly broadcast his arrival with repeated cries and grunts, followed by the even more annoying clatter of his staff. This he took and deliberately struck repeatedly against the stone walls or veranda planks with all his might—any place which would make a loud noise. He would then pause and yell "Hah!" at the top of his lungs.

It is most disconcerting to be in the middle of some dream about winning the 50,000-meter run by a full ten minutes on Sports Day when, suddenly, just as you are closing in on the finish line, you are jolted awake by the sound of a stick being hammered repeatedly against the metal tool shed behind Sandes. The hammering would be immediately followed by a loud series of lung clearing whoops. Then a moment of silence, during which you grope for a clock and find it is two-thirty in the morning. Following the silence there would be throat clearing, and sniffing sounds, and then vigorous spitting noises. Enough people complained about this to the dorm administrator that something should have been done, yet it went on.

The people most amused by this show were the kitchen staff, who lived in staff quarters just above Sandes. Hearing the din which he raised every night, they fancied this new chowkidar to be some sort of half-wit. The cooks invited him into the kitchen in the early mornings and asked the chowkidar why he saw fit to produce these outbursts all night long. They explained to him that there had never been a problem with burglary here, and that it wasn't necessary to scare away thieves that weren't there. The chowkidar looked at them with disbelief and explained that he wasn't trying to scare away burglars, but was making all the clatter to protect himself from the *churdail* which he had been told lurked about in the woods.

According to local folklore, a *churdail* was a kind of forest demon—the disembodied spirit of a woman who had died in childbirth. This apparition, according to our chowkidar, stood over ten feet in height and had the physical strength of ten men. The *churdail* had limbs on which the hands and feet were backwards, so the toes pointed behind rather than in front, and the left hand was on the right arm, and vice versa. It was clothed only with its own hair, which hung in long and hideously knotted masses all the way to its ankles. In addition, the *churdail* had teeth which pointed straight out of its mouth, and it sustained itself on the flesh of men. It could not abide light, so it preyed upon foolish men who dared to wander the woods at night. The other thing which the *churdail* could not abide was loud, sudden noises. Thus, all the clamor as our chowkidar made his rounds.

It is possible that this fantastic story could have been planted in his brain by the outgoing chowkidar, or by locals who resented the change in personnel at Sandes, and who may have wished to cause some difficulty for anyone who attempted to replace the old watchman. Perhaps this new man brought this wild notion with him from some previous situation. At any rate, by the time we got him, the picture had reached gigantic proportions in his mind. He was possessed of an unquenchable terror and persuaded to a complete certainty that such a being lurked in the vicinity of Sandes Home. The cooks were so amused by this tale, that they repeated it to any listening ear, and this included a few of us boys.

It had reached the point with the boys in the dorm where the constant banging about at night was disturbing too many people's sleep. After several weeks of inaction, several of us decided the time had come to correct the problem ourselves. Clearly, this chowkidar was an intolerable choice for the position. We would have to devise some means by which he could be persuaded to stop all of the nocturnal brouhaha, or be permanently removed.

Our plan was inspired by the cooks' stories, and we were confident that we could encourage him to move on by assisting the fulfillment of his wildest fears. I suggested that we get two guys, one sitting on the other's shoulders, to dress up as a *churdail* and chase the man all over the hillside. This idea was quickly withdrawn from consideration when it occurred to us that, rather than turn and run, someone who is terrified and cornered will often attack. We didn't wish to risk being bludgeoned to death by a hysterical chowkidar. Instead, we decided on a more sophisticated tactic. We would give him the proper stimulus and let his imagination do the work for us.

Behind Sandes Home, near where the short-shortcut begins at the garbage pit, is the most isolated corner of the building. On one side is the thick, *churdail*-infested forest, and on the other side, the high stone walls of the back terrace. To the left, a lonely, unlit stretch of driveway leads to the front of Sandes Home; to the right is an extremely steep slope. To get around this requires taking a path through the edge of the forest to the playing field in the back or traveling through a tight walkway leading to the kitchen. Over the entire area there was only one light, a single bulb fixture about twelve feet above the ground, situated close to a small window looking out from one of the basement bedrooms.

As daylight was fading, the chowkidar began his rounds by turning on all of the outside lights. He was easy to locate, because of his decibel level. He would have done just as well to tie a string of tin cans around one of his legs. After he had turned on this particular light, and once the darkness of the evening had deepened and the night became silent, two of us went outside. Standing one man on the shoulders of the other, we unscrewed the light bulb—ever watchful, lest the chowkidar should come up from behind and mistake us for a *churdail.* Chicken fighting was a popular pastime on swimming parties to the Intercontinental Hotel in Rawalpindi, but not at night in the dark with a frenzied chowkidar brandishing a stick.

Some of the guys positioned themselves with a loudspeaker in the window adjacent to the outside light. The sound effects tape we had selected included a one-minute segment of warbling, computer-generated noise that sounded like flying saucers crashing. All of us thought it was the most bizarre thing we'd ever heard; it seemed reasonable to conclude that our chowkidar probably would think so, too. The rest of us went down to a doorway about twenty feet from where the chowkidar would be standing while trying to figure out where the light bulb had gone. From that position we would have a clear view of what happened.

It wasn't long before the approaching clatter let us know that the chowkidar was on his way. We shut off all of the inside lights, and waited for him like spiders anticipating the arrival of a fly. He rounded the corner at a good brisk pace, and must have immediately noticed that the outside light was out. The whole area was shrouded in a silent and sinister darkness. He slowed, and paused. After a moment of hesitation, he drew back and beat his staff against the rocks of the adjacent retaining wall, and followed this up with a mighty "Hah! Hah!" Routinely, he would only emit a single "Hah!," so we deduced that his imagination was already kicking into high gear. He edged forward toward the light fixture, and finally stood directly below it, glancing upward. In the darkness, he probably couldn't see that the bulb was missing. But he didn't spend long squinting at it to find out. Once or twice, he glanced over his shoulder at the woods which were behind him, as if he expected something to emerge, or as if he were being watched by someone.

At that moment, the guys with the loudspeaker went into action, flooding the area with other-worldly noise. An unanticipated echo reverberated weirdly off the stone walls of the narrow alley, redoubling the delightfully nightmarish quality of the sounds.

Human imagination is a wonderful thing. Our chowkidar most certainly had no idea what he was hearing, but he wasn't going to spend any time figuring it out. He bolted straight up the grassy slope leading to the playing field behind Sandes, completely ignoring the pathway, and did so in about five or six seconds.

He took the four-foot retaining wall at the base of the slope in one flying leap. The slope itself, with numerous shrubs and brambles on it, and steeper than forty-five degrees, appeared to have no effect on our chowkidar. He was a motivated man at that particular moment. It seemed as if his body had been catapulted on a low trajectory, and he was simply moving his arms and legs in some perfunctory semblance of activity as he hurled forward. There was a brief tearing and cutting sound as he encountered the resistance of the brambles, but he punched his way through like a bullet through a plastic bag. Once on the playing field above, he simply vanished from sight altogether, leaving us to wonder if we had in fact really seen him at all.

We all thought the whole thing was terribly funny. But our degree of success had so greatly exceeded expectations, that we also felt a bit disappointed at how quickly it was over. One wishes to savor such moments.

After a few minutes of silence, we heard our chowkidar once more, but this time he was far off. He had covered a great deal of ground in a very short time, and now produced a series of five or six "Hah!" calls in a row. This was truly unprecedented. And it indicated that he was highly agitated about whatever he imagined that he had heard down by our dark corner. Also unprecedented was the fact that no one heard another sound out of the chowkidar all that night. It was the first undisturbed sleep we had enjoyed in some time.

The next morning, the cooks were laughing much louder and more frequently than normal. On the breakfast line, as I went up to get more French toast, they told me that Mr. Calderwood had gone looking for the chowkidar before sunrise that morning, and had been unable to locate him at any of the usual spots. I guess he had also noticed that the night had been devoid of the usual racket. Finally, he went to the chowkidar's quarters, and found him locked inside, fast asleep. Once the chowkidar had been roused, he came to the kitchen where the cooks were preparing breakfast. He told the cooks that he had been chased by a *churdail* the night before, and that it had emerged from the woods and shrieked at him just behind Sandes. He had outwitted it, though, by escaping to his quarters, locking himself in, and making a lot of noise to scare it away.

That afternoon, our chowkidar was paid a visit by the boarding administrator, and we heard from the cooks later that he had decided to leave. I guess one close call with a *churdail* was enough.

CHARLIE

Jhika Gali was the crucible in which many of these fiendish plots were hatched. Three or four nights of the week we went down to Jhika for tea. Sometimes large groups would go, but two to five guys was the norm. One tea shop, which we called Joe's, had a back balcony that offered a little extra privacy. A door prevented a direct view of the balcony from the street, while the porch itself had no lighting whatsoever. The balcony was a haphazard structure of boards, poles, and flattened old kerosene tins. It sagged down toward the outer edge, it had no rails or roof, and there were holes in the floor boards. The entire structure was coated with a layer of blackened dirty grease, the accumulation of years of spilled food and foot traffic. But from here, one could enjoy the view at night, and not be seen by anyone who might be passing through town looking for people who shouldn't be there.

From the edge of Joe's balcony, it was about twenty feet to the ground below. And so, provided the company was not mixed, if one felt the urge while dining, all one had to do was stand up and aim out over the abyss. In the whole town of Jhika there was not one bathroom; the area behind the buildings served quite adequately for this purpose. Unfortunately, many of the townsfolk seemed to favor the slope behind Joe's tea shop, and many a fine evening's fellowship was ruined by the foul aroma of someone relieving themselves directly below us.

Of all of the establishments in Jhika Gali, one that reached preeminence was the tea shop operated by a gentleman named Ghulam-e-Rasool. The name Ghulam involves the use of a guttural "g," which is unfamiliar to most anglophones. Besides, most of the MCS students were unconcerned with the particulars of Pakistani culture, such as language, and did not care to know the names of most Pakistanis with whom they associated, much less their proper pronunciation. To avoid this indelicacy, we had given most of the shopkeepers of Jhika Gali new names, such as Joe, or Bozo, who ran another fast food business on the Sandes side of Jhika. But Ghulam-e-Rasool was the best and most favored place in town. We all knew him as Charlie. In fact, the other places usually filled up with tea- and *paratha*-hungry MCSers only once Charlie's place had reached its capacity.

Charlie had established himself in this position of favor by being the most gregarious, tolerant person in the entire town. We were accustomed to going into Charlie's for all of our tea-drinking and omelet-eating contests. Tea cup size would vary from one place to another, and a recognized standard for such orgiastic undertakings was necessary. Charlie became the standard because whenever some-one would go in and ask for a thirty-egg omelet, or one hundred cups of tea, no questions would be asked. The product was delivered at a regular pace without any incredulous looks, or any questions about one's sanity. He apparently understood the type of mentality under which we were operating, and felt it was a good business proposition to give the *Ungrez* (English) what they wanted without having to understand why they wanted it. No other establishment offered us such privacy, or such unquestioning respect and service.

Our fondness for Charlie's willing attitude led some of the students to make a special sign to hang outside his door. Using Old English lettering, the words "Charlie's Tea Shop" were carved into stained wood and it was unique among all of the signs in the town. Charlie was quite taken with it, and displayed it proudly until the local Muslim cleric complained. The *maulvi* was adamant that the sign not be displayed since it contained the letter "C," which he said stood for Christ. The Maulvi ran the only mosque in town, and he didn't want any competition. It was enough to conduct commerce with Christians from foreign places, but Jhika was not going to become a staging area for conversions. The "C-word" had to go. Charlie took the sign down, but kept it. And the same students made him another sign which had no "C." It read "Ye Olde Tea Shoppe," and was still hanging there when I left in 1978.

PATAKAS AND KUCHIES

Ever since our walks with Auntie Inger as Little Boys we had been intrigued by the deep, tubular holes in some of the giant boulders beside the road. About the diameter of a broom handle, these holes had been drilled by the army, we eventually learned, to pack dynamite in (presumably, in the process of carving the road out of the side of the mountain). We saw no reason why we shouldn't use these holes in a similar manner. One such hole—ideal for directing the force and sound of an explosion outward in one direction—could be found in Elephant Rock on the way to school. A single *pataka* would not do justice to such an opportunity. We pooled our gunpowder and stuffed it into a small jar, forcing a crude fuse through a hole in the lid. We found some incredibly stupid and foolhardy person (no shortage of volunteers) to light it and drop it in the hole. We stood to the side, covered our ears, and then counted the echoes off the hills. We were not disappointed.

Contrary to the folklore, however, which I understand has branded me as the great pataka raider of my era, my firecracker use was strictly limited to areas away from school or Sandes. Besides, I favored the golas (wedding bombs) over patakas (cherry bombs), because golas packed more bang for the rupee. The problem with pataka raids was that no matter how successful the raid, the perpetrators were invariably found out. While raids in general were frowned upon, pataka raids were strictly forbidden and viewed, therefore, as a direct affront to school authority. Consequently, the reaction tended to be more harsh than to other forms of mischief. It's a long way from school to Sandes, and identifying empty beds was easy. One solution tried was to use cigarettes as time-delayed fuses. Only a few patakas actually exploded, but the engineers of this novel approach were more than pleased with their efforts.

I did execute one pataka raid, when I was a junior, and while it did not occur anywhere near the school, it certainly was a direct affront to those at the receiving end. I failed to appreciate the significance of this at the time, of course, but the event was quite enough to persuade me that pataka raids were simply too much excitement for normal people to handle.

It was during the summer of 1977, just prior to my brother's graduation from MCS. Our family was living in Jungle Din, just above Camp Mubarak. Every day we had to walk down the hill, through Camp Mubarak to the Sunnybank road about half a mile below, where we caught the bus to school. During the summer months, the Kuchies, or gypsies, would migrate with their flocks through the foothills on their way to higher pasture, often stopping for a time in Murree. Sometimes, if they found the accommodations to be sufficient, they would remain in their encampments in Murree all summer long. One such group had established itself on the side of the road below Camp Mubarak, and as the summer came on it became a most unpleasant experience to walk past their camp each morning.

Kuchies have a reputation as cannibals and kidnappers of children. When I was very young, our cook used to tell me that they regarded the children of the *Ungrez* as a delicacy, and that if I wandered too far from the house, I would wind up in their dinner pots. In reality, Kuchies sustain themselves on a largely vegetarian diet, as do most of the poor people in that part of the world. They are rapidly mobile, fiercely independent, always armed, and live by the code of vengeance. Of course, we were foolish children, and didn't worry about such matters. To us the issue was the smell of the excretory functions of their goats, which came to permeate the area of their camp at a distance of 100 feet in every direction. It was most unsanitary in every way, and we decided to make the accommodations uncomfortable for them as a subtle way of encouraging them to move on.

That summer, the Sherbecks were staying for a brief time on the same side of the hill. The Sherbeck brothers were great fun, since they all had a certain genius for mischief, and my brother and I spent more and more time with them as the summer passed. Of course, when the Sherbecks and the Baileys got together, there was a certain synergy which rendered the result to be twice as bad as the sum of all of our separate actions. I'm sure that Murree has never since seen a summer like it. When we disclosed our desire to unnerve the Kuchies to the Sherbeck brothers, that explosive combination found a wonderful opportunity to express itself.

We decided that a pataka raid would be a superlative means to achieve our objective. Dennis Sherbeck happened to have a large supply of patakas and golas on hand, and he had a burning urge to use them before he left for the States, rather than to give them away. In addition, there were certain strategic factors that filled us all with a brash confidence in our own ability to pull off such a daring raid and escape unscathed. Directly above the Kuchie camp, at the top of a cliff-like embankment, stood the concrete shell of an abandoned building. It offered an excellent vantage point overlooking the camp, and was the perfect spot from which patakas could be effortlessly lobbed down onto the encampment below. The concrete structure offered complete concealment, and it was on a direct path to Camp Mubarak. We calculated that we could quickly pelt them with dozens of patakas and escape undetected before they ever realized what had happened.

As we planned the tactics which we would employ, one in our company, Dan Cutler, decided that the venture was foolish, and that he would not participate. He told us it was dangerous. The thought seemed ridiculous to us. How could he imagine it to be dangerous? Were they going to kidnap us and eat us for dinner? In the darkness, they wouldn't even be able to tell who it was, much less catch us. So, discounting Dan's concerns, off we went to execute our daring plan. In order to return home, however, Dan Cutler would have to pass directly by the Kuchie camp, at the very same time that we would be skulking high above the camp with our patakas. In respect for Dan's personal safety, we agreed to allow him to pass by before bombarding them.

It was pitch black that night. For the purposes of concealment and assured escape, we could not have chosen a better night for our adventure. As we neared the concrete structure from which our raid was to be launched, we were overcome with the urge to urinate. For some reason, perhaps as a last opportunity to consider the wisdom of actions one is about to undertake, God has ordained that this urge will inevitably arise during moments of nervous strain. (It was also another reason for Rule One of our boarding school raid policy— never include women.)   Once this urge had been satisfactorily resolved, we found ourselves looking down upon the peaceful camp below.

Four or five large tents were pitched in a half circle on the concrete flooring—ideal for the impact of patakas—which surrounded an old bungalow. For some reason, the landlord had been unable to rent it that year—perhaps due to the fact that the gypsies were occupying half the grounds and proliferating the stench of their animals throughout the building. Once we saw our objective before us, all thought for anything else, including poor Dan Cutler, was forgotten, and we instantly began to hurl great handfuls of patakas down on the sleeping gypsies. As it turned out, our assault began at the very moment that he was walking by their camp.

The first explosions triggered in each of us a wave of hysterical giddiness. I found myself almost paralysed with laughter. Of course, the more we threw, and the more frequent the explosions became down below, the funnier it all seemed to us. I recall glancing sideways at Tim Sherbeck, who at that moment was virtually apoplectic with laughter, while furiously hurling great fistfuls of patakas between spasms. He (like myself, I'm sure) had a wildly excited look on his face, as if he had been stabbed with something, and his hair seemed to be flying about his face as he threw.

It is amazing how much commotion can be raised in just a few seconds.

Only our certainty of escape could have permitted us to perpetrate such an outrage on our neighbors. We were taking delight in it *because* it was an outrageous thing to do. Had we been able to devise a more outrageous act and still be certain of escape, I have little doubt that we would have done it. When I glanced at Tim, at that moment I saw primal man revealed in all his glory, unrestrained by conscience, and freed to the impulses of his will, even if only for a brief moment. It was just such exhilaration, such moments of epiphany, that made raids such an essential part of my Murree experience.

Once we had discharged our ordnance, we turned and ran blindly down the road to Camp Mubarak, greatly warmed and fulfilled by our complete triumph, but breathless from the exertion.

On our way down to conduct the raid, we were seen by the Pakistani watchman at Camp Mubarak. He seemed an affable fellow, but we didn't know him very well, and certainly not well enough to tell him what we were up to. In fact, we made our best effort not to be seen by anyone—which is the second rule of raids. But this watchman was better than we were, and he not only saw us going down, but he heard the ruckus down below at the gypsy camp. When we came running back through Camp Mubarak just moments later, at full tilt and laughing hysterically, he deduced that we were somehow connected with the ruckus he had heard. It is our extreme good fortune that we *were* seen by him that night, for had he not intervened on our behalf just minutes later, we would probably not have survived the incident.

As we were running through Camp Mubarak, still laughing, we heard what sounded like a pataka exploding. We all stopped to listen, since this was the brouhaha we had all anticipated down in the gypsy camp. We figured that they must be examining the remnants of our patakas, and found one that had not exploded. As we listened to the yelling, barking, and disorder which we had produced, there came another explosion. How was it possible that so many of our patakas had failed to explode? Then we heard voices coming quickly up the road toward Camp Mubarak, and a series of six explosions. It was gunshots.

Our laughter stopped, transformed into the horrible realization that we were being hunted by a group of highly agitated men who had a clear disposition to use their guns as a means of retaliation. We heard them yelling something about "*Ungrez*," and all hope of escape vanished. A creeping hot fear replaced the cathartic rush of the raid. Somehow, they had figured out who had attacked their camp. We turned and fled, each to his own house, and said not a word to our parents. Instead, we busied ourselves with the quiet domesticated tasks of well-behaved children, such as homework, while we waited for the armed party to arrive. Time crawled by.

Quite late that night, just after we had gone to bed, the watchman from Camp Mubarak arrived and asked for my father. A few minutes later we were summoned from our beds, and heard the rest of the story. Just after we fled from the camp in fear for our lives, the gypsy party arrived at the gate, and entered the camp in hot pursuit. The watchman met them at a narrow stairwell which they had to pass through. He asked them what they meant, coming into the compound with guns. They told him that the children of the *Ungrez* had attacked their camp, and that they were going to set matters straight. He asked them how they knew it was us. Who else but the *Ungrez* would do so stupid a thing, they responded.

At this point the watchman began to sing our praises—what well-behaved children we were, and that he himself had known us for some time, and we were not the sort to be out late at night. Besides, he would certainly have seen us come through the camp on our way to do such mischief had we, in fact, done as they said, and he had seen no one. He mentioned that there were other children living just up the road, who were little *shatans* (satans), and more likely the sort to do such things. They were not *Ungrez* at all, but local children. And so it went, for some time, until finally they were persuaded by him.

My father was under no illusions as to our capabilities; he didn't even ask for an admission from us. We were told that this had to be the stupidest thing we had done yet, and we were grounded for a week. I guess that my father realized by the narrowness of our escape, and by our solemn demeanor, that the experience had taught us something. He had no doubt that we would not repeat our foolishness, at least not in this fashion. And he was familiar enough with our recklessness to understand that survival is often the most one can hope for in teenage boys.

THEIR COUNTRY

It is amazing to me how well the Pakistani people tolerated us foreign intruders. Despite our many and most grievous violations of acceptable conduct, they seldom displayed annoyance. The inevitable conflicts that arose from the differences between Islamic and Western cultures were met most often with a patient wisdom. Many Pakistanis even seemed to enjoy our ability to violate their rules, and get away with it *because* we were foreign. It was frequently explained to me, when such conflict situations arose, that I was a foreigner and therefore expected to behave differently. As a guest in their country, they wanted me to enjoy my visit. To my mind, this is a far more enlightened view than usually encountered by Asians visiting our home countries in the West.

Another explanation regularly employed to account for our different behavior was the loony factor: We were simply insane, and had to be tolerated for that reason, for no one but an insane person would do the things we did. At other times, there was no explanation at all—only dumbfounded silence.

One such situation arose on a high school camp-out near Attock, along the shores of the blue Indus River. Camp-outs offered a chance to cut loose and get rid of built up stress; for this reason they were the most highly anticipated event in the social calendar, perhaps even more than the annual spring banquet. Among other reasons, the girls looked forward to camp-outs as rare opportunities to try out their new swimwear and to work on their fading tans. The fellows looked forward to the camp-outs for the same reason.

The countryside, however, was often filled with unwanted spectators. Here, the seemingly minimal allowances of MCS culture (as we experienced it) confronted the prohibitions of Pakistani culture against the public display of any female anatomy. Attock was particularly vulnerable to this problem, and eventually this otherwise choice location had to be abandoned: our camp site was situated below a broad overview where the Grand Trunk Road ran parallel with the river for awhile before winding its way toward Peshawar and the frontier.

The G.T. Road was the main artery for truck traffic between all major cities, and the most notoriously aggressive truckers were the Pathans (natives of this mountainous frontier province). This reputation was certainly not limited to their driving. It stood to reason, therefore, if a trucker were driving by this overview, and he noted a few brilliant white women in scant swimwear, that he would be inclined to stop for prayers, and for coffee. If he were a Pathan, he might wish to wander down to the waters of the Indus far below in order to wash. So, after a few hours of midday exposure, a high school girl could expect to collect both a painful sunburn and a crowd at the shore line—the latter, needless to say, being the less desirable.

We high school boys were called upon in such situations to "deal with" the problem, for it was considered inappropriate for women in that society to talk to men they didn't know. The dress code and social guidelines at MCS assured that its girls would always be discreet in public. At all outdoor sporting events, and even during practice, the girls were required to wear the regulation "greenie"—a modest outfit of white slacks and a long-tailed shirt (to cover the derriere) of lurid green only faintly similar to the school colors.

Greenies were certainly not regulation on camp-outs, however, but most of the girls made some effort, despite the lax decorum, to be conservative in their immodesty. Then there were those who sought to outshine even the brilliant light of the Attock sun. One girl, in such an effort, paraded herself in a pink two-piece that was risque even by Western standards. At a distance, this outfit had the enhancing effect of blending with her flesh, so that her more distant admirers would be led to see her as having nothing on at all. This only added to the consternation and amazement of the crowd of onlookers at the Grand Trunk overlook. By early afternoon, their numbers had grown thick, so they appeared like crows perched for a hundred yards on the retaining wall at the edge of the road. This was particularly disturbing to the girls, and some of us who spoke Urdu were asked to make an appeal to the gathered throng to please be considerate of our privacy and move along.

Brian Calderwood and I were elected to this ticklish task, and we slowly ascended the incline to the edge of the road. At our arrival, not a man stirred from his perch, but we had the sense that all ears were tuned in our direction. We made some perfunctory greetings to the row of middle-age truckers squatting closest to us, inquiring as to their health, and the health of their children, as the rules of etiquette required, and then we plunged right in.

"We have been asked by the women with us to explain to you that what you see is not unusual in our country."

From weathered faces under great swaths of turban came a few grunts, and nods of acknowledgement, and some broad smiles as well.

"In our country, however, it is considered highly insulting to stare at anyone," I continued.

Then one of the company, who obviously comprehended the direction of the conversation, spoke up: "But in our country, it is not considered rude to look at anything which is seen."

"Yes, I understand that very well. But we ask that you consider that to us it is seen as an insult. The women below are upset that you are looking at them."

"If they are upset, they should come up here and say so."

This retort brought much laughter and many sidelong comments. The conversation had now become more interesting to many of the truckers than the girls on the sand below, and the truckers began to gather more closely around us.

"Ah, yes, but they *have* told you," I pressed, smoothly. "They have sent us to tell you that it disturbs them that you gather to stare at them."

"But why would they go out in full view if they wished not to be looked at? And we are just stopping here on our way to Peshawar or to Rawalpindi. Should we drive without rest?"

Brian and I began to get flustered. The men were clearly of no mind to be persuaded to move on. What would we do now?

"When we go among you we try to respect your women, and not bother them," Brian tried. "We have rented the Government Rest House on the river because we, too, wish to rest. Have we ever stopped in your villages to stare at your women?"

"But our women do not display themselves like yours do, running naked for everyone to see."

The insurmountable logic of this last retort so stunned both Brian and me that we were left without anything to say. We asked their leave, then turned and descended the embankment. Once at the bottom again, we were astonished to discover that while we were making our way down the slope to the river all but a very few of the truckers had returned to their vehicles and left. Clearly, they had not done this out of any compelling sense of self-consciousness or shame, but out of simple courtesy. In spite of what must have been a pretty compelling spectacle, in the end, it was their own sense of hospitality that prompted them to leave us in peace.

Senior Highs and Goodbyes

___

Amy Jo (Inniger) Boone '89

I will always remember Debby Rupe—a godly example, wonderful housemother and, best of all, a true friend. Deb truly cared about each one of us and was sensitive to us as individuals. Ever ready with a cup of coffee, she took time to listen to us, to our joy and our sadness. Her door was always open and we'd sometimes hang out in her room late at night, arguing with Deb about the no-dancing rule, or skirt lengths, or how late seniors could stay up. We tried our best to give her a hard time, but usually she just threw back her head and laughed at us.

One thing Deb was known for was her alter ego—Bill Skitch. She would slip out of the room and a minute later Bill would appear. He looked remarkably like Deb, except for his buck teeth and black moustache. He would always say, "Where's that cute Debby Rupe? I love her more than life itself!" Then he would go off in search of Deb, who would soon reappear as herself. When we told her Bill had been there she would be so disappointed. He was the love of her life, but she had never had the chance to meet him!

Deb had another unusual talent: playing "Blue Moon" on the piano. She would happily play it whenever we asked—and we would often ask. I've never heard the original version of the song, but I'm sure it never matched Deb's version in terms of the performer's emotions and audience appreciation.

The Annual Staff-Student Tea was a highlight of my last few years at MCS. Each year the student council would choose a theme for the party, attended by the senior high students and all staff

members. My sophomore year the theme was the Mad Hatter's Tea
Party, and everyone was encouraged to dress up as characters from
fairy tales. Marge Montgomery and Auntie Rosie Stewart came as
Tweedledum and Tweedledee (they were sisters, and both a bit
"well-rounded" already); Angela Smith zipped herself up in a sleeping bag and hopped around as the caterpillar in *Alice in Wonderland*.

The next year the theme was An English Tea Party, set in the
British raj of 1930s India. Everyone had a wonderful time impersonating pompous aristocrats and delicate ladies. It was fitting that
the party was held in Sandes Home, a former rest home for British
soldiers.

Finally, my senior year, we chose the theme, "The Arabian
Nights." A big, colorful *shamiana,* a Pakistani tent, was set up in the
school gym and rugs were rolled out. Various Eastern personages
gathered for the celebration of the marriage of the local sheikh and
his lovely bride (Mr. and Mrs. Murray). Harem girls, bodyguards, a
missionary, a beggar, a terrorist, tourists, and many others filled the
room. We were all a bit mystified when Mr. Wood showed up in a
yellow raincoat, until he explained that he was a worker on a North
Sea oil rig; there must have been a connection there, somewhere . . .

Another highlight of my senior year was winning the girls'
interschool basketball tournament by one point. In the final game,
against Lahore American School, Murree was ahead by one point in
the last minute. Then Lahore's best free-throw shooter was fouled
and got two shots. Amazingly, she missed both; then their star
player got the rebound and shot twice, missing both her shots, too.
Murree repossessed the ball with just seconds left, and won the game.

The annual Spiritual Emphasis Weekends were a chance to focus on God and our relationship to Him. Speakers would challenge
us to think how our faith could be brought to bear on the day-to-day
situations in our lives. My senior year God really worked in the
hearts of many of us there. At the very end of the weekend our
speaker, Al Lowrie, a missionary from Multan, said this: "If you
don't remember anything else I've said this weekend, remember this:
Living for Jesus is the *only* life worth living!"

Of course, some people got more out of these special weekends
than others did. But, MCS did offer many such opportunities for
spiritual growth, for those who wanted to take them. Most
importantly, I think, MCS demonstrated the principle of
community, of the joys and struggles of living and working together,
with Christ as the foundation of it all. Community isn't meant to be
easy. Living at MCS wasn't always easy. But I think MCS was a

good example of the diversity of the Body of Christ, and of the importance of commitment to one another.

My senior year, on the night of our Spring Banquet, the boys honored us with one final raid. We had gotten up the hill from Islamabad at two a.m., arriving back to a completely dark hostel: the *bijilee* was off again. The guys had gotten off the bus at Sandes. When we got to the hostel we were all exhausted and went straight to bed. An hour later we were awakened by noise in the hall. Our doors were quickly opened, something was thrown in, and then the guys were gone as quickly as they had come. Our rooms were full of fluffy, peeping little chicks! As the *bij* was still off, we got our flash-lights and tried to gather them up. They had been dyed different colors—pink, blue, green, orange. In the confused darkness I heard my friend, Holly, yell from across the hall, "He's pooping in my Reeboks!"

We began to notice that all the chicks were numbered, apparently one through a hundred. So as we collected them we counted to make sure we got them all. Sure enough, five or six were still missing. We searched and searched and finally gave up. We put the little peepers in a trunk in the hall and went to bed. The next morning we gave them away to the little kids. Later, we found out that the boys had deliberately skipped a few numbers to keep us confused!

It was a night I'll never forget.

Darlene Liddle '87

INVOCATION

Tin rain clinking down. Thunder sawing through clouds like waves pounding on the shore. Flickering slashes, cannon flashes. Furious raging blackness hounding at the door; dazzling blindness icily etching whipping branches, lashed by erratic force. Whistling, rasping, sandpaper voice rising in proud boast of distant destruction; threatening, faraway rumble of mud and rock . . . road block. My room glows shaky-bright then dark again as silver-stencilled pictures leap from the night. Spray spiralling in streamy aftermath.

EDUCATION

Twenty hot bodies crowd suffocating into a stuffy room. As a soft drone comes from the direction of the grayboard, the flaking paint in the corner of the ceiling and the marked grooves in the desk become objects of intense fascination: "I love Lois." (I know who wrote that.) "Hi!" "I HATE French!" "Math Stinks!" K.C.+J.T. (in a heart-shaped border) "C.J. wuz here" — all provide insights into a relevant history totally unrelated to the unification of Germany and the Treaty of Frankfurt. The class suddenly comes alive. The structure of DNA is lost, as an enthusiastic discussion evolves: Should monitors be given more privileges in return for their many services to the school? Exam time! Blank paper becomes a source of dismay as the time bomb ticks steadily past C and D to F. Tears gush in frustration as "2 cos (a + b) = sin a sin b + cos a cos b" eludes its allotted slot among millions of brain cells, and floats irresistibly into "don't know." A friend offers much-needed encouragement, and correct diction and grammatical accuracy barely cross the mind. "You're gonna be alright. There isn't nothing God can't help you through." Hours of careful examination of the French imperfect, conditional, past historic, and future perfect verb tenses lose their place in the exciting world of "Je t'aime." It is the time spent with friends talking, laughing, and crying that makes parting difficult— not the missionary journeys of Saint Paul. I remember the Biology field trip to the valley of Swat from a year ago—the rocky potato fields, their pocked-brown expanse smelling like old people's skin, and the icy streams bouncing joyously down green mountains, the sun sparkling a xylophone melody off the water—but I cannot remember the area of a polygon rotated around the x-axis from yesterday. Yet, that was education.

GRADUATION

Walking dazed out into the cold night air. Face unseeing and numb. Choked throat, gritted teeth, ragged emotions, searing pain. Leaving, saying goodbye—a part of me is withering, dying. My friend is gone: the hand on my shoulder; the eyes that understood; the words of comfort; the heart that opened to me with trust and sharing. Why must paths part? My heart is screaming. He is gone and I must return in three weeks—the one left behind. The tears fall silently on the hard ground.

The very word "graduation" evokes painful emotions. Graduations at Murree were like funerals for me, especially the ones when I was not the graduate. My friends at MCS were my second family, my brothers and sisters, and yet at graduation, they left to scatter across the globe, likely never to be seen again in this life. It was like they were dying. The "weeping line" (at the reception) was the equivalent of the last moments by the side of a loved one about to leave this world to enter the great unknown: The one staying is sobbing; the one leaving is sad and scared, but also excited by the new life ahead. The paths part. It was a heartbreaking celebration and the night after, an annual agony.

My Dad, the Principal

Elaine Roub '75

There are two things about my parents that I remember most from my childhood. One is that they always had time for me, no matter how busy they were. The other is that they were praying people, and I knew this both by their words and their example. How many times I burst into my mother's room just before school in the morning to find her sitting up on her bed, Bible open beside her, her head resting on one hand, eyes closed. I knew she was praying for her world and mine—the world of MCS, Pakistan, her family, and her extended missionary family. And more than once I ran down to the school early in the morning to see if Dad wanted to go into Murree for breakfast. I would peer through that one clear pane of diamond-shaped glass in the door to the principal's office and see my father on his knees in front of his desk chair, praying. I guess they both knew how much they needed God's help.

Our house was always grand central station—for students, staff, and the missionary community alike. We hardly ever got through a meal without being interrupted at least once by someone at the door or on the phone. Besides the drop-ins, my parents did a great deal of entertaining, taking special care to include single staff members in their dinner parties and outings. Apart from the missionaries, staff, and students they entertained, we were often visited for tea by Pakistani army officers from up the road. Dad always liked that, because then he had an excuse to slurp his tea, Pakistani style, in front of Mom—something he never dared do when on his own with her. The soldiers always slurped their tea; Dad would slurp and then glance at Mom, his brown eyes twinkling, and she would give him the expected, tight-lipped, disapproving look. The army men never knew what silent games they inspired in our home!

●

Dad and I used to walk together at night. I'll never forget the security of my hand being held in his large, warm one, or the foundation of trust he gave me by letting me share my heart with him. But perhaps the greatest gift he gave me was to trust *me* with some of *his* heart. He never "unloaded" his burdens on me, but sometimes we would talk about the things at school that troubled him, and I could feel a shadow of the weight he carried. Dad has always been very committed to everything he does, and with the school he took his responsibilities very seriously. There were so many issues and people and opinions to be dealt with continuously. Finding and sticking to the right policies for the school could not have been easy, with so many different missions involved. If a whole mission didn't complain about something from their positions on the school board, individual parents would. Dad's work days were long, and sometimes he'd be trying to find a few quiet hours in the evening to catch up on work, only to have a troubled staff member drop in on him and bend his ear for two hours instead.

That he never broke, openly at least, from the unrelenting demands placed on him can only reflect the depth of God's marvelous grace in his life—and Mom's, too. I doubt if many people could have borne so cheerfully and freely the constant intrusions into their personal and home lives.

Sometimes, however, the overlapping requirements of his position could be comical. I remember one time in high school I was helping him with filing in his office. An American staff member came in to talk to Dad while he was talking to Allahdad, the bus driver. Dad started talking to the American in English and to Allahdad in Urdu. But as the two conversations went on and the talk got faster and faster, my dad got mixed up with his languages: he turned to the American and spoke rapidly in Urdu (not understood by the American) and then to Allahdad and spoke in English. He didn't even realize he'd done it at first, until he saw the blank looks on the faces of the other two, and then we all laughed. My dad was never at a loss for words, though which language to speak them in was sometimes in question!

Mom was always quoting the Bible verse that says, "Whatsoever thy hand findest to do, do it with all thy might," and as hard as Dad worked, he also laughed and played and enjoyed life to the full. Family vacations were hard to get away to, but once we did they were wonderful. It didn't take Dad long to "feel like a millionaire."

Dad was always so frustrated when it was time to leave for a holiday: "*Why* did I think I could get away today? Look at all this stuff still to be done, and a half a million other things that I ought to do before we go!" And of course, the work always waited for him—and seemed to multiply—while we were away. Yet, when we were together as a family, somehow that fact never made us feel that he was only there in body and somewhere else with his mind. I always felt that I had his full attention, even during work hours. When my sister Rachel and I were small, it was often Dad who would plaster Band-Aids on our cut knees and dry our tears when we'd fallen.

We didn't even have to be far away from home for Dad to step aside from the pressures of his position. A summer evening eating a dish of ice cream on the porch at Firco's, overlooking the colorful, well-peopled mall in Murree would be enough for Dad to look at Mom with this expansive grin on his face and say, "Doesn't this just make you feel like a millionaire, Honey?"

I don't mean to make it sound like Dad was perfect, because I know he wasn't. He is of course his own worst critic, and there were times when I saw the things that he now accuses himself of as he looks back: impatience, not delegating enough, not always having clear priorities. There are certainly times when Dad got really discouraged, but he is an eternal optimist, and when he was down, Mom was a great encouragement to him. It was difficult, in their position, to share the deepest things with others because so many things needed to be kept confidential. I couldn't say who their closest friends were.

Yet, when I recently asked my mom, Eloise Roub, what she remembered most from twenty-five years at MCS, it was the good relationships they had as a staff. That's what she enjoyed the most. Other than a few "irregular people," they really did have good fellowship. Since poor relations with other missionaries is one of the top reasons for missionaries coming home prematurely, I guess there's a lot to be said for the warmth and communication the MCS staff had amongst themselves. I know there were really difficult times with staff, but the "veterans" weathered those difficulties well.

Mom also really enjoyed the kids. She began teaching typing in that little storage room off the side entrance into the school. She had never taught before, but they needed a teacher, so she ordered the books and covered the typing keys with white tape and began. Every time I sit down to write something, even now, I still remember: *"feet flat on the floor, posture erect."* I am sure there are hundreds of MCS students who will never forget these lessons—as well as Mom's typing parties and sticky buns.

Of course, she also worked as the school secretary for years and saw a lot of kids coming in and out of the office. Mom was a listener—to my Dad, to high school girls, to other staff members. She was also a pray-er; she is credited with "praying in" a lot of husbands for staff missahibs!

The hardest thing for her to adjust to in Pakistan was the dirt, and in Murree, the dampness—never being able to get anything really clean or dry. The Pakistani servants were horrified the first time they saw Mom down on her hands and knees trying to scrub her cement kitchen floor. It was totally unacceptable for a missionary memsahib to do such a thing, and after a couple of times she gave it up. The summer monsoon season was especially frustrating, with the constant dampness and the scorpions and spiders that came with it.

Mom remembers the pain of taking her first child to boarding. My older brother, Ron, was only in first grade. This was before our family moved to the school when Dad became the principal; Becky and I, and Rachel, were always "staff kids." Mom still doesn't like to talk about it much, but she was always grateful to God for that experience of putting her own child in boarding because it gave her a deeper understanding of what parents were going through all those years. One time she walked up to the school library and met a parent who had just left his little girl in school and was heading for the plains. He had tears in his eyes, and she felt so deeply for him, though she hardly knew what to say to comfort him. What is there to say in a situation like that? I know a lot of parents didn't let their children see their emotions during the goodbyes, but there's no doubt in my mind that for 95% of the parents—if not 100%—it really did tear them up, and they never thought of their children as unimportant in comparison to their work. Boarding was just the way things were done, and not many people considered the alternatives.

Reunion

Carol (Patzold) Berg

It is Friday morning, July 2. The house is full of cots, beds, and mattresses; the basement is filled with tables and chairs; the fridge and freezer are full of food; and my heart is full of anticipation and excitement.

Slowly they begin to arrive—and the momentary awkwardness of twenty years apart quickly fades into hugs, laughter, and "Babu" English! I am reminded of years gone by when we returned to boarding after winter vacation—how we awaited and greeted each arrival, till all were safely back and settled in their bunks. We had, then, a sense of looking out for each other. Our hearts were heavy at having left our parents at home, and somehow we knew we had to "pull together" to support and care for each other in their absence. That same spirit of connectedness envelops us again, twenty years later, as we reminisce, share our stories, and meet spouses and kids. It is a gathering of 38 people; when we graduated in '73, we were only eleven!

Roy Montgomery

There was never a question in my mind whether or not I would go to this reunion, but as we were driving into that congestion called Minneapolis, I got cold feet, thinking, "*What on earth am I doing here and what do I expect to have in common with these people after all these years?*" It may sound crazy, but it hadn't occurred to me until this moment that we would now be strangers. I fancy that I have changed considerably since I left those chilly halls of learning twenty years agone, but the curious wonder was that those other clods had changed not one lick!

Upon our arrival we were greeted by Auntie Ruby Patzold, Carol's mom. Imagine my surprise at seeing that she had not visibly aged a day since she just as warmly wished me all the best at graduation as she now welcomed us to John and Carol's house. Was I some sort of Rip Van Winkle in reverse or what? Had I dreamed twenty years of living, only to awaken to the fact that it was just one afternoon nap?

I was the first of the class-fellows to arrive; Carol was hiding somewhere. Thus, I was able to greet each old friend as they arrived. I was wondering who all the old folks were that they had brought to the party, when it dawned upon me that I had been greeting the off-spring, and these old cripples were actually my chums! No joke. It was absolutely incredible to see such clear reflections of old blocks in young chips. Naturally, this dawning realization explained beaut-ifully to my senile bewilderment how my fast friend Dave Addleton had suddenly become two lovely young ladies, in their distinct per-sonalities both so like their old man. Needless to say, those vintage relationships required no renewal—we just picked up where we left off. Spouses and children were instant friends.

Of special pleasure to me was sharing with one another our spiritual pilgrimages to date, and putting childhood memories into perspective. The staff at MCS had to be jolly good sports! Some of them were not long out of high school themselves at the time, though to us they seemed antiquities of unfathomable vintage. It was rather shocking to realize that we're older now than the majority of them were then. I wonder now how many of them went out to the "mission field" with romantic ideals of caring for proper children of saintly missionaries, respected and appreciated by their grateful little charges. I hope that they have the grace to see now—as they may not have then—that the grief we gave them was mostly growing pains, not meanness, and the pranks deviously wrought against them were more sport than devilment.

We all remembered the notorious "magic seat" in the hostel dining room, a sinisterly roving, unmarked spot—known only to the staff—that offered an enviable award for mannerly behavior at table. I can't remember a male ever receiving the prize! It's just as well. It'd likely have gone ill for the poor blighter back in the barracks for breaking faith with disorderly traditions. I recall thinking how beast-ly unjust it was as I watched yet another prim schoolgirl collecting a sixteen-inch pencil topped with a whistle. Why, I'll bet that ever did get blasted to full potential.

cle Paul Davidson from New Zealand was a great one for entering into after-school play. At one point we had a rather elaborate dinky-car development out behind the Middle Boys' house at Sandes. Quite regularly Uncle Paul got as muddy as the worst of us. Hiking with us, swimming at the river and later camping at Rawal Lake and on the Indus, impersonating the fierce Maori warrior, reading Hardy Boy stories aloud to us at bedtime, bringing treats home to us from his day-off excursions—these memories far outweigh less pleasant ones of his size-thirteen slipper, not to mention his abominable cough remedy. And who will ever forget his oft-repeated admonitions of *"Don't moan,"* or *"Ay-kie, lawds, let's pry."*

I noticed that it was miles more easy to talk about fondly remembered personalities than my own feelings. I was curious about other people's experiences—how they validated or challenged my own. And what did it all mean for who we were now? "Roots" is such a treacherous word when you come up the way we have, in my case, Jordanian by birth, Scots-Irish/American by parentage, Pakistani at heart, Canadian by choice.

With all our experience at saying good-bye, saying it again after two days together was still a wrenching ordeal. If I'd not had my loving family to accompany my departure, I honestly don't know how I'd have managed. I'm still somewhat in a state of amazement that the whole thing actually happened. Trying to relate the experience to friends back in Alberta has been like trying to explain a Canadian winter to a tropical *jungli,* so I have found myself resorting to brief, stupid descriptions like, "awesome!" "Fantastic!" Or worse—"moving," and "memorable." We spent, as it were, a short time in heaven and now, brief as that was, living on earth has required some readjustment.

Patty (Irwin) McGarvey

When we arrived, Roy Montgomery and Doug Walsh were already there with their wives and children, as well as Scott Kennedy, who had to leave his wife Nora and two toddlers in California because the boys were sick. But he paid for a ticket for Tim DeHart to fly out from Maine, ensuring that we could all be here. And Auntie Ruby Patzold was there to greet all of us, too—she had been my first boarding mother! She had cooked Pakistani food ahead for our supper on Saturday night and came each day to help Carol. Shortly after we arrived, Glenn and Peggy Hamm drove in with their three kids. Leslie (Christy) Valencourt and her husband Rene drove in Saturday morning from where they were staying with friends in the city; Val (Lundgren) and Bryan Weinstein flew in from New York. David and Liv Addleton drove in Saturday afternoon with their two girls, having left Atlanta, Georgia, on Friday morning.

We *all* made it! Except, of course, Tom Ketcham, who died just last year; and we missed him. I think this must be some kind of record for an MK reunion—after twenty years! And those years just seemed to fade away as we talked and reminisced. We were still the gang who had made it through the fun and tears of years together, and I felt as at ease with them as I had in high school—maybe more, because we weren't dealing with the self-conscious hang-ups of adolescence anymore.

Friday evening after dark, Carol's husband John built a bonfire in their huge back yard and we sat around and swapped memories. It was midnight before we all went to bed. Saturday morning we sat around and talked while the kids played, and greeted the rest of the gang as they arrived. Saturday evening, after our feast of pea pilao, chicken curry, *naan,* and *desi chai* made by Tim, who had brought Brooke Bond Supreme (a Pakistan classic) with him, we went outside and had a picture session—the whole group, then by families. There were lots of cameras clicking, and Ruby took pictures of the group for all of us. We also took some of just the class—including one that reduplicated a class picture from our senior yearbook: we posed on the steps leading down from Carol's deck the same way we had posed on the steps leading down to the school from the Roub's house.

We watched slides that Glenn had brought of Pakistan in general and of his visit back the summer of '76 when several others were also back. Several had brought their class yearbooks (the *Kahani*) and photo albums, so there was much sitting around looking at and reading those. We got the kids to bed by midnight, and then the class stayed up talking till after two! All our spouses eventually gave up and went to bed. We did a *lot* of laughing at stories of fun weekends and pranks.

Camping trips must be one of my most favorite memories, spanning junior and senior high. As an adult now, I thoroughly admire the courage of those who risked taking us on these trips. I remember camping at Pindi Lake where we arrived once after dark and just unrolled our sleeping bags wherever on the ground. The next morning I woke up to find my sleeping bag full of ants—I'd slept on a large ant hill! But I also remember that the sunrise that morning was brilliant over the lake, and so peaceful.

An especially memorable trip was up Mirianjani after dark, hiking for what seemed like hours before finally arriving at a resthouse. The moon was huge and yellow on the horizon until it set, then it was pitch dark. Cindy Webster fell off the path and tumbled down the mountainside. Someone helped her back up, and the next day, retracing the path to find her glasses, they saw that if she hadn't been stopped by a tree stump she would have tumbled over a cliff, hundreds of feet down. God certainly had his hand on us!

Once in government class, Mr. Nygren went into the closet— the one under the steps up to the science lab. On the spur of the moment, I leaped up and shut the door, locking him in! (And I was never one to do that sort of thing—I guess I was considered a "goody-goody" sometimes.) We would have let him out soon, of course, but who should stop by the classroom just at that moment but Mr. Roub, looking for Mr. Nygren! He was shocked, and Mr. Nygren was so angry his face got very red. Another time, our class made him a "birthday cake" with a water balloon inside, icing on the outside. He was a good sport.

I remember playing in the woods in grade school and sliding down a slope covered with pine needles, just like in "The Faraway Tree" by Enid Blyton; getting all sticky with sap from climbing the pine trees; and on cold mornings, pulling the clothes we had laid out the night before under the bed covers to warm them while we had our Quiet Time before getting dressed.

Our kids can't believe that we would find Saturday night "walks" to be exciting weekend entertainment; they think we're nuts. But those junior and senior high walks in the dark, sometimes so dark you couldn't see your hand in front of your face, were filled with relationships and romance, watching who was walking with whom, or getting to walk with the one you wanted to walk with. On clear nights we could see the great mountain ranges outlined in the distance, and bright and silvery moonlight filled the crisp, measureless sky.

Glen Hamm

What a great class to not give up on me even if I never wrote a letter to one of them in those twenty years. It took a little planning to get this thing to go—Hats Off to Carol and her mother for all their efforts, and to others who wrote to encourage us to come. Perhaps Tom's death and Carl McGarvey's illness brought us to the realization of our own mortality, and the shortness of our time here.

Perhaps it is just a natural thing to think about as we enter mid-life (and it is a crisis for some of us). At any rate, we did all show up, and that fact says a lot.

I drove from Pennsylvania with my wife and kids, anticipating the reunion with some curiosity and a comfortable feeling of peace. But as we neared the Twin Cities I grew a little frightened, that maybe I was doing something very foolish. I wanted to back out. I'm not sure what I was afraid of: not being accepted, not knowing what to say, not liking anyone, that I wouldn't measure up, or that the others would think that I had turned out strangely. But the reunion was nothing like the movie. My fears were dispelled as soon as we arrived. I may have lost more hair than any of the others, but I didn't have the biggest belly. I still couldn't play basketball, and I wasn't quite what I used to be at soccer.

Some of us have changed very little, others a lot. We have all grown from where we had been at MCS, though I can't say it has been easy. It was good to see each of us working with what we had been as high school students—products of the boarding experience, products of the religious indoctrination—to become adults who each grew from that to something more. You could still see snatches of the old kids, especially during the soccer match, but no one was the same, really. Still, even with the changes, we were family in a very real sense. We had been together through a lot; and though we hadn't been taught to express our feelings, or to trust, we understood each other without the explanation, *"Well, I grew up in . . ."* This must be what it is like for foster kids. I had, in fact, spent more time with these people than with my birth family.

It was good to be in that group, and though we didn't have as much time to work at issues as some of us needed, it was a start. It was a time to remember, a time to wonder what we've done with our lives and where we have come from, a time to reflect on the way we were raised and look at the way we are raising our kids, a time to reassess our values and goals.

Some hard questions came up:

1. Would you do what your parents did? Four out of the ten of us had done at least short term mission work.

2. Would you put your kids in boarding school? Try zero for ten.

3. Would you change your experience if you could go back? One said, "No, it was great." The rest of us were not so sure.

4. Did our parents have a choice? Can we blame them? The consensus was in favor of the parents, showing that this crowd has

matured, has worked this stuff out and isn't blaming anyone—*or*, they are denying everything through their teeth.

5. Can we still sing the Hallelujah Chorus as well as we did in high school? The answer is "No." (I'm not sure we really did sing it that well in high school anyway.)

6. Are we all happy with the way boarding was run? One "yes" and five or six "I'm not so sure."

I think individual growth was most apparent in Roy. His loving spirit and understanding were fabulous. His inner peace was evident, and his love obvious. Some of the rest of us were less together, still with a lot to work out.

My older sisters, Kathy and Patty, were two of the original eight kids when the Presbyterians started the school at Sandes Home in 1956. My first memories of Murree are those of going to Rock Edge for Kindergarten. The building was perched on the edge of a rock, as its name implies, thus beginning my long-standing love of paper airplanes. I'm not sure that I learned much else that summer.

My sisters had warned me about the second grade teacher and THE RULER, and I was terrified to begin that class—even after having to repeat first grade. Patty had been crying one day soon after school started. Miss G. made her come to the head of the class, hold out her hands, and then smacked them with a hard wooden ruler. The lesson was very clear to all of us: "You don't cry in this class." I think it carried over into many other things, because we learned to hide our feelings very well.

No sooner had I escaped second grade than I was confronted by THE READING CONTEST in third. All across the cupboards at the back of the room was a great blue sea upon which our little construction-paper boats were to sail. Unfortunately, the only way we could get the boats to move forward was to read books. Here, the ultimate embarrassment—the whole class could now see that I couldn't yet read. That became clear to Miss Cunningham, too, as she had me and two other kids down to her apartment in Ash Wing after school to practice reading for what seemed like hours. Those were some very long afternoons, as this was right in the middle of the handkerchief parachute phase of boarding.

Fifth grade introduced me to real poetry, and to another dreaded reading program—SRA. I never did learn to memorize well, but I can still remember parts of "The Charge of the Light Brigade" and "The Village Smithy." The SRA (for "Scholastic Reading Aptitude," I think) became an unintentional social marker. The smart kids who read fast got to take cards from the back of the box, with the maroon color, while us slower kids had to take the ones from the front, with the red edge. Thus, everyone could see you were at the bottom of the class by what color card you took back to your desk.

I had sixth grade in the States, while our family was on furlough. I found that I could tell old MCS jokes and still get a laugh; I could work not too hard, and still be the teacher's pet; I learned about the "neat" kids and the "gross" kids, and managed to socialize with both.

Seventh grade was highlighted by Wood Shop and low-lighted by French. When it came to foreign languages, my inability to memorize got the best of me. Fortunately, however, I finally felt I had some company. Poor Miss Haugen. She certainly "earned some jewels for her crown" putting up with us. I'm not sure how many times we drove her from the room in tears.

All these memories came flooding back during that weekend together. And others that I hadn't thought of for many years—like when our homeroom was under the library and paper airplanes would occasionally come floating down through a hole in the ceiling (where the "bay" for one of the long cathedral windows caused a gap in the library floor above us). And Joni, with all his immaculate pencil drawings of airplanes in their dog fights across the page. That poor boy took so much abuse from us; I sure hope it didn't permanently damage him. Uncle Paul Davidson's camping trips and lake outings, and his *"Wakey wakey boys, rise and shine to meet the day!"* That great flat-bottomed canoe we built in junior high Shop. Mr. Murray's *"Get a grip there lads!"* Girls. Quarantine for mumps. Measles. Mono epidemics. Monitors. Chai. Boats and Sailors. Sunday night walks. Tea shops. Bicycles. Physics . . . .

Leslie (Christy) Valencourt

Boarding trunks . . . fire drills . . . monkeys . . . cow-pies . . . Deodar ringing the bell for every class period . . . chapel . . . evacuation suitcases . . . Army convoys . . . train party . . . Pakistani *ayahs* giving us baths . . . inspection . . . Ovaltine at recess . . . *suji* for breakfast, and little round red Upjohn vitamins . . . five-minute silence when things got too noisy in the dining hall . . . yellow jello . . . tea-time . . . blisters from the old wooden monkey bars . . . buckeyes . . . Mr. Lawrence's Urdu fruit chart . . . Mrs. Roub's typing class . . . Mr. Murray and his flying chalk . . . flying squirrels . . . wads of gum lining desk lids . . . Saturday night "movies" . . . water shortages . . . flannel sheets . . . huddling around kerosene heaters . . . field hockey—and "greenies" for gym class . . . cheerleading "very carefully" so as not to offend the culture or "harm our witness" . . . study hall . . . Charlie's . . . Jhika Gali Burka Babes (old maids' club) . . . Skip Day . . . Sports Day . . . choir cantatas . . . having three or four different teachers for French—all with different accents . . . monsoon rains on a tin roof—and school plays that had to stop for awhile because it was impossible to hear . . . rain dripping into buckets all over the classroom floor . . . pressure lamps hissing and fuming . . . jackals howling . . . *"The bus is leaving!"* . . . carsick kids on bus trips to Pindi . . . water balloon raids . . . pataka raids . . . midnight feasts . . . Chopsticks . . . piano recitals by kerosene lamp . . . roller skating parties . . . skirt check . . . flashlights . . . UFOs seen on every night walk . . .

As the reunion approached, I didn't have much time to ponder or worry about it. I just looked forward to it abstractly. But when the day came, I thought to myself, How do these people remember me? As the sarcastic little snot that I was back then in high school? Surely not, I hoped. Much tempering has occurred over the ensuing years and I hoped it showed, without my having to prove it.

Once we were all together, anxieties quickly evaporated. Here were people who knew me, loved me and accepted me. Not only were they school mates, but soul mates in a rare sense. As Roy so aptly stated, here among friends we can be who we are without fear of censure. What freedom.

We haven't really changed all that much, except for being refined and matured. A few gray hairs don't mean much when we all have them. There is a lot of laughter, many long forgotten stories recalled. (The puddle under Patty will *never* evaporate!) But also there are shared tears, easily shed. We have such a rich heritage, some of it painful, yes, but see who we have become as a result! Sensitive people for the most part, caring people. God has been faithful.

All too soon, the weekend is over. The lump in my throat melts into tears at the pain of saying goodbye, reminding me of graduation night and the grief of separation. Who could have known, back then, that twenty years along our journey we would be together again? In our reunion we have found a sense of belonging and roots, we have felt a healing and a home-coming.

David Addleton

Tom Ketcham died from an overdose of unprescribed painkillers on March 19, 1992, little more than a year before our class reunion. He was thirty-six years old. After three marriages, numerous jobs, and years of wandering through a spiritual wilderness, he seemed to have turned his life around. He was committed to a twelve-step program —in fact, had been dry and drug free for the last six years—and relished his new role as a father. He had returned to church and had just finished medical school. Shortly after Tom's death, I wrote down some thoughts about my friend and high school roommate—a sort of private eulogy, which I subsequently was able to share at the reunion.

[excerpts] *I don't pretend to know how to make sense of it all. I look to my life for the first reference point, to my individual biography and unique landscape extracted from the vast reserve of memory each of us uses to define ourselves. Tom and I shared at least something of a common past, first and perhaps foremost, a missionary upbringing in Pakistan, and a lingering sense of disconnectedness reaching back to our first encounter with America.*

Later, when we began our adult lives in the United States, Tom and I did not spend much time together. Yet, even after years of absence and change, we still experienced a kinship and intimacy that seemed impossible to find anywhere else. I can't explain or defend how Tom lived his life or the way it ended. Tom hurt a lot of people and he charmed a lot of people—often simultaneously. And he was never more ruthless than with himself. He had a compelling openness about him that many found threatening, even in its most gentle forms. Selfish, self-indulgent, and idealistic, Tom was above all else honest about his passions. And ultimately, regardless of what the coroner reports, or what his family chooses to believe, it is this honesty that killed him.

Our coming of age coincided with the Vietnam war and the passions it aroused. Some learn enough about passions to fear them; others become farther and farther removed so as to become completely in-different to them. If our passions threaten us, we call our pastor, priest, or rabbi; or, more commonly, our therapist. We avoid our passions, and with them our desires and compulsions, at every turn, even when reading Scripture. Our allegories miss the point of the Song of Songs, not because they hear divine resonance in its lovers' language but because they cannot hear a spiritual melody in the earthy passions which that epic so beautifully celebrates.

Having tamed our passions, we no longer even try to hear God speak to us. We content ourselves, instead, with an artificial substitute for the actual Voice: our own act of making Scripture relevant. No one really comprehends the depth of our passions, much less the role they might play in addiction. And yet to experience them must be to begin to experience God, for God has marked us with them almost as if they were his icon, his image in us, from the beginning of time.

It is Good Friday as I write this, and again I am struck by the restrained solemnity with which we celebrate a story called "The Passion." Jesus' compassion—his "COMrade-ly PASSION"—for drunkards, prostitutes and lepers put him at the edge of society. If the Song of Songs can be summed up in its climactic phrase, "Love is strong as death," then the Gospels can be summarized as "Love is stronger than death."

Perhaps we are too easily satisfied with what religion and society tell us about ourselves, about God, life, and death; about our passions, desires, and compulsions; even our attitudes toward the people who live at the edge. Perhaps we compulsively escape our passions and desires with an artificial "soft" drink of humility, charity, or personal sacrifice so that we won't find ourselves there at the edge, too. Tom may have lingered too long with Job and his unanswerable questions. Maybe he found—despite all outward appearances—that his community, church, profession, job, and family could not in the end satisfy his deepest desire for something more. But when he left he was perhaps farther along that passionate journey many of us fear even to begin.

It is hard to describe my emotions when meeting my classmates again and discovering at an unexpected level how much more each of them meant to me than I could comprehend when we said our farewells those twenty long years ago. Everyone (except Tom) was there; and we all remembered him, each in a different way. When Carol's mom, whom we affectionately called "Grandma" that weekend, mentioned Tom in our Sunday morning meeting, I could not hold back my tears of loss and grief.

We also laughed and played, joked and sparred with one another almost as though we'd been transported back in time to 1973. Saturday afternoon we played a soccer match. Everyone except Scott and Tim managed to bring their families, and our kids played with us. Doug's son, Matt, at fourteen was the same age as Doug when Doug first arrived at MCS. I played "*fool*-back," the position Ian Murray gave me to play twenty-two years ago because I "fancied" playing it. When Matt came barreling down the "pitch" next to Carol's house, he looked and felt to me as though he were Doug himself. When Scott's mocking wit turned to relationships between physicians and attorneys in the USA, we found ourselves jousting again, not over high school sport or academic performance anxieties, but over anxieties we'd learned from our respective professions.

Shortly afterwards we posed for a group picture. Scott remained with our spouses taking the pictures, behind his camera. We all were ordering him to join the group when someone remarked, "Scott thinks he can run faster than light!" I added, "He always did think pretty highly of himself." Consciously meant as a joke, the quiet that met my comment gave me a guilty feeling. I had stepped beyond the bounds of kindness we had hoped to experience again—and did experience—from each other during our reunion.

Those of us in our class who'd grown up together in boarding school, and some of our spouses who had, likewise, been raised in boarding schools, found our memories and conversations drifting into the early 1960s, when we were the ages of our own children, now. Glen's wife, Peggy, mentioned that her boarding school in Ethiopia actively discouraged sibling relationships; and while we could not remember any conscious policies on the subject, we all recalled feeling cut off from our siblings when we entered boarding school. Roy remembered how his older sister would sneak into his room to kiss him good-night, until he learned to prefer his peers' acceptance over the security his sister offered. I remembered learning not to cry in public, after watching an older boy verbally savage a younger one for being a "cry baby." When I mentioned that I could and did cry alone, Carol quickly added, "Where no one was around to comfort you."

I remember Catherine Nichols as the kindest, most caring of all my boarding parents. I remember Roy's kindness to me during the first recess I spent with the class of 1973, when I started fourth grade for the second time. Carol put it best, I think, when she said that we relied upon one another for love and caring which our surrogate parents, even in the best of worlds, could not possibly provide to all of us. I left Minneapolis with an experience of kindness that I've rarely felt since leaving MCS. I think we tried to give to one another during the weekend of our reunion a taste of the same kindness that sustained us as a class at MCS.

I think we largely succeeded. I write *largely* because I cannot honestly write that we said everything to one another that we might have, because some of us left things unspoken. Leslie said to me as we parted, "We act as if we hardly knew each other!" We all are trying, each in our own way, to know and love one another; we won't ever get it exactly right. Back then, sometimes, we got it almost right; and now, sometimes, because and in spite of what we learned back then, we get it almost right again, with our wives, husbands, children and friends. And when I get frustrated at not getting it right more often, I think that this must have been at least partly what Saint Paul had in mind when he wrote, "Now we see through a glass darkly; then we shall see face to face." I am grateful for our class's reunion, for there, briefly, I glimpsed again, through as clean a glass as I've ever seen, the dearest people I've been privileged to know, and felt for a weekend what it's like to more often get it right.

Postscript

John Young

"There's a good article in the *Jhika Journal* you should read," says Lindsay on her way out the kitchen door. What *Journal?* I didn't realize it had arrived; by the afternoon post, apparently. Lindsay brings it through for me to look at—the MCS alumni newsletter. I glance through it: photos, names . . . an old familiar knot begins to pull in my stomach. Tighter and tighter. I put the *Journal* down.

I've gone quiet. Lindsay soon notices. Sometimes I go off on these journeys into the past. Lindsay says she can tell because a scowl appears on my face. There are parts of my past that make me scowl. It's not that I hate them, it's more that scowling is the only way I can deal with them. I remember so many names of fellow students from the Sixties and Seventies. Names my sisters often mentioned. Names of people I knew myself. People with whom I endured first and second grade. People I sat in class with, queued up with, ate lunch with, played soccer with, walked to church with, and walked home to Sandes with. People I remember well. Would they remember me?

It took me two years to fit myself into MCS. In Gujrat I had my Pakistani friends. We spoke Punjabi together, went to weddings together, stole sugar cane and tomatoes together; made clay models, pumped water, and sat in church together. MCS was an alien world at first. A world of two-tone golf shoes, denims, and strange American place-names whose familiarity was taken for granted. It took me a year to realize that "the States" and America were the same place.

I remember getting my third grade reader and straight away looking up the stories at the end. That's where the patriotic ones always were. What would it be this time? The Boston Tea Party! The story of "The Stars and Stripes"! Why did my parents have to be British? I spent the length of the book waiting to get teased. Why weren't my parents with the UPs, or with TEAM? No one seemed to have heard about the Church of Scotland. But I got there in the end: I ran the fastest on Junior Sports Day; and by then I could sound as American as the rest. Slowly I found my confidence growing. Slowly I made friends, and began to enjoy the better side of MCS life. By the end of fourth grade I was beginning to relax.

Then we went home. "For the sake of your education," my parents said, and I accepted this. My two older sisters had been home for two years already. New school, new culture, new accent; begin all over again. And don't bother bringing up your past. Just get on with your life.

Three years later I was twelve years old, and at long last I was going back to Pakistan! The land of happy memories. Not for good —just to spend the summer holidays with my parents. I remember the drive up to Murree from Guj. Familiar sights, sounds, smells. The Wazirabad level crossings—no, there's a bridge there now; the Gujrat level crossing; the Jhelum bridge; Gujar Khan; Pindi . . . the memories came flooding back. On our first Sunday at church that summer, at Holy Trinity on the mall in Murree, I remember thinking, "I've been away, but I'm back. Remember me—John Young?"

But it wasn't the same. All my good friends were gone. The school was different. There was a new hostel now. I felt a forgotten person. People had moved on. Memories that were important to me were buried in their fourth-grade past. Scowl, John, scowl. Hide the disappointment. Hide your bitter envy of those Scots who had stayed on, who were still part of things, whereas it was too late for you now. Who needs MCS memories anyway? You're much better off where you are.

Six years later I am in Pakistan again, visiting my friends on the plains. A friend of my parents offers me a lift to Murree; their son is to be graduating—the class of '74. "I'd love to come," I say, having forgotten all about that knot in my stomach. But it soon comes back. Chuck Roub remembers me. I have to stand along with other former pupils. "John who?" What am I doing here? Why on earth did I come? A couple of alumni from the year above me recognize my name. My class would have been the class of '73. But I wasn't there to graduate. I have no one to have a reunion with.

Now, twenty years later, I find myself thinking back to a visit we paid Ian and Isabel Murray when they were on home leave in Edinburgh not so long ago. Fellow Scots, they have been teaching at MCS since I was a student there. The talk has come round to our memories of school, and I suddenly realize how fragile I am feeling.

This is ridiculous! I'm thirty-eight years old. I have my own family, and we've all spent a while working in Sind. We've been back to Murree together. Lucy even went to kindergarten at MCS. Why do I still feel that knot inside?

Ian has dug out some old *Kahanis* for everyone to look at. "When did you leave, John?" he asks. "Oh, I left the first year MCS had a yearbook. It came out that year, but my picture wasn't in it." That was what I had heard, and that was what I had always thought. Ian Murray never gives up. "What year was that again?" he asks. He pulls out the 1965 *Kahani,* and there, staring me in the face, is the fourth grade picture. I manage to smuggle the copy out of the room and sit in a quiet corner staring at it. There they all are. The familiar names and faces that were my MCS memories. And there, in the back row, was me. John Young. I exist after all. I was there.

The knot in my stomach is beginning to go.

Acknowledgements

This book first began to come into focus at The Writer's Center in Bethesda, Maryland. Thanks especially to members of Sara Taber's Spring 1994 workshop—Angela, Brian, Isabel and Kit—who generously read multiple versions of some early chapters. I am grateful to the APEL Program at American University for "priming the pump"; to the Washington Biographer's Group for sustaining me (especially Judy Nelson and Marc Pachter for sustaining the group!); to Louis Spirito, Joanna Arnold, and Mary Edwards Wertsch; and to my father, Alan Seaman, and Yoma Crosfield Ullman, both of whom proofread the manuscript and provided valuable feedback.

I am honored by the trust of many former students from Murree Christian School who shared their deeply personal stories and reflections with me and allowed them to be included here. A special thanks to Roy Montgomery for "lending" me one of his early memories where mine had grown dim. Eileen Powell's close editorial reading resulted in significant improvements to the book in its final stages; no one could ask for truer friends than her, Raymond Washington, and Margie Deane Gray. Amidst everything else, I rejoice in the gift of Rosalie, who provided steadfast encouragement for this project and whose companionship greatly enriched the process.

I am always delighted to hear from readers interested in sharing their thoughts. Write to me c/o Ruth Freeman, RD 1, 80 Van de Bogart Rd., Willseyville, NY 13864; tel. 607-272-2478. Or contact me through Cross Cultural Publications.

My first book—intended as a companion volume to this one—presents a larger selection of reminiscences and commentary on life at Murree Christian School, including contributions by former staff and teachers, as well as essays on the history of MCS and an evaluation of the impact of such an upbringing. *Far Above the Plain: Private Profiles and Admissible Evidence from the First Forty Years of Murree Christian School, Pakistan (1956-1996)* is available from the publisher (William Carey Library, Pasadena, California), or may be purchased directly from me for US $20.00 postpaid. Add one dollar per copy for orders outside the United States.